ON THE FRONTLINE

ON THE FRONTLINE

True Stories of Outstanding Bravery by British Forces in Iraq and Afghanistan

NIGEL CAWTHORNE

JOHN BLAKE

Published by John Blake Publishing Ltd,
3 Bramber Court, 2 Bramber Road,
London W14 9PB, UK

www.blake.co.uk

First published in hardback in 2007

ISBN: 978-1-84454-510-0

British Library Cataloguing-in-Publication Data:
A catalogue record for this book is available from the British Library.

Design by www.envydesign.co.uk

Printed in Great Britain by William Clowes Ltd, Beccles, Suffolk

1 3 5 7 9 10 8 6 4 2

Papers used by John Blake Publishing are natural, recyclable products made from wood grown in sustainable forests. The manufacturing processes conform to the environmental regulations of the country of origin.

CONTENTS

Introduction   VII
1 Into Kabul   1
2 Up Against the Elusive al-Qaeda   19
3 Under Scuds in the Gulf   39
4 Assault on Al Faw   51
5 Umm Qasr and Beyond   79
6 With the Yanks at Nasiriyah and Rumaylah   97
7 Taking Az Zubayr   109
8 The Battle of Abu al-Khasib   125
9 Into Basra   147
10 Red Caps at al-Majarr al-Kabir   169
11 Actions in Al Amarah   173
12 Into the Triangle of Death   187
13 Death in Basra   199
14 Helmand   211
15 The Return of the Marines   229
   Glossary   273
   Bibliography   277

INTRODUCTION

The world is undoubtedly a dangerous place. But we in Britain are fortunate. Fighting for us on the frontlines are the men and women of the world's elite armed forces. The American army may have greater numbers and more equipment, but no one can beat the British troops for training and tradition. The Princess of Wales's Royal Regiment (PWRR), which recently saw action in Iraq, can trace its history back to 1572 and it won its first regimental colours at the Battle of Tangiers in 1662. And the Royal Marines, who were one of the first regiments into Afghanistan and Iraq, celebrated their 342nd anniversary in Helmand Province. They had been around for 111 years before the United States of America came into existence.

As you read this book you will be left in no doubt about what superb fighting forces the British Army and the Royal Marines are. Nor can you fail to be impressed by the troops' dedication and bravery. The stories of the daring exploits of these young men and women – often in

---

their early twenties – show them to be individuals of astonishing maturity and fortitude in the face of extraordinary dangers. Every day in action, they faced death or injury by bullets, mortars, rockets, rocket-propelled grenades (RPGs), improvised explosives, car bombs and suicide bombers. They have to put up with poor food and appalling living conditions. They may be billeted in bombed-out buildings, or sleep in holes in the ground. For weeks on end they may be out on patrol in the desert, so short of water they cannot wash or shave. Then there are the snakes and insects to cope with, along with diseases unknown at home. And they are forced to fight in places strewn with toxic chemicals, radioactive waste and industrial pollutants.

On foot patrols, troops face potential snipers around every corner. Their armoured vehicles are rocked frequently by explosions. Their bases offer precious little safety and are repeatedly attacked. Even rear echelon troops find themselves in the frontline when the Scuds and 107mm Chinese rockets are flying. But the men and women of our armed forces react to this not with anger or despair, but with a gentle sardonic humour. Whatever catastrophe befalls them, whatever the odds, they get on with the job. This, they say, is what they signed up for.

Whatever the rights or wrongs of the wars in Iraq and Afghanistan, remember the brave boys and girls who have gone out there to fight them, because they had been asked to do so by the government – ultimately on our behalf. They have acquitted themselves magnificently and have done themselves, their regiments, the armed forces, their nation and its people proud. And those who died fighting them should be honoured and remembered for evermore.

CHAPTER 1
INTO KABUL

It began with the events of 11 September 2001, when hijackers deliberately crashed two commercial airliners into the twin towers of the World Trade Center in New York. Another hit the Pentagon. A fourth, on its way to another target in Washington, crashed in rural Pennsylvania when the passengers fought back against the hijackers. In all, some three thousand people died. The perpetrators were affiliated to al-Qaeda, an Islamic terrorist group based in Afghanistan. It was led by Osama bin Laden, a Saudi Arabian millionaire who cheerfully claimed responsibility for what became known as the 9/11 attacks. The US government repeatedly asked the Taliban, an Islamist group who ran Afghanistan at the time, to extradite bin Laden, but they refused. The US, with British support, then launched Operation Enduring Freedom as part of what President George W Bush called his 'war on terror'. The British and Americans began bombing the terrorist training camps in Afghanistan and providing substantial logistical support to the Northern Alliance, a group of Afghan warlords opposed to the Taliban. Then US and UK Special Forces moved in.

On 15 November 2001, an advance party of UK military personnel was deployed at Bagram Air Base, 48 kilometres (30 miles) north of the Afghan capital, Kabul. Although the UK Joint Rapid Reaction Force was on reduced notice, no decision had yet been made to deploy anything more than a token force. With the Taliban in full retreat there was no talk of taking them on. However, British troops were readied to distribute humanitarian aid and support the United Nations and other agencies on the ground.

Units on standby included elements of 3 Commando Brigade of the Royal Marines and 16 Air Assault Brigade. The men of 45 Commando, Royal Marines and the 2nd Battalion of the Parachute Regiment, along with support elements including Royal Air Force transports, helicopters, engineers, explosive-ordnance-disposal (EOD) experts and logistics teams, were made ready to move at short notice. More than a hundred Ghurkhas who had reinforced 2 Para since 1996 and were due to return to their parent unit, the Royal Ghurkha Rifles, were retained for the duration of the crisis and 118 reservists were called up, while 40 Commando of the Royal Marines were also put on a high state of readiness.

Following 9/11, 40 Commando had been moved from Cyprus, where they were training, to Oman to prepare them for desert warfare. After a brief sojourn on Diego Garcia in the Indian Ocean, home to one of the biggest American bases in the world, they boarded the assault ship HMS *Fearless* under a veil of secrecy, which, its commanding officer said, was 'broken only by CNN and most of the British press'. Half of Charlie Company were flown back to Oman, ready for deployment in Afghanistan.

Then began the frantic job of re-equipping them for operations in cold weather – it was winter in Afghanistan. The Royal Navy task force sent to the region was led by the aircraft carrier HMS *Illustrious*, supported by a large Royal Fleet Auxiliary, and HMS *Fearless* carrying the rest of 40 Commando as an in-theatre contingency reserve force.

On 23 November, elements of C Company of 40 Commando were flown by C-130 Hercules transport to Bagram Air Base, now the site of the UK Forward Operating Base. They were greeted by row after row of wrecked planes, burned-out Soviet-era barracks and spent ordnance. The valley where Bagram sits had been taken by the Northern Alliance just ten days before, after a fierce battle with the Taliban. The runway was pitted with small craters made by mortars. Spent cartridges lay everywhere and the Marines had strict instructions not to stray from paved areas because of the danger of mines.

Work began on securing the airfield. Field defences and stand-to positions were quickly erected and sentry routines drawn up. Then Bravo Company of 40 Commando arrived and were sent on to Kabul. Their job was to provide a British presence in the capital. On the evening of 21 December, they escorted key political figures through Kabul, and appeared at the inauguration ceremony of the Afghan Interim Authority on 22 December. This was the first time troops in foreign uniforms had entered Kabul since the Soviet occupation of the 1980s, and there were worries whether the Marines would be greeted as liberators or invaders. As it was, the reaction was favourable. The Marines acted as a deterrent to any remaining Taliban sympathisers and demonstrated the UK's commitment to the new administration.

Afterwards, B Company Group conducted regular mobile patrols in and around Kabul, extending their range on Christmas Day out to Kabul International Airport. Media interest in the Marines was intense. When asked, 'How long do you envisage patrolling the streets of Kabul?' Warrant Officer Second Class Pearce, Company Sergeant Major of B Company, replied, 'As long as it takes to make the streets safe enough for 2 Para.'

Christmas was celebrated in the mess with a 'Bin Laden Night'. No fewer than 14 Osamas turned up.

On 27 December, B Company Group secured a building in central Kabul opposite the US Embassy. This was to be the headquarters of the International Security Assistance Force. Defensive positions were established and patrolling began from this new location. On 30 December, the Marines began joint patrols with men from the Afghan Ministry of the Interior Police. Soon after, the rest of C Company arrived to support the deployment of the International Security Assistance Force (ISAF). Then, in mid-January, B Company handed over their patrol duties to D Company of 2 Para, who were flown into Bagram in C-130 Hercules.

The flight from England took over a day with stops at Cyprus and Oman. All arrivals and departures from Kabul took place at night, since it was not safe to fly during the day because the country had yet to be pacified; there was a certain trepidation as the troops neared Afghanistan.

'The last hour of the flight to Kabul focused everyone's mind on the fact that this was a peace support operation like no other,' said Captain Guy Gateby of 2 Para.

As they neared the border, an announcement came over the Tannoy: 'Right, gentlemen... we will be over Afghanistan in 20 minutes... all the lights will go off... put your flak jackets on... they have been welcoming us into Kabul with tracer.'

On the runway, the Hercules kept its engines running because it had to leave before daybreak. The temperature outside was minus 17°C (63°F) and there was a biting wind. In these conditions, batteries left outside ran down and jerry cans of water froze.

As the sun came up it grew warmer, but, every so often, the peace and quiet was shattered by a massive explosion as EOD teams set about destroying mines. These posed a major problem. Twenty years of civil war and war against the Soviets had left an estimated 10 million mines in Afghanistan. They create new casualties every day. British troops were shocked to see the number of amputees in the streets of Kabul. The job of clearing the mines, starting with those around Bagram, fell to the sappers of 9 (Parachute) Squadron of the Royal Engineers, who were flown in from Aldershot.

The Royal Logistic Corp had already arrived in Bagram to fix up relatively comfortable quarters. Tents were heated and the soldiers slept on camp beds or cots, but washing and showering facilities were basic. In many places, only a plastic bowl for a quick wash down was available. Cleanliness was made more difficult by the thin black dust that covered everything and clogged sensitive equipment such as cameras and laptops.

'It was not like Kosovo or Bosnia, where you had nice "Gucci" showers,' said Signalman Craig Smith of 30 Signal Regiment. 'Here it's shower bags from water heated in burners and hand-washing of clothes. Your admin has to be spot-on.'

Others were not so lucky.

'This was what I call a "dot" deployment,' said Staff Sergeant Steve Symmonds, also of 30 Signal Regiment. 'By that I mean we had to do everything from scratch because there was nothing here when we arrived. We had to build our own accommodation, our showers, toilet, kitchens – everything. The soldiers we've brought out on their first tour couldn't have had a better start to their careers.'

Decades of war had left the Afghan capital with little in the way of infrastructure. Power was provided by an ancient hydroelectric plant. This was hardly very effective as there was a drought at the time and it provided only around three hours of electricity a day.

Troops were attached to ISAF's headquarters, which had been secured by Bravo Company of 40 Commando. The building was the former Afghan officers' club, built during the Soviet occupation. It had since been used by the Taliban as an interrogation centre and the building had to be swept of unexploded ordnance and mines before personnel could be moved in.

'Initially the Royal Engineers had to clear the area of mines,' said Corporal Rob Anderson of 3 (UK) Division Signal Regiment. 'The buildings were full of UXOs [unexploded ordnance] and on our site we had to move armoured personnel carriers and even a T-54 tank before we could start putting up the tents.'

For the lucky ones, there were Spartan rooms in the club itself, but most lived in the tented village that had sprung up outside. The four-man tents equipped with heaters and thermal linings kept out the winter cold. Engineers were continually working to improve conditions, wiring the area with power and lighting, and building washing and toilet facilities. But showering for the most part took place under portable shower bags in purpose-made tents.

An old winery became the headquarters of 16 Air Assault Brigade, while the British logistics team set up shop in an industrial complex with the German battle group that had joined the international effort. Troops from 2 Para, who patrolled the streets of Kabul day and night, used old schools as patrol bases, winterising them so that they could be given back to the local people in good shape when they left, while the 1st Battalion of the Royal Anglian Regiment (RAR, or the Anglians) lived in their fortified patrol bases.

'Sarajevo in 1995 was harder,' said Corporal Rob Harvey of 3 (UK) Divisional Headquarters and Signal Regiment (DSR). 'I thought we'd forgotten how to rough it, but we hadn't.'

After weeks of boil-in-the-bag or ten-men ration packs, cooks from 3 (UK) DSR began providing three hot meals a day and have even experimented with the local cuisine.

'Afghans who help in the kitchen have been dropping hints about how to prepare curries,' said Corporal Stuart Brierley. 'We trialled the famous local dish called *mantoo* one night and that seemed to go down well.'

According to Staff Sergeant Daz Scott, who led the catering team of 3 Close Support Regiment of the Royal Logistic Corps, soldiers of other nations chose to eat in British cookhouses.

'As a chef, our day-to-day job remains pretty much the same, no matter where we find ourselves serving,' he said. 'But here it seems more rewarding, and sustaining our troops with three excellent meals a day provides them with a morale boost in a harsh and unforgiving environment.'

A Royal Air Force mobile unit provided meals at Kabul airport, the aerial point of debarkation (APOD), for ISAF operations. Although they only had rations for 300 people a day, their eight chefs often had to cater for an extra 100, as well as providing a 24-hour a day mess service to cater for those flying in and out at night. Warrant Officer Second

Class Andy Clement, the regimental catering officer for 1 RAR, paid tribute to the chefs.

'They were always coming up with new ideas, from improvised equipment to theme nights and barbecues,' he said. 'They also took an active part in the battalion tasking, including food and vehicle patrols, visiting orphanages and raising money for local schools.'

But even catering was not without its dangers.

'When a rocket aimed at the APOD flew overhead, mess personnel looked at each other and carried on,' said Warrant Officer Clement. 'It was like something out of *Carry On Up the Khyber*.'

Resupplying ISAF had to be done mainly by air and by night, and the bitter winter caused delays when snow and ice closed the runways. Mail from home normally took between five days and a fortnight to get through, but most soldiers had access to the Internet and handheld satellite phones to call home. They were allowed 20 calls a week. And soldiers could usually get their hands on a newspaper that was only a few days old.

The 1st Battalion of the Royal Anglian Regiment had arrived in Kabul to take over from 2 Para in March 2002 as part of the British-led ISAF in Operation Fingal. At that time, the Afghan capital was one of the most dangerous cities in the world. After dark, the streets were full of armed gangs and opportunist criminals. Twenty-three years of war meant that life was cheap; with random murders, armed robberies and brutal rapes commonplace. In the Afghan police force, corruption was endemic. Its officers had no uniform and no pay. The Taliban had kept order in their own brutal way, but after their fall the crime rate soared to a level that threatened to destabilise the nascent democratic state.

'Armed crime was plaguing the city and its population when we first arrived in Kabul,' said Lieutenant Colonel Phil Jones of 1 RAR. 'There were some brutal murders going on and gangs of up to 30 people were operating with complete freedom. Every crime was being politicised and it became obvious to us that this plague of criminals posed as much threat to the peace as any remaining Taliban or al-Qaeda.'

The 550-strong battalion found itself in charge of the security of the south-west of the city, an area that had been levelled by rocket attacks during the civil war in the early 1990s. They put the experience they had gained in Northern Ireland to good use and began patrolling the streets 24 hours a day, seven days a week.

'The foremost function of our patrols was to deter armed crime,' said Lieutenant Colonel Jones. 'We went out aggressively to show the criminals that we meant business and in the first month we had five or six direct contacts with them.'

The first part of the plan was to take back the nights. In the first days of 1 RAR's tour, nearly two-thirds of the patrols went out after dark, emptying the streets and turning the city into a ghost town. Acting on information from local people and intelligence from both overt and covert observation posts (OPs), the Anglians swamped areas where the gangs were operating. Their activities were not unopposed. At the end of April, C Company set up an observation post in one of the city's western suburbs after reports that bandits had moved into the area. One night a group of around 30 armed men fanned out on open ground and advanced on the OP.

'Challenges were issued by the guys on the OP, but the group of 30 opened fire and a number of rounds came within six inches of hitting soldiers,' said Captain Olly Brown of 1 RAR.

There was a prolonged firefight. As the gang began to disperse, a quick-reaction force went in to make arrests. Seven men were taken into custody – five of them turned out to be policemen.

'That act of getting right up face-to-face with these guys, knocking them over in the streets and arresting them, really spelt the end of the plague of armed criminality in Kabul,' said Jones. 'The whole area went unbelievably quiet in terms of criminal activity after that incident. We would like to think it sent a shockwave through Kabul's underworld and that it was the reason why the three or four other gangs which have been operating stopped doing so.'

But that did not mean the danger was over. When the team leader, Bombardier Mick Tunnacliffe, of 19 Regiment of the Royal Artillery – part of the Royal Anglian Battle Group – turned a corner in Kabul he found himself confronted by seven armed men, brandishing guns, at close range.

'The team commander, in a very brave act, rushed the lead man, who was armed with an AK-47,' said his commanding officer, Captain Brown, 'and knocked him to the floor. He disarmed him and they arrested the seven individuals. In the situation he faced, under the rules of engagement, he could have opened fire and killed all those guys. It was a very brave act to rush the guy rather than having six or seven dead people lying in front of him.'

Such incidents were not unusual.

'After 23 years of civil war virtually everyone owns a weapon of some description,' said Captain Brown, 'but local people say this is by far the most peaceful, stable and secure environment in which they have lived in all that time. They are delighted to see us here and they feel secure that we are patrolling. They are very friendly towards us and from that perspective our mission is going very well indeed.'

Eventually, casual shootings and armed raids even ended in Barjay, a district notorious for its high levels of crime and ethnic tension.

'Barjay was one of the busiest areas in the theatre, and when we first got there crime levels were very high,' said Corporal John Kitson, a patrol leader with B Company. 'A lot of incidents happened during the early hours of the morning when the traders went to work. Criminals were constantly trying to jump them and steal their money, so we flooded the area and closed it down completely. We had men constantly out on patrols and the criminals were not expecting us to be there and did not expect to be challenged. The police had always been too nervous to take on the gangs but, as soon as they saw that we always came forward and attacked, they calmed down.'

Determined to have some sort of lasting effect on the troubled city, the battalion also set about finding an Afghan solution to the problem of crime. They spent several months working with the police force to improve their professionalism. Until then, when the Afghan police were not actively involved in crime, they cowered in their police stations.

'As a matter of policy we encouraged the police to accompany us on our patrols,' said Jones. 'It dragged them out of their bases, made them patrol the community and made them confront reality. Previously, their method of interaction with the public did not involve dialogue and was done at the end of a 12-inch stick, so we tried to show them by osmosis how they should conduct themselves. It also meant that, when we arrived on the scene of the crime, we could force them to take responsibility for the investigation as the appointed force for justice.'

The Anglians also called on the expertise of 160 Provost Company of 3 Royal Military Police (RMP), embedding a service policeman at each of the company's patrol bases to act as a liaison officers and offer the Afghan police low-level training programmes. According to Sergeant Nigel King of 3 RMP, this was long overdue.

'A lot of the Afghan police are former soldiers who had joined the police force with no training,' he said. 'Their idea of an investigation was an interrogation and a lot of them could not even read or write. How are you meant to take a statement when you can't write? They were not so much addressing crime as coping with it, and they were certainly not dealing with it as a trained police force with a court system about them would. The police were acting independently and, if a policeman thought a punishment needed handing out, then he would deal with it.'

But a little training worked wonders.

'We have noticed a dramatic change in the way they do things,' said King. 'Those who can write now take notes. They collect evidence – albeit in their own unique way – and there are now vehicle checkpoints all around the city. They're a long way off becoming as professional as a European police force, but we have made a start.'

As the weather improved in the spring and the temperature started to climb, the troops in Afghanistan faced new dangers – the extreme cold of the Afghan winter kept numerous endemic diseases in check. Decades of war and neglect had left the country without the most basic facilities such as clean drinking water and effective sanitation. As a result, the country was ravaged by cholera, typhoid and dysentery, so army medics set about trying to win hearts and minds by providing clinics and helping to improve the main hospital.

There was also a high incidence of insect-borne diseases such as malaria and leishmaniasis – a disfiguring skin disease spread by sandflies. The World Health Organisation estimated that there were 20,000 cases of leishmaniasis in Kabul alone. Visiting troops also had to look out for the ten species of venomous snakes found in Afghanistan.

It was the job of the Environmental Health Team (EHT) of HQ 3 (UK) Division, based in Bulford, Wiltshire, to protect the troops of the 17 nations that make up the ISAF from these health hazards. They regularly tested the quality of the water provided by 521 Specialist Team, Royal Engineers, and checked on the quality of the food provided by the caterers. The team discouraged sampling local food, which could result in serious cases of gastrointestinal illnesses. They also put an emphasis on personal hygiene, but the EHT found it hard to get the troops to wash their hands in the Afghan winter, when water froze in the jerry cans. The cold also dried out the soldiers' skin and a respiratory condition called the 'Kabul cough', caused by the dust, was common.

Then there were the psychological dangers of being in a war zone. Captain Ben Campion, a community psychiatric nurse, was on hand to offer colleagues support after four Americans in an EOD team were killed in an accident in Kandahar on 15 April 2002. However, up until that point, disease and non-battle injury rates were surprisingly low at just 1.1 per cent of the force per day.

Despite the precautions taken by the EHT, 13 medics came down with a 'winter vomiting virus' that caused fever and diarrhoea. Some were flown out for treatment in Germany and the UK. As a precaution, 34 Field Hospital of the RAMC from Strensall, outside York, was closed to all but similar cases after its staff contracted the disease.

Medical teams from 19 Air Assault Medical Squadron (AAMS) and 16 Close Support Regiment, both of the Royal Army Medical Corps (RAMC), provided medical help for the locals. It was badly needed. When they turned up at the village of Gulbaz, outside Kabul, for example, more than a hundred people – a fifth of the village's population – turned out.

'Clinics for local people were held once a week and were extremely well attended, with problems ranging from simple skin problems to old gunshot wounds,' said the regiment's adjutant, Captain Ian Robertson. These were so popular they had to put on extra clinics.

Captain Andy West of 19 AAMS said that he quickly became an expert on leishmaniasis, which he found was treatable using lotions and injections at the sight of the infection, though it usually left a scar.

'This has been a opportunity to encounter medical conditions that we would never see back home,' said Lieutenant Colonel Martin Nadin.

Despite the dangers, British troops mixed with the locals as Kabul began to throw off its war-torn image and return to the thriving market town it once was. Suddenly, fresh-fruit stalls and even a shop selling second-hand bicycle tyres flourished.

'British soldiers are not afraid to talk to the Afghans,' said shopkeeper Ahmed Hiwali, 'especially in a World Cup year.'

The Ghurkhas were particularly popular, as their native language is similar to that spoken in Afghanistan.

As World Cup fever gripped the country, a football match between Afghanistan and an ISAF team was organised in the stadium that had been used by the Taliban for public executions the previous year.

'Standing in Kabul's Olympic Stadium listening to Afghanistan's national anthem, and looking up and seeing snipers lining the roof gave me one hell of a rush,' said former Spurs captain Gary Mabbutt, who was coaching the ISAF team. The Afghan team was coached by former Southampton boss Lawrie McMenemy.

Tickets for the match sold out within hours of going on sale and on the day of the match more than 30,000 spectators turned up.

'There were also about ten thousand fans outside the ground and there were a few problems before kick-off, with people trying every means possible to get into the stadium and be part of the occasion,' said Mabbutt. 'It was nothing more than overexuberance really, and fortunately no one got hurt. The forces did an excellent job of keeping the ticketless fans at bay.'

The ISAF team adopted a British style of play, while the Afghans used a more continental style.

'When Kabul opened the scoring with a spectacular scissor kick, the whole stadium erupted,' said Mabbutt. 'It was a magnificent sight. Under Taliban restrictions supporters weren't allowed to cheer a goal and so they went absolutely crazy.'

But the ISAF team had the advantage of being bigger and fitter. Skippered by Captain Jonny Croof of HQ 16 Air Assault Brigade, they rallied in the second half, winning the match 3–1.

There were more serious dangers than those presented by rioting football fans however. Captain James Cameron led the Specialist Monitoring Team of the Joint Nuclear, Biological and Chemical Regiment into the house in the suburbs of Kabul where Osama bin Laden and a Pakistani nuclear scientist had discussed making a 'dirty bomb'. This was the first time the Joint NBC Regiment had deployed operationally. Their job was to check the rooms for anthrax and radiological hazards. The house was clean, but intelligence recovered left no doubt about al-Qaeda's intentions.

The eight-man team were experts in detecting nuclear, biological and chemical weapons as well as radiological and toxic threats from industry and other causes. They used highly sophisticated detection equipment that could identify 129,000 chemical compounds in the air, soil or water. Devices around Kabul collected samples every six hours and tested them in-country in a £2.5 million mobile laboratory flown in for the purpose.

The NBC team also had to deal with the antiquated X-ray machines in Kabul's hospitals, which were a potential source of lethal radiation, and had to check out reports of veterinary anthrax. One of the worst hazards they had to handle was a batch of Cobalt-60 – a highly radioactive isotope that emits high-energy gamma radiation – the team found in a disused hospital. It had been intended for use in radiotherapy for cancer sufferers but, left unattended, posed a serious hazard.

Cameron was alarmed at the Afghans' relaxed attitude to potential hazards. 'I saw an Afghan sucking up anthrax through a straw to provide a sample,' he said, 'and a Mujahideen who kept a Russian chemical shell on his mantelpiece above the fireplace.'

Cameron used Radio Afghanistan to warn the locals of potential dangers, from messing about with old shells that the Russians left behind to children playing in ponds polluted with agricultural fertiliser. Sometimes, to deal with these hazards, they had to turn out in full NBC suits.

'One of the best things has been seeing the reaction of the locals,' said Sergeant Pete Brookes of the Joint NBC Regiment. 'They look very nervous when we turn up in full protection kit with respirators, but they're relieved when we give them the all-clear.'

Working in full NBC kit soon became particularly unpleasant as the weather turned warmer and the team were in danger not simply from chemical, biological, radiological and nuclear hazards, but also from unexploded ordnance and armed insurgents.

In July 2002, when Turkey took over the lead of the ISAF from the British, 1 RAR withdrew and headed home to their base in Pirbright in Surrey. They left behind a contingent of about 400 British troops to support the ISAF forces. These including a squadron of Royal Engineers and British staff officers at ISAF HQ, ready in case British forces had to be deployed in Afghanistan again. Then, in early September 2002, 40 soldiers drawn from the Territorial Army's Lancastrian and Cumbrian Volunteers went into Kabul to provide additional protection for the 400 British troops remaining there on Operation Fingal. Based at Camp Souter, near Kabul Airport, they were tasked with providing security for the headquarters staff, the Royal Engineers and other units working around the city. They also conducted foot patrols into Kabul, particularly along the route to the British Embassy.

'Tensions were high during the period around 11 September and after a recent car bomb in the city centre,' said their commander, Captain Graham Heap, a fitness instructor from Barrow-in-Furness. 'There have been several scares involving suspect vehicles around the base, but no serious threats to our lads. One foot patrol discovered an unexploded mortar bomb close to a school and called in the Italian EOD detachment to dispose of it.'

Things in Kabul would remain calm, for the time being. The action was to move to the south and, once again, the Royal Marines would be involved.

CHAPTER 2

UP AGAINST THE ELUSIVE AL-QAEDA

In early 2002, 45 Commando took over in-theatre when HMS *Ocean*, a helicopter carrier, relieved the aircraft carrier HMS *Illustrious*. They were to be deployed in Operation Veritas, supporting the Americans against the remaining pockets of al-Qaeda and Taliban resistance in a combat role completely separate from the British participation in the ISAF. The battle group also included 7 (Sphinx) Commando Battery of 20 Commando Regiment of the Royal Artillery, armed with 105mm light guns and, like 45 Commando, based in Arbroath near Dundee; 59 Independent Commando Squadron of the Royal Engineers; a detachment from the Commando Logistics Regiment, including Royal Marine, Royal Navy and Army personnel; and RAF Chinook helicopters from 27 Squadron of RAF Odiham.

Back in the UK, Alpha and Delta Companies of 40 Commando were also being prepared for deployment with gruelling physical training and briefings, including one on the 'Soviet Experience in Afghanistan' by Steve Walsh of the Defence Studies Department at Sandhurst. Then, at the beginning of February, A Company were sent to the Persian Gulf to take part in commando-raiding exercises in the United Arab Emirates, involving amphibious landings at night, which would come in useful two years later.

After that, A Company flew on to Afghanistan to relieve C Company, who had been away from home for six months. They were housed in a huge hangar on Bagram Air Base and began their duties in sangars – sandbagged firing positions – and observation posts, where they still found the nights painfully cold. But the action began to heat up. Operation Anaconda – a US-led operation to destroy al-Qaeda and the Taliban in their heartland in Paktia province – began in early March. Remaining elements of C Company were put on standby, ready to deploy on the ground to assist in the evacuation of any wounded Americans. One of the first tasks fell to teams under Corporals Conway and Cole, who were to provide force protection for two Chinook CH-47s – one carrying a field surgical team, the other a backup. They were deployed on the ground ready to receive American casualties and soon found themselves digging defensive positions. It wasn't before long the lads wondered whether these were dug deep enough when they heard over the net that, according to US forces, 300 al-Qaeda were heading for their position. Casualties began coming into the field hospital, but soon the Americans and their Royal Marine protection 'bugged out'.

In March, Major Rich Stephens, commanding officer of Zulu Company of the 45 Commando, had told his men – as they boarded HMS *Ocean* bound for Djibouti – that they would not be going to Afghanistan. The rumours were that the Paras were going to be sent in to deny al-Qaeda and the Taliban their sanctuaries in eastern Afghanistan instead, so the Marines left their cold-weather kit and mountain boots at home. However, it turned out that the Royal Marines had been chosen to undertake Operation Jacana and they then got the call telling them to fly to Bagram and prepare for a new offensive against al-Qaeda and the Taliban in Paktia province.

A team was sent in to reconnoitre the area in mid-March. On the way back they were stripped of their hexamine cookers on the grounds of flight safety. This particularly distressed the ops officer, Major Huntly of the US Marine Corps, though he could never get his to light anyway. After a stopover in a fleapit hotel in Karachi, the team returned to HMS *Ocean* in the North Arabian sea for a debrief. Then an advance party flew forward to Bagram via Kandahar, a seven-hour journey by CH-47. Some 250 Command Support Group (CSG) ranks were deployed to provide specialist support. The Brigade Patrol Troop were deployed to Afghanistan in early April, closely followed by Y Troop, the electronic-warfare specialists, and quickly settled into what was going to be their home for the next 90 days at Bagram Airbase. Whisky Company of 45 Commando arrived in Bagram among a press scrum about a week later, followed by the rest of the *Ocean* group on 11 April.

'Bagram had certainly seen better days,' said Captain Stew Tulloch of the CSG. 'A sprawling mass of Soviet military hardware in various states of decay adorned the mine-strewn fields that surround the main runway.'

Every new arrival underwent mine-awareness training. Although extensive mine-clearing operations had been undertaken by the Royal Engineers, the danger had by no means gone away. Five Coalition and local troops lost limbs while the Royal Marines were there.

Next the Air Defence Troop (ADT) flew in from Kabul aboard an aircraft whose crew had plainly seen too many Vietnam movies. They sat at the open doors, popping flares, smoking and playing Jimi Hendrix loud on the PA system. Once on the ground, the ADT reconfigured to provide two security troops.

With two companies of 45 Commando now in-country, they began zeroing their weapons and packing their 'bergen' rucksacks, ready to move out on the first part of Operation Jacana, which was called Operation Ptarmigan. This was to take over where Anaconda had left off, clearing al-Qaeda and the Taliban-and their defences, weapons caches and infrastructure-from Paktia Province. The Marines were to search and clear the mountain valleys there, where the enemy were thought to be operating.

The Brigade Reconnaissance Force, the Tactical Air Control Parties and elements of Y Troop were inserted with 45 Commando. They were also supported by 7 (Sphinx) Commando Battery of 29 Commando Regiment RA, armed with 105mm light guns, and 59 Independent Commando Squadron of the Royal Engineers. Transport was by helicopter, one of which had seen better days; according to Tulloch, 'Y Troop were the guests of "Mr Stinky", who had come off worst in a futile engagement with a US AC-130 Spectre gunship.'

The terrain was far from ideal. The Marines soon found themselves operating in snow at altitudes over 3,000 metres (10,000 feet). At night, it was not uncommon for them to get into their sleeping bags wearing everything they had.

'The threat of the altitude was not as great as some pundits – notably a former Royal Marine ML [Mountain Leader] officer – would have had it,' said one Marine.

'Apart from the lung-searing pain and a heart rate that would not have disgraced a Para in a maths test while ascending, it was of no great concern.'

On top of that, they faced fearsome daytime temperatures. 'The fitness of the observation post parties has been tested to the limit as the terrain proved exceptionally challenging,' said Captain Chip Bryant of 148 (Meiktila) Commando Forward Observation Battery. 'In addition, the climate constantly fluctuated between snow, rain, electrical storms and freezing temperatures to seething heat. On top of that, each man was weighed down with small-arms ammunition scales, grenades, enhanced body armour, helmet and surveillance equipment.'

And the troops had no time to acclimatise. Some had arrived in Afghanistan only 48 hours before being sent out on Operation Ptarmigan. Gunners from 148 Battery were inserted with the Brigade Reconnaissance Force, and three days later a troop of guns flew in by CH-47 to support the infiltration by 45 Commando Royal Marines with Tactical Group of 7 Battery.

Although it was not for want of trying, 45 Commando made no contact with the enemy. However, they did find and destroy some of the enemy's ammunition and equipment, and removed articles of intelligence interest for analysis. The Marines were not best pleased that, midway through the operation, they were afforded the opportunity to host a party of media, as one Marine put it. This meant that they had to haul their way to the summit of Takur Gar – 'the scene of some previous unpleasantness' – where they welcomed a ten-strong group of UK and international press. They were, the Marine said dismissively, 'A motley group complete with the obligatory blue helmets plus a bergen containing overnight kit'. Whisky Company looked on as the press party 'struggled manfully down the ridge and took advantage of the chance to ditch their bags in the care of a party from AE Troop, balanced on the edge of a ridge'. Their Royal Marine host said, 'That some of the press found, on collecting their bags, that the weight had increased significantly was purely circumstantial and the rumour that rocks had been added to their bags was groundless.'

During the operation, Zulu Company's fire positions found themselves perched on a series of knife-edge ridges to give fire support to Whisky Company as they cleared the valleys below. Supported by guns, mortars and US A-10 attack aircraft, as well as direct fire from medium and heavy machine guns, Major Phil Joyce's company staged an assault on a cave complex, which they found had been abandoned.

'If there were an enemy in the vicinity they would have taken note both of the significant combat power that we could wield and our enthusiasm to use it,' said one artillery observer. 'No chances were taken and the assaulting troops made full use of the firepower at their disposal. Watching from an anchor OP, it was a textbook application of force.'

Officially, it was said, 'Ptarmigan reinforced many themes and, although it allowed us the opportunity to practise our co-ordination with other elements of the Coalition Joint Force, it was also a very valuable opportunity to run through internal procedures, skills and drills.'

During their sweep they captured communication equipment, documents, weapons and ammunition. During these operations gunners from 7 (Sphinx) Battery of 29 Commando Regiment RA fired more than 120 shells from their 105mm light guns. According to Captain Bryant, although coalition forces had previously cleared the area, there was a real threat that al-Qaeda and Taliban forces had remained dug in amid the numerous caves and bunker complexes. Those on a ridgeline called the 'Whale' had previously been at the centre of heavy fighting during Operation Anaconda. After five days, 45 Commando Group returned safely to Bagram.

Following the success of Ptarmigan, 45 Commando switched their effort into a longer operation, called Operation Snipe, in late April. This was a 16-day, thousand-man search-and-clear mission in a remote and uncharted mountain region not previously visited by the coalition forces, and thought to have been a base for the Taliban and al-Qaeda. Their task was to make the area safe for humanitarian operations. Chinook helicopters of the RAF's 27 Squadron carried the Marines to the extreme south-east corner of Afghanistan, where they found themselves exploring what one Marine called 'the dusty tracks and detritus of a failed Soviet venture of not long ago'.

With all forces now in the theatre, Air Defence Troop managed to get in on the action as the Forward Operating Base (FOB) protection party, with Major 'Lucky' Green in command.

'During this period, they provided camel-herding parties and a tripwire display team, head by Marine "Crabstick" Rossiter,' said Captain Stew Tulloch. 'Lucky's usual reporting, late at night, on the Force Command Net began with the phrase, "Hello, Zero. This is P44. We are under attack." He normally forgot to mention that the rockets were landing nearly two kilometres [1.25 miles] away.'

Y Troop were then ensconced in an American Special Forces safe house in the main town of the area of operation, where it quickly became apparent that, if they wanted to blend in, they would have to become ZZ Top lookalikes and change their names to Randy or Jimbo.

'This area can only be described as grim,' said Tulloch. 'Local pastimes include drive-by shootings and launching 107mm rocket attacks on a weekly basis. According to locals, however, these were not attacks, but wedding celebrations by guests who just happen to bring heavy ordnance to help the lucky couple celebrate their nuptials.'

Y Troop was tasked to provide Radio Reconnaissance Teams to support both 45 Commando and the Brigade Reconnaissance (or 'Recce') Force (BRF) throughout the entire operation. This meant that their numbers had to be bolstered by ranks from the UK. Three hapless security troop members were sent to become communication technicians overnight, or so they thought. They were soon bamboozled with the arcane jargon of 'spinning and grinning' in the 'Sigint kitchen'. They found that their first training in the relaxed world of electronic warfare involved being shown how to turn a light switch on and off, so the communication technicians could get their heads down. Later they discovered that their true role was to be as human pack animals when the radio reconnaissance teams went out into the field.

While Operation Snipe was in full swing, the rains came. 'Not so much as an extra egg cup full of rain was necessary for a re-enactment of the Somme,' said one veteran, 'and it became common practice to attempt to elevate all possessions above the rising tide when the rain sentry called "storm ahoy!"'

(The regimental sergeant major maintained that Operation Snipe should have lasted an extra day to allow the water level in his tent to go down enough so he could remove his flippers and snorkel. Nevertheless, between downpours there was bright sunshine and the BRF were the battalion declared sunbathing champions.

Yankee Company of 45 Commando had also been flown into Camp Gibraltar at Bagram for Operation Snipe. They were give a couple of weeks' acclimatisation before they were airlifted forward into the mountains. As they ran from their Chinooks, they cocked their weapons, scanned arcs and adopted firing positions. For the next two weeks, Yankee Company covered more ground on foot than any other company. Some time was spent picketing the high ground that often rose to over 3,000 metres (10,000 feet). Then they would switch to clearing low ground. In one operation, they cleared a valley 20 kilometres (12.5 miles) long. Sometimes they would find themselves scrambling through narrow ravines. At others, they would be strolling through villages on the wide flood plain.

The culmination of Operation Snipe came when the BRF discovered 20 to 30 truckloads of munitions hidden in four caves in a remote valley. There were more than a hundred mortars of various calibres, more than a hundred recoilless anti-tank guns, several hundred RPGs, two hundred anti-personnel mines, hundreds of artillery rounds and rockets, and countless small-arms and light anti-aircraft ammunition. The ammunition had not been stored well and was thought to be too unstable to remove from the cave complex, so it was destroyed in place. Yankee Company provided a cordon while the engineers moved in to carry out what was thought to be the largest controlled explosion since World War Two. The blast was so large that the topography of the area was substantially altered.

Although, again, no contact was made with the enemy, Second Lieutenant Waite of Whisky Company, 45

Commando, answered what he called the 'armchair critics at home who decried our efforts' in Operation Snipe.

'Snipe was not as bloody as they may have liked,' he said, 'but it did allow us to dominate some very hostile terrain. It therefore meant that we denied the enemy freedom of movement in an area known to have been use by them in the past, preventing a resurgence of al-Qaeda and the Taliban in what had been their heartland. It was also a good chance to test our soldiering, fitness and command and control.'

A spokesman added, 'That we didn't kill any of the bad guys was, and is, a source of disappointment for the Marines. It is partly ameliorated by the impact on them of live operations in a challenging and very hostile environment, and the opportunity to see at first hand how the enemy had done his business in the past.'

The operation ended as suddenly as it began and 45 Commando were withdrawn to Bagram, tired, bearded and in much need of some fresh food. At Bagram, the chefs worked tirelessly in temperatures of up to 65°C (150°F), attracting other coalition troops to what was said to be the best food on the base. But Marines preferred to gorge themselves with American junk food, particularly Spunkmeyer's muffins and Pop Tarts. They would 'power-bronze' on the part of Camp Gibraltar that looked like a beach – minus the sea and bikini-clad women – covering themselves with animal fat and adjusting their shorts when the sun was hottest.

'It was pleasing to see the dedication of the lads in rehearsing for their leave,' said Waite.

The quality of life at Camp Gibraltar was markedly improved by the construction of a TV room with a DVD player and makeshift gymnasium. Although scantly furnished, the gym offered the Marines the opportunity to throw heavy weights around and get 'beach fit'. Meanwhile, the gunners integrated their Mamba artillery-locating radars into the system defending the airfield to provide vital data on any indirect fire attack. The system was coupled to a battery of guns ready to provide immediate counter-battery fire if they came under attack. Another Mamba outfit was deployed in Kabul to protect the ISAF.

The promise to provide power to all the tents was not fulfilled, nor did the mobile shower block for the accommodation site known as the Hacienda materialise, although this did not detract too much from daily life. Generators began to provide power for some tents and, eventually, a steady supply of shower bags ensured a decent shower for all – or at least for those who had not already discovered the American shower block. There were fears that being too long in camp would make the Marines stale and remove some of the focus they had built up in the field, so the planners got to work on Operation Buzzard.

After Ptarmigan and Snipe, it became clear that a different approach was needed. The sweep and block operations that had been conducted so far had not brought the troops into contact with the enemy. In Buzzard the plan was to conduct a classic counter-insurgency operation to move further to the south in an area known as the Khowst Salient, close to the border with Pakistan. But before Buzzard began, an opportunity for action presented itself closer to home.

On 16 May Captain Stringer of Yankee Company was relaxing in his tent at Camp Gibraltar when a runner stormed in. He told the captain that an Australian Special

Air Service patrol had made contact with the enemy in the mountains of Paktia Province. Apparently, the Aussies had been engaged by another heavily armed 'wedding party' – complete with RPGs and fixed Soviet DShK (Dushka) 12.7mm heavy machine-gun positions – who seemed intent on holding their wedding celebrations on the Aussies' turf. There was a lengthy firefight and air strikes were called in, inflicting casualties on the enemy. The quick-reaction force had been deployed to chase them, on what was known as Operation Condor, but they needed 45 Commando as reinforcements. As soon as the Marines heard that the Australians had had a contact in their area of operations, their fighting spirit came flooding back. This was the news they had been waiting for. Six hours later three companies were on the ground, yomping towards the contact area.

'We were all glad that the Australians have been able to extract themselves without incurring casualties,' said Lieutenant Waite, 'and we all hoped that we could catch those responsible for the contact. Unfortunately for us, this opportunity came amidst a mysterious outbreak of the dreaded lurgy.'

A number of commandos had been admitted to 34 Field Hospital with some very serious symptoms, in the form of vomiting and diarrhoea. This started off as a small-scale localised event, but soon spread. Some fell so ill that they had to be evacuated back to the UK.

'This impinged on our deployment into the field as a case occurred in one of our tents only a couple of hours before the helicopters were due to take off,' said Waite. 'Tragically, this included my own radio operator, which led to a panic search for a new "wets monkey".'

More than 50 men were packed into each helicopter as they set off. When they reached the landing zone and the ramp lowered, they expected to meet the withering rate of fire witnessed in the opening sequence of *Saving Private Ryan* [Steven Spielberg, 1998]. But the valley they set down in, though hot and dusty, was free of the enemy.

'We were given the relatively simple task of yomping two kilometres [1.25 miles] to a harbour for the night,' Waite said. 'Having yomped over very steep terrain on previous operations, this might have seemed an easy prospect, but the heat made dehydration a real concern. The lower altitude and the onset of summer made this operation a lot hotter than the previous outings.'

By 18 May, all four companies of 45 Commando of the Royal Marines were in position, along with their supporting Royal Artillery battery, flown forward by RAF and US Army helicopters. They then proceeded to sweep the area around the location of the terrorist attack. But again it was now clear of enemy presence. Munitions were discovered and disposed of. Sergeant John Simpkins of Yankee Company recce team spotted what he thought was an enemy hilltop position in the distance. A dismounted night attack was planned, but it turned out that the 'enemy' were in fact local forces involved in a dispute with a neighbouring village, who had mistakenly fired on the Aussies.

Yankee Company spent the next week securing the area with a number of challenging yomps up precipitous valleys. This was made all the more difficult as they had carried only the equipment necessary for a 48 hour deployment.

Although the Marines did not encounter the enemy, the operation was judged a success as the Australians encountered no further opposition.

'It's amazing the effect 500 commandos can have on local attitudes,' said Lieutenant Waite.

In one village, the Marines detained a man suspected of being an al-Qaeda/Taliban sympathiser who had been turned in by his own mother. They also discovered and destroyed a considerable amount of ammunition, though the Marines who found it were rewarded with a dose of scabies for their trouble.

Operation Condor – the action in support of the Aussies – delayed the start of Operation Buzzard for a few days. When the operation got under way, the Marines found themselves deployed on the flat plain and low foothills to the south and east of the town of Khowst, an area not visited by Coalition troops before, in searing heat.

The aim of the 29-day operation was to prevent the members of al-Qaeda and the Taliban who had sought refuge in Pakistan returning, and leave the Pakistani authorities to deal with them. Whisky Company were the close-combat company and took a one-hour trip forward by helicopter. This left them with a long walk from the landing zone to their objective. The stand-off companies X-ray and Zulu went in by vehicle for the first time in Operation Jacana. The journey took the heavily armed convoy two days.

'For this last op, we climbed into our vehicles,' said Lieutenant Colonel Chicken, commanding officer of 45 Commando Group. 'It was an impressive sight to see two company groups hit the road for its trip south. Anyone wanting a fight would have got it – in spades – from the motley assembly of combat power that flooded the area.'

During the initial phase of Buzzard, Afghans in a vehicle engaged a patrol under Sergeant Mick McCarthy.

'Apparently they were on their way to another wedding,' said Captain Tulloch. 'Although under effective fire, it was allegedly only when Mick McCarthy saw a Rangers scarf waving out of the vehicle's window did he order his patrol to return fire.'

Corporal Matt 'Lucky Shot' Hughes placed an M203 40mm round through one of the car windows. A second vehicle approached waving a white flag, so the Marines ceased fire, allowing them to recover the casualties. McCarthy's patrol were unscathed and were taken back to Bagram for debriefing.

Next, the Marines were deployed to conduct intelligence and hearts-and-minds operations in villages close to the Pakistani border. They then had to yomp through the mountains to Zhawar Killi. A cave complex had been constructed by the Mujahideen at Zhawar Killi during the Soviet occupation. It was an impressive feat of engineering, extending over some 30 square kilometres (11.6 square miles) and including tunnels over a kilometre (0.6 mile) long. These had been hardened to resist bombing, with electricity and plumbing built in.

'Small wonder that the Russians captured the area for only a few hours in three attempts and were unable to prevent their continuous use by the Mujahideen,' said Lieutenant Waite.

The Marines' task was to find out whether the caves were still being used by al-Qaeda and the Taliban, recce their full extent and destroy selected facilities that might prove useful to the enemy. The caves proved to be unoccupied and, once again, there was no contact with the enemy. But a lot of useful intelligence was gathered. The engineers duly blew up a number caves, along with large quantities of hidden ammunition, and 45 Commando's presence denied the enemy freedom of action in the vicinity.

A year later, Marine Liam Armstrong discovered that he had won the Military Cross during the operation. As part of Zulu Company, he had been conducting vehicle patrols when his troop came across a building that aroused their suspicions. As the patrol halted, the local people around the building ran inside and locked the doors. Armstrong and two other men tried to kick the door in but failed. Then he and Marine McCann pulled down a 1.8-metre (6-foot) block wall, making a gap big enough to squeeze through. Once inside, they began to clear the house.

Having cleared the adjacent rooms, they moved on to the main part of the compound, where they found a cache of weapons and ammunition, weighing 45 tonnes in all. In this main area, Armstrong was confronted by nine armed men. He forced the men to surrender, thereby protecting the rest of the patrol, who followed them into the building.

'It has been unbelievable to receive such a high accolade, as I just went out to Afghanistan to do my job,' said Armstrong of his award. 'I can't really put into words how happy I am at the moment. I definitely feel this award is for everybody in Z Company who were there at the time, because everyone worked just a hard as I did and should be recognised equally for their contribution.'

Marine Irvine from the Mortar Troop was also commended after he managed to dissuade a local militiaman from using his light machine gun for crowd control. But, again, there was no serious contact with the enemy.

'If there wasn't any opposition,' said Lieutenant Colonel Chicken, 'it wasn't for lack of our searching for it. We were well known across the areas where we operated, so much so in the last operation that we were received in much the same way as the victorious allies were in the Europe of 1944. Cries of "How are you?" from across the age range of the local population accompanied our passage. We'll probably learn subsequently that this, in

Pashto, means "sod off" or some such. Countless numbers of children were bombarded with boiled sweets and there is probably a generation of Pashtuns who, like us, cannot abide treacle duff.'

Using their helicopters, Whisky Company went on to conduct snap searches of suspect vehicles, a technique perfected in Northern Ireland involving what were known as 'eagle' vehicle checkpoints (VCPs).

Yankee Company also went out searching for caves and providing a cordon when the EOD teams blew them up, denying them to the enemy for future use. During this operation the Marines had a chance to get to know the local people. The Pashtuns, they found, though extremely poor, were friendly, cheerful and generous. Y Company also had an opportunity to play cricket on a rather suspect wicket and sample various local culinary delights.

'Operation Jacana was a fascinating tour,' said Captain Stringer of Y Company. 'Although it has been frustrating not having had contact with the enemy, every man in the company has learned a lot. After all, we had now done it for real – expeditionary campaigning in the mountains and wadis of Afghanistan.'

The operation was supported by the Commando Logistics Regiment, whose equipment-support elements were deployed in vehicles along the Afghanistan–Pakistan border. They also found the local Afghans very friendly, pointing out possible dangers and offering to put them up. To supply the forward troops with stores and ammunition, the Fuel and General Transport Troop made countless trips to Kabul and back. During Operation Snipe, they also carried ammunition from the FOB to 45 Commando and the guns of 27 Commando, as well as fuel for the RAF. One convoy narrowly missed a rocket attack, when Afghan forces discovered rockets trained on the FOB. Another cause for concern was the state of the ageing vehicles, and most drivers found themselves being given a practical course on vehicle repair.

On 20 March 2003, the eyes of the world turned to Iraq, but operations against insurgents in Afghanistan continued. While war in the Gulf was reignited, 126 more British soldiers were sent to support the ISAF on Operation Fingal, designed to bring law and order to Kabul. Nearly half of them were Territorial Army soldiers from the Royal Rifle Volunteers and the East of England Regiment reinforcing A (Lincolnshire) Company of the 2nd Battalion of the Royal Anglian Regiment.

The TA troops were initially marked down for the monotony of guard duty, but the company commander, Major Simon Etherington – realising the quality of the men he had been assigned – decided to integrate them into all aspects of the operation. They were sent out on foot patrol in Kabul and provided personnel for escort duties and the quick-reaction force when things hotted up.

Platoon commander Lieutenant Xavier Griffin of A (Royal Green Jackets) Company, a doctor in the Accident and Emergency Department at Oxford's John Radcliffe Hospital, said, 'This is a fantastic opportunity for these guys. They'll take a wealth of experience back with them, which can be passed on to the rest of the battalion.'

And they were close to the action. At around 11 pm on 13 April 2003, Camp Souter, the British Army HQ and home to the British contingent, was shaken by two massive explosions. Afghan insurgents had detonated a remotely controlled bomb as the ISAF convoy passed by on the main Kabul–Jalalabad road about a mile from the camp gates. One vehicle was bringing a Royal Air Force crew in from the airport. Another blast shook the camp seconds later. The RAF crew were shaken but, miraculously, unhurt. The convoy sped on to the camp, where sirens were wailing. Soldiers who had been sauntering back to their rooms from the shower block raced for their weapons, helmets and body armour. The numbers at muster points swelled and the quick-reaction force was swiftly on the scene of the incident.

'It goes to show the worth of having experienced British troops on the ground,' said Captain John Leevers, duty operations officer of A Company of the Royal Green Jackets. 'Everyone knew where to go and what to do. All their training paid off.'

CHAPTER 3

UNDER SCUDS
IN THE GULF

In the build-up to the second Gulf War in 2003, the scale and pace of the deployment of men, machines and *matériel* to Kuwait from Germany stretched the British Army's logisticians to its limits. Within just a few weeks, an entire armoured division with its support had to be shipped some 12,900 kilometres (8,000 miles). Twenty-three trains were needed to shift the force to the port of Emden, in the largest move in Germany since the first Gulf War in 1991. There, specialists from 623 Vehicle Troop of 6 Supply Regiment of the Royal Logistic Corps (RLC) loaded 1,029 armoured and 2,926 wheeled vehicles, as well as 215 pieces of engineering and specialist kit, onto 19 ships, which then sailed from Germany to the Gulf. More than a hundred people alone were employed upgrading the armour of the fleet of Warrior armoured personnel carriers and painting them in desert camouflage.

As the last vessel packed with armour, vehicles and equipment sailed out of Emden, RAF and civilian charter aircraft began flying logistics personnel from Hanover to meet the ships when they docked in Kuwait. Up to 900 soldiers were flown out per day, ready for Operation Telic, as the British called Operation Iraqi Freedom. (Unlike the Americans, the British do not give their operations descriptive code names, reasoning that it rather defeats the object.)

Meanwhile, logisticians at Marchwood Military Port near Southampton put in almost twenty thousand man-hours in a 40-day period at the height of the movement of vehicles, stores and ammunition to the Gulf. The RLC had to handle more than three thousand deliveries by truck and six trainloads of freight. The soldiers loaded 4,350 vehicles, ranging from armoured personnel carriers and reconnaissance to Land Rovers, plus 2,400 trailers and 1,700 containers, onto 32 ships dispatched from Marchwood, and another eight from Southampton. In addition, they carried 3,000 tonnes of ammunition and 55,000 tonnes of freight, including 4,800 items of cargo from bridges to helicopters. Then a regiment of Territorial Army soldiers had to be sent to the Gulf to meet them at the dockside.

By early March 2003, the Royal Marines' Commando Logistic Regiment had to move from Camp Gibraltar to Tactical Assembly Area (TAA) Viking in Kuwait. Their job was to supply all UK land forces during the early stages of the deployment. The forward recce team consisted of B Echelon's Company Sergeant Major Mark Wicks and the Motor Transport Team's Sergeant Major Andy Coventry. They were getting ready to receive the rest of the Echelon in the designated area of the desert when they were suddenly engulfed in a sandstorm, which they compared to a Norwegian whiteout. At this point, the Echelon arrived and a night of chaos began. But, being typical Bootnecks, they managed to get themselves established by first light, though they suffered a 'severe sand-blasting', according to Sergeant Bri Rosary.

TAA Viking was some 12 kilometres (7 miles) south of the border with Iraq, close enough to be at risk from an NBC attack by Iraqi Scud-B, Frog 7 and 122mm Multi-Rocket Launch Missiles, as well as an array of Iraqi artillery. That evening, Scuds and Seersucker/Silkworm missiles started heading their way, giving the squadron live practice of getting their NBC gear on and into the trenches as quickly as possible. Nevertheless, morale remained high and even the notoriously dour garrison quartermaster sergeant, Colour Sergeant George Fowler, was seen with a smile on his face.

Once the invasion of Iraq was given the green light, the Communications Squadron joined them from 45 Commando at Camp Rhino.

'Camp Rhino was home to the circus,' said Warrant Officer Second Class Cluetts. 'We call the Brigade Command "Post Billy Smart's". It's because it's a very big tent and it's full of clowns – so one of the Marines told me.'

Cluetts was not pleased with the Communication Squadron's new posting. 'It was strange being within artillery range of the enemy,' he said. 'What was more uncomfortable was the fact that throughout the intelligence briefings we were told that the only thing, apart from the smoking barrel, in which the Iraqis compared with or bettered our weapons specs was their artillery. So the phrase "dig deep" really hit home. Scud alerts became second nature and I had my NBC suit on for more time during this op than during my previous 23 years' service.'

Vital to the success of the invasion of Iraq was the Royal Marines' UK Landing Force Command Support Group.

But before departing for Christmas leave the ops officer of the group had told his men, 'No matter what happens, we will deploy to Norway after leave.' It was only when they got back from leave that the Brigade Recce Force were told of their new destination: they were going to the Gulf as part of Operation Telic.

The Naval Task Group – including elements of the Brigade Patrol Troop (BPT), 148 Battery and the Tactical Air Control Party – were sent to Cyprus to conduct low-level training before joining 40 Commando on HMS *Ocean*.

'When we eventually embarked on HMS *Ocean* with the remainder of the Task Group and headed for the Persian Gulf, we found ourselves within Command Company as attached ranks to Recce Troops,' said Sergeant 'Gaz' Veacock of the BPT. 'For seven weeks we prepared ourselves for the eventual assault on the Al Faw peninsula. Overall, this was an exceptional period with a well-structured programme, followed by countless rehearsals before we disembarked onto Kuwaiti soil for some final battle preparations.'

Then, from Plymouth, the main body of the Royal Marines moved out to Kuwait and took up residence in the newly constructed Camp Coyote, though there were still plenty of trenches to dig and sandbags to fill. This large patch of dust doubled as a training ground, where they did weapons training under Sergeant Joe Gillespie, along with practising vehicle recognition and doing quad-bike courses. The NBC drills were augmented with Scud alerts – mostly false – and warnings of suspected suicide-bomber attacks.

'Even someone shouting "Gaz" – misinterpreted as "gas" – would have everyone fully gas-masked up,' said Veacock. 'And Marine Luke Coleman, who unfortunately had his respirator proffed [stolen] prior to an NBC warning, made a good effort on becoming the BRF's [Brigade Reconnaissance Force's] human budgie.'

NBC and Scud attacks were not the only dangers that awaited British soldiers in the Gulf. There were flesh-eating spiders, packs of rabid wild dogs, venomous snakes, and scorpions that can cause paralysis with a single flick of their tails.

The worst of the lot in the eyes of the squaddies was the camel spider, which is unique to the Arabia desert. Many had first encountered these eight-legged carnivores during Exercise Saif Sareea in Oman two years earlier. The palm-sized arachnid is falsely reputed to inject an anaesthetic before feasting on its numb – often sleeping but still living – victim. According to Warrant Officer Second Class Adrian 'Hippo' Humphries of 1 Close Support Medical Regiment, a member of the Army's Environmental Health Team in Kuwait, the camel spider was responsible for numerous cautious glances around tented accommodation before the lights went out at night.

'There were lots of stories going around about a guy getting up in the morning to find no skin on his arm, and another waking up to discover that a spider had eaten his leg,' he said. 'Fortunately, they were just stories and an exaggeration of a very minor threat. Camel spiders, like most of the other nasties in the desert, will usually only bite you if you go out of your way to upset them. The worst case I've ever seen of a spider bite is when somebody lost a bit of flesh the size of a five-pence piece from their face while they slept, but it's amazing how word quickly gets round, and one bite victim miraculously becomes 50 overnight.'

As a medic, Humphries insisted that soldiers should be more wary of a far more familiar pest: the common fly. In the heat of the Gulf, flies breed quickly and lapses in the standards of hygiene, coupled with poor field skills, could put the British Army's most important asset – its soldiers – out of action.

'Flies can go from being eggs to egg-laying in a week, so it's easy to see how a camp could quickly became infested if rubbish, waste water and the like are not disposed of properly,' he said. 'Flies are directly linked with the spread of gastric illnesses such as diarrhoea and vomiting, and once this begins it can be difficult to snuff out. Thankfully, this message was taken on early by soldiers arriving in the field, and, because we had environmental teams already on the ground, we were able to ensure the right ethos. Troops in the Gulf have quickly got into the habit of looking after themselves in the right way.'

Other dangers included the extremely venomous horned vipers that hide under the sand in the heat of the day, scorpions that lurk in the sand and inflict a lethal sting, and sandflies that suck blood and cause leishmaniasis.

Some of the first men deployed in the Gulf were environmental health officers, who arrived in Kuwait in January 2003 to assess the potential health hazards troops would face north of the border.

'The onward threats in Iraq we have been particularly concerned with are in the field of environmental industrial hazards,' Major James Fletcher, HQ 1 (UK) Armoured Division's staff officer 2, Medical Intelligence and Environmental Health Officer. 'The southern oilfields, gas and oil separation plants and petrochemical industries present a number of chemical threats. If they take a hit we could end up with oil heads on fire and a lot of smoke in the air, which is why soldiers have already been provided with two dust masks each.'

Also on its way to the Gulf was 9 Assault Squadron of the Royal Marines, who were specialists in amphibious landings. In mid-January HMS *Ocean* began embarking elements of 40 Commando and 845 and 846 Naval Air Squadrons. Within 72 hours, 646 personnel, 22 aircraft, 40 vehicles, associated trailers and eight light guns were embarked, along with 24 low loaders of helicopter spares and ship stores for a six-month deployment. During the passage to the Mediterranean, the squadron began to work on the system to launch two company groups in an amphibious assault simultaneously. Arriving at Cyprus, the squadron began a period of six weeks of intensive practice that would see the ship run up more engine hours than in the whole of the previous year. They were to become the tactical control of 539 Assault Squadron, who trained beside them. Operation Telic was to be the first wartime operational fighting deployment for 539 Assault Squadron, which was formed in 1984. During the exercise, the Assault Supply Team under Colour Sergeant Nixon began practising offloads with the aim of becoming the most efficient flight deck team in the theatre.

After passing through Suez, the Red Sea, the Gulf of Aden and the Straits of Hormuz, 9 Assault Squadron began another exercise with 539 Assault Squadron off the United Arab Emirates, delivering most of 40 Commando from *Ocean* to their training areas. The highlight of the exercise, apparently, was the arrival of the landing craft LCVP N2 at the forward operating base that day at 03.00 hours, which was heralded by Marine Baker crying, 'Whoa, Mick!' This was followed by an almighty crash, though luckily there was no damage.

A2 Engineer Section on HMS *Ocean* came in for particular praise during the exercise. They worked around the clock on the craft, which had problems with reliability, notably with their hydraulic steering gear. Without Marine Engineering Mechanics Lamb and Taylor, who deployed with the boats, and the leadership of Chief Merrigan and Petty Officer Strowdger, it was said it was unlikely there would ever have been more than one working boat in the water.

Once in the northern Gulf, HMS *Ocean* provided a platform for 40 Commando and the Air Group to work from. The Commando Group went ashore for four days for mission rehearsals, before returning to *Ocean* to rest and reservice. Each offload provided another opportunity to get the boats in the water and practise navigation and drills. On 15 March, 40 Commando offloaded for a final time. With the Australians, 539 Assault Squadron and 9 Assault Squadron conducted an 11-hour operation over 27 kilometres (17 miles).

Once the various elements of 3 Commando Brigade had arrived in the theatre, operational command was transferred from the Commander-in-Chief of the Fleet to the Commander of 1 (UK) Armoured Division. At that point, 3 Commando Brigade RM took two additional elements under its command – the US Marine Corps' 15th Marine Expeditionary Unit and a squadron of light tanks from the Queen's Dragoon Guards (QDG). These were integrated into the brigade throughout the intensive training in Kuwait. Then the Brigade moved forward to assembly areas in the final days before 20 March 2003.

Although they had sailed into the theatre with the Amphibious Task Group, 40 Commando remained ashore, leaving only D Company aboard HMS *Ark Royal* in case poor weather prevented reinforcements flying in from Kuwait. The initial plan was to offload the QDG onto the

Al Faw peninsula – the Iraqi promontory nearest Kuwait – using US Marine Corps hovercraft, so the QDG also remained at sea aboard the USS *Rushmore*.

Although 45 Commando were omitted from 3 Commando Brigade's initial deployment in the Gulf, they supplied 34 individual reinforcements to other brigade units and a total of 395 men in company groups to Operation Telic – about 490 deployed on operations all told. Virtually all their light-wheeled vehicles and about three-quarters of their firepower was also sent to the Gulf.

In the build-up to the assault, 7 and 8 Batteries of 29 Commando Regiment of the Royal Artillery were joined by eight AS-90 self-propelled guns and a battery of American 155s to form an offensive support group OSG. This OSG moved forward from mainland Kuwait to Bubiyan Island, with a plain view across the Khawr Abd Allah – also known as the Khawz al-Arab – waterway to the Al Faw peninsula. There, on 18 March, they established gun lines to support 3 Commando Brigade in their assault on the southern part of the peninsula.

Not far away were Detachment 4 of Y Troop, who had been moved up to the demilitarised zone established between Kuwait and Iraq after the First Gulf War.

'Everyone settled quickly into the routine of "det life",' said Lance Corporal Harle. 'Apart from the frequent Scud and gas alerts, they were able to get on with the job of providing the brigade with position fixes for Iraqi forces.'

Y Troop were the UK Landing Force Command Support Group's electronic warfare unit, who provided intelligence and warning of enemy movements to the brigade.

'As an Arabic linguist stuck behind a desk for the last year,' said Lance Corporal Harle, 'the chance to go out to

Iraq to do the job in an entirely different environment was too good to miss.'

The 1st Battalion of the Royal Irish Regiment were with the Coalition forces massed at Fort Blair Mayne in northern Kuwait. Their commanding officer, Lieutenant Colonel Tim Collins, delivered a rousing speech that was said to be unscripted.

'We go to liberate, not to conquer,' he said. 'We will not fly our flags in their country. We are entering Iraq to free a people. The only flag which will be flown in that ancient land is their own. Show respect for them. Iraq is steeped in history. It is the site of the Garden of Eden, of the Great Flood and the birthplace of Abraham. Tread lightly there. You will see things that no man could pay to see and you will have to go a long way to find a more decent, generous and upright people than the Iraqis. You will be embarrassed by their hospitality, even though they have nothing... As for ourselves, let's bring everyone home and leave Iraq a better place for our having been there. Our business is now north.'

After that, the final preparations were made. All land troops about to cross Kuwait's northern border into Iraq were ordered to 'pack light' for the trip. They were stripped of mobile phones, wallets, passports, photographs and letters from home. The only personal items they were allowed to carry in their pockets and bergens were an identity card that bore a list of the laws of armed conflict and details of the Geneva Conventions, issued medicines and an emergency morphine injection.

'This sanitisation process was enforced by sergeant majors and platoon sergeants,' explained Major Andrew Taylor of the Royal Welch Fusiliers, a staff officer with 1 (UK) Armoured Division. 'Soldiers were cleansed of any personal information just in case the unthinkable happened and they became prisoners of war. Items such as personal letters can easily be exploited by interrogators. The mention of your wife or your child's name during an interview would come as a huge psychological blow and could cause someone to divulge more than the permitted big six – name, rank, number, date of birth, blood group and religion.'

He also pointed out that it was vital that mobile phones should not be carried. They could be tracked. Most store the last ten telephone numbers of received or dialled calls and people tend to keep their phone books stored on them.

'The last thing we want is for friends and family back home to receive a text message or telephone call saying their loved one has been captured,' he said.

CHAPTER 4
ASSAULT ON AL FAW

By 19 March, the Commando Logistics Regiment had ensured that all British land units were fully equipped for the operation. That evening, the second Gulf War began with an unsuccessful missile and air attack on a site believed to be occupied by Saddam Hussein. This was the first of a number of such attempted 'decapitation' or assassination strikes, aimed to kill Saddam and end the war.

Around 80 men of the Australian SAS were already on the ground to prevent missiles being fired from the 'Scud line' in the western Iraqi desert, where launchers had bombarded Israel from in the first Gulf War. They stayed in-country for 42 days, suffering no casualties but taking more than 2,000 Iraqi prisoners, including members of the elite Republican Guard and specially trained counter-Special Forces troops.

Two British soldiers from 216 Signal Squadron were among the first troops outside Special Forces to enter Iraq. Less than eight hours after the first shots of the conflict were fired, Corporal Russ Sharp and Signalman Dan

Seager joined an American armoured convoy and, to the accompaniment of heavy-artillery fire, headed north to the centre of Iraq's wealth, the Rumaylah oil fields. Their job was to set up a forward broadcast station for 16 Air Assault Brigade.

'We always knew that we would be among the first to cross the border,' Sharp said. 'But it still came as a bit of a shock when we received orders to move so soon after the American marines had entered Iraq. I'd be lying if I said I wasn't a little nervous and, when we were told we may encounter some resistance bypassed by the Americans, it certainly gave us plenty to think about.'

Signalman Seager said, 'There was artillery fire going over our heads in both directions, but I was too busy concentrating on the road to worry too much about anything else. We were travelling in darkness with no lights and the thick black smoke from burning oil made driving pretty difficult.'

Meanwhile, the British 3 Commando Brigade were sent on to seize the Al Faw peninsula at the mouth of the River Tigris. They were to seize intact the oil facilities there and provide a land flank to open the Khawz al-Arab waterway, the sea route to Umm Qasr, Iraq's only deep-water port. Then they were to take Umm Qasr itself, as it would be vital to supply the invasion force.

After days of bad weather, 40 Commando and the US Marines landed on the peninsula on the night of 20 March. But soon there were problems.

'The initial insertion phase went well enough,' said one Royal Marine, 'but when we landed that's when it went tits up, to put it bluntly. It was pitch black where we were, and, apart from some lights in the dim and distant, there was nothing to see. Some of the lads had NVGs [night-vision goggles], which is just as well, as they were the ones who spotted the fucking mines that were near us. The boss shouted for us not to move, as he wanted us to wait until first light, which made sense to me, as I couldn't see fuck all – and I'm sure he couldn't, either. Also, I don't like mines. I found a spot to lay up in, which was a beach with a small raised bit – the theory being it would give me some cover if we had contact – but if we were mortared, then I was going to get FUBARed [fucked up beyond all recognition]. For me it was the longest four hours of my life.'

Nevertheless, the Marines on the ground had a bit of a laugh – until they were ordered to be quiet, because they were on tactical duty.

'Picture the scene. Here we all are, sat put, on account of these mines – with helicopters whizzing over us all night long to the west, jets whizzing over us to the east – and this numpty wants us to be quiet. If the Iraqis didn't know we were here now they never would.'

The main body of 40 Commando were coming in on helicopters. Their job was to secure the oil facilities – the pipelines that took the oil out to the tanker-loading platforms 40 kilometres (25 miles) offshore in the Gulf and the all-important Manifold Metering Station (MMS) on the Al Faw peninsula. One of the coalition's main efforts was to keep the oil infrastructure undamaged, because it represented the nation's wealth. If it had been blown up, any new Iraqi regime would have found itself without the money it would need to reconstruct the war-damaged country. If well fires were started – as they were in the First Gulf War – they would slow the coalition's advance, and smoke and possible oil spillage would have caused an ecological disaster. So the oil facilities had to be taken intact.

'The operation sounded pretty simple on paper,' said Marine D Martin of Charlie Company. 'All we had to do was land a few helos – toppers with Bootnecks – right in the middle of the MMS. Easy peasy, apart from the enemy in company strength with armoured vehicles in positions around it.'

The task was to be carried out jointly with the US Navy SEALs, who had undergone specialist training to operate and shut down specific areas of the MMS. C Company had several objectives to clear and secure, including buildings and areas of land with the codenames 'Plymouth', 'Taunton' and 'Arbroath'. Each troop had its own objective. With satellite imagery and other intelligence they knew where every window and door of their designated building was, along with the enemy strengths and positions.

For weeks before the operation, Charlie Company had run through endless rehearsals in a remote desert area with imaginary buildings and models of the objectives they were to secure. As H-hour (the term for an appointed time for a military event, such as an attack) drew nearer, aerial photographs were scanned for the last time and final SOPs (Standard Operating Procedures) were talked through. Finally, after being sandblasted again at TAA Viking, they got the call.

'We heaved on our day sacks, weighed down with enough ammunition to sink a ship,' said Marine Martin. 'Plenty of jokes and maybe a bit of nervous laughter were exchanged as we stood ready to board the helos.'

A painful ride followed. Laden with kit and combat body armour, the men had very little room to move or stretch. Anti-aircraft fire or even a few stray AK-47 rounds were on everyone's mind as they flew into Iraqi airspace. The men were standing on the Chinook's ramp as it flew over the objective. Catching sight of the installation itself made all the rehearsals come vividly alive.

As the Chinook hit the ground with a thump, everyone felt a profound sense of relief. They disembarked quickly, as the pilot showed no sign of wanting to hang about, and set about their task.

'It was a bizarre feeling seeing the buildings and land we had studied in photographs and realising that we knew exactly where we were,' said Martin. Another Marine described the action as 'surreal'.

They made their way through ankle-deep mud to link up with the SEALs. Once their objective was secured they moved on to the first building, their eyes searching for snipers, mines and tripwires. None of them were prepared for the huge weight of fire that came from the US A-10 ground-attack aircraft and AC-130 gunships circling above, but the men of Charlie Company found it reassuring that friendly aircraft hammered anything that moved near their perimeter. Nevertheless, as the recce troop set down near the MMS, they found their mobile support group embroiled in a firefight close by.

The BBC's Asia correspondent at the time, Clive Myrie, came in with 40 Commando on a Chinook. He noted that the troops were silent for the 20 minute journey. Myrie, who was usually based in Singapore, remembered thinking, 'What the hell am I doing here? Have I gone crazy? We're flying low in order to sneak beneath Iraqi radar, making us sitting ducks for anyone with a decent rifle. And we're going to land right on top of our intended target, the main southern Iraqi oil installation on the Al Faw peninsula. We're not landing a few kilometres away so we can then advance towards it: we're actually going to land right on top of it! I must be crazy; we're *all* crazy!'

Military manuals called this method of attack a 'vertical envelopment manoeuvre'. It was high-risk strategy, especially if the enemy had anti-aircraft guns. What it had going for it was the element of surprise, and the way should have been clear. The US Navy SEALs had gone in an hour before to identify Iraqi troop positions and direct Coalition artillery and air attacks. The enemy should have been keeping their heads down, but the Chinook in front of Myrie's had come under attack as soon as it had landed. For ten to fifteen minutes, Myrie's helicopter had to hover above the landing zone while the Royal Marines already on the ground fought what turned out to be the first firefight of the war.

Tension mounted as Charlie Company approached the first building of Taunton. Six Troop were in the middle of a noisy contact not far away at Arbroath and enemy movement had been spotted in one of 7 Troop's buildings. Nobody knew what would be behind the door at Taunton when they kicked it open. Grenades were posted and the assault team swept through and secured the building, just as they had in rehearsals.

The raid was a huge success. Just five hours after H-hour, the area was secure and the oil facility intact. There had been no friendly casualties and a number of prisoners had been captured. However, the enemy threat still existed and C Company spent a sleepless night in their new defensive positions.

Despite marginal flying conditions, the initial waves landed on the three objectives as planned, but it quickly became evident that the enemy had greater numbers than expected. They would have to be dislodged before the Marines risked bringing in any more men by helicopter. It was then that they received news that the intended deployment by 42 Commando in a blocking position to prevent the Iraqis reinforcing had been delayed. This left the men of 40 Commando on the ground vulnerable. However, Delta Company on HMS *Ark Royal* were ready to ride to the rescue.

'All thoughts turned to my family and friends and what they would be feeling watching events unfold on the news,' said a Marine from D Company. 'I desperately tried to push these thoughts to the back of my mind. It was the same for everyone in Delta Company, from the most junior Marine, right up to the OC. Despite personal feelings, we had to focus on the job in hand. As we lined up in our chalks to board the helicopters, the tension and strain began to show, fuelled by not knowing what to expect when we got off at the MMS. Thankfully, everything went according to plan and in the early hours of the morning the MMS was secured.'

The next phase of the operation for Delta Company was an 'advance to contact' to the south of the MMS down three axes, clearing the area of enemy. Enemy numbers were not known, but there were confirmed reports of numerous enemy bunkers and a major military installation.

Throughout the night, there were a number of fierce, sporadic firefights with the enemy on the periphery of the three objectives, and it was not until well after first light that the immediate environs of the oil installation could be deemed secure.

That night, Corporal Peter Watts, section commander of the 40 Commando, Royal Marines' Manoeuvre Support Group (MSG), which went in with the first wave, won the Military Cross. His section were tasked with clearing and blocking the northern approach to the installation. Despite difficult terrain and the loss of expected US support, Watts led his men towards the enemy trenches, using textbook contact drills to win firefights with the enemy. According to the citation, his section was then selected to lead an assault on a well dug-in enemy force and, 'demonstrating great courage, little regard for his own safety and never shrinking from the action, he led from the front, generating sheer aggression and momentum that won the battle'.

Having taken the initial trenches, Watts immediately regrouped his section and began clearing further positions until they reached the inter-unit boundary. The magnitude of the enemy position they had attacked became apparent only at first light when 60 Iraqis from the depths of their defences surrendered, on top of the 25 captured in the action.

Alpha Company of 40 Commando had a long wait in northern Kuwait before they went in.

'The combination of Scud launches, the heat and an increasing anxiousness to get on the task led to a strange feeling around the camp,' said Second Lieutenant Buczkiewicz. 'We watched as the other companies began to file past our positions and out to the helos, counting down the minutes until it would be our turn.'

As Alpha Company sat waiting in the darkness, the timing of the operation began to slip. Word spread that Charlie Company and MSG were in contact with the enemy at the MMS. This upped the adrenalin level and, by the time Alpha Company's turn came, everyone was raring to go.

'After what seemed like an endless helicopter ride,' said Buczkiewicz, 'we landed at the MMS, only to discover that there had been a change of plan.'

Because of the delay of 42 Commando, they were unable to put out a screen to the north and Alpha Company found themselves protecting this flank. The three troops then moved to clear the area where the MSG had been in contact with the enemy the night before, but it soon became clear that the AC-130 Spectre gunships had done their work.

'All that was left to do was to take prisoners and pick up the pieces of bodies blown apart by the aerial bombardment,' said Buczkiewicz.

Bravo Company's task was to secure the Pennzoil and Quaker State pipelines, which run along the southeast coast of the Al Faw peninsula. They were augmented by the US Navy SEALs, engineers, forward observers, reconnaissance parties and other support groups – 144 men in all – who were landed by US MH-53 helicopters in two positions around the target area.

'Almost immediately, both locations were in contact and tracer rounds were filling the night sky,' said a Heavy-Machine-Gun Sergeant with B Company. 'The feelings that I had during the insertion, of apprehension and concern for the well-being of the men around me, were gone as the training and adrenalin took over. Each man knew his job and carried it out with the utmost professionalism and determination to succeed.'

The initial insertion onto the ground was well rehearsed. Despite resistance and counter-attacks, the mission was hugely successful.

Following B Company down 'Broadway' were the Signal Troop, whose job was to keep the channels of communication open with Commando Main.

'We felt extremely vulnerable as one of the unit's key communications assets,' said one of the signallers, 'knowing that if we were taken out the unit's comms could fail.'

Royal Engineers were also on hand, and Captain Pete Young of 1 Troop of the 59 Independent Commando Squadron of the RE was with 40 Commando Group when their Chinooks touched down on Al Faw.

'Industrial oil tanks could be faintly distinguished,' he said. 'To the south, a mortar line opened up and to the north the rattle of small arms, suppressing the enemy outside the compound, focused the mind.'

During the attack, the engineers were attached to fighting companies. Their initial tasks included blowing their way into buildings, breaching barbed wire and other obstacles with explosives such as Bangalore torpedoes, and supporting the infantry. 'Although the enemy had largely been neutralised by artillery bombardment and close air support synchronised with the landings,' according to Captain Young. Once the oil infrastructure was taken, again with no friendly casualties and the minimum loss of enemy life, the mission moved into the defensive phase. The engineers started clearing areas and vital routes of mines. Sappers also advised on sangar construction and set claymore mines. A water point was set up for the Field Surgical Group and obstacles were placed around it to restrict enemy access.

With the oil installation now in Coalition hands, control of the facility was handed to 17 members of the 27 strong 516 Specialist Team of the Royal Engineers (Bulk Petroleum) – known as 516 STRE(BP) – embedded with the combat teams of the 5th and 7th Regiments of the US Marine Corps, who arrived just hours after the assault troops. They had been on exercises with US Marines on sand models of the installations they planned to secure, and had followed the combat troops across the border on the night of 20 March. Their job was to shut down the key oil installations in southern Iraq. This was one of the most vital and, potentially, most hazardous operations of the war. Consequently, another two members of the team remained behind in Kuwait to provide backup if needed.

Oil experts had predicted that, if Iraq's petroleum infrastructure was not sabotaged, it could function unattended for up to two days. After that, storage facilities and pipelines would be overburdened and would begin to rupture at weak points. The mission of 516 STRE(BP) was to prevent this happening. EOD teams cleared predetermined routes before the 516 troops moved in to shut down pumps and turn valves to safe mode. Once they had closed down the pumping station at Al Faw, they followed the troops advancing into Az Zubayr and Rumaylah, and closed down the pumping stations and gas–oil-separation plants (GOSPs) there. In addition to their primary task, the specialists shut down a well-head in the southern Rumaylah oilfields and isolated a burst pipeline that was flooding a vital supply route with crude oil. Five days after the operation began, the bulk petroleum team were back in Kuwait, their mission completed. The most important oilfields had been captured and shut down with minimal damage.

By first light on 21 March, the Royal Marines had fanned out across the area, encountering fresh resistance. There were around 1300 Iraqi troops in the area, against some 900 British commandos. On such a mission, military commanders like to outnumber the defenders by three to one. In this case, the odds were not in their favour. However, it soon became clear that the Iraqis were ill-equipped and poorly trained. They were no match for the elite of the Royal Marines.

In the early-morning light, the BBC's Clive Myrie could

see a bunker just 30 metres (33 yards) from where his Chinook had landed. It had been shot to pieces. A dead Iraqi soldier lay nearby in a pool of blood. At the tiny observation post alongside, the light was still on. There was food and coffee on table. Clearly, the element of surprise had worked in the Coalition's favour.

Another bunker further away was still manned. A psyops – psychological operations – team were called in. They carried a tape recorder and speaker in backpacks. This boomed out in Arabic, 'You're surrounded. Surrender. You won't be harmed.' But the Iraqi defenders took no notice and fired back. The bunker was mortared and shelled. When the British finally went forward, at least six Iraqis were dead. Another lay groaning on the ground. His right arm had been pretty much shot off and he had shrapnel wounds in his chest and legs. Royal Marine medics rushed forward to try to save him. They inserted a drip to keep him hydrated and tried to staunch the bleeding. An Iraqi bystander looked on, puzzled. Just a few minutes before, the Marines had been trying to kill this man. Now they were trying to save his life. As it turned out, he died later.

The Iraqis in other bunker positions saw what had happened and decided it was not worth fighting any more. They began to come out with their hands up or waving white T-shirts and surrendered to the Marines, who made them lie on the ground until they had been searched in case there were suicide bombers among them. The fighting in this little part of Iraq was over for now. But there was plenty more to come.

After seven weeks kicking his heels in the deserts of Kuwait, the invasion had come not a moment too soon for Corporal Sheraton of 42 Commando, who was in the next wave. In the dead of night on 20 March, Juliet Company had moved to the helicopter landing site adjacent to its dusty desert camp, which was already heaving with American CH-46s, CH-53s, Hueys and Cobra gunships. As H-hour approached, everything seemed to be going according to plan and Sergeant Briggs of UMST, the training unit attached to 42 Commando's Lima Company, found the buzz of anticipation there almost unbearable. After a short wait, a guide led Corporal Sheraton and the rest of 3 Troop to a CH-53. Inside, under the dim green light, each man checked his equipment. The light went off and the huge rotor started to turn. The aircraft shuddered, but did not lift off. After what seemed like an age, the light came back on and the boss signalled that the mission had been aborted.

'Nobody believed it,' said Sheraton. 'Months of training and waiting seemed wasted just minutes from H-hour.'

The engines shut down and the troop got out. An American pilot then informed them that one of the smaller CH-46 helicopters had crashed. L-hour, the time when the first elements were to have landed on the Al Faw peninsula, had been set for 23.50 Zulu (local) time. However, within eleven minutes of the first wave's landing, one US Marine Corps (USMC) Sea Knight helicopter crashed over northern Kuwait, killing all four of its USMC aircrew and its eight 42 Commando Group passengers – the HQ element of 3 Commando Brigade Reconnaissance Force.

'Nobody said a word initially,' said Corporal Sheraton. 'We all had friends onboard the other helicopters. All thoughts of the mission abort had been temporarily suspended as we contemplated the tragedy and made our way back to the admin area.'

Few in the unit slept that night.

'Of the many enduring memories of success and triumph, the loss of our eight brothers-in-arms will be something none of us will ever forget,' said Lieutenant Roger Green of 42 Commando. 'It was undoubtedly the point where the whole focus of the Commando changed. This was for real and no longer an exercise.'

There followed a tense eight-hour delay while plans for the helicopter lift were hastily rewritten. At first light the next morning, the waiting Commandos got news that the RAF were supplying eight Chinooks for the insertion on Al Faw peninsula. At 08.00 Zulu, the operation was relaunched. The Marines were now raring to go.

'The events of the previous night meant that everyone of us was up for a fight,' said Corporal Sheraton, who admitted he was not the hardest man in 3 Commando Brigade, but liked to think of himself in the top five.

They were then picked up by RAF Chinooks and flown across the Iraqi border, not under the cover of darkness as originally planned, but in broad daylight.

'Although we had been told that the landing zones had been secured, there were butterflies in everyone's stomach,' said Briggs. 'But soon the Chinooks touched down on enemy soil and the campaign to liberate Iraq was well and truly under way.'

Following the loss of the Sea King and BRF's HQ element, the original landing site became untenable. Captain Christopher Haw, who had now assumed command, was forced to find an alternative. This led to confusion on the ground, made worse by the boggy terrain, the threat of enemy action and limited visibility due to dust and the smoke. After quickly establishing control of the situation, Haw won the MC for his actions at the landing site.

The 3 Troop was divided. Corporal Sheraton and his section were flown in separately – he was to lead his men to a predetermined troop RV (rendezvous). From the landing site, they had to trudge through knee-deep mud, carrying what felt like a house on their backs. They moved to the co-ordination point for their pre-arranged linkup with 40 Commando, who had flown in the previous night with the US Navy SEALs. There, they relieved themselves of their bergens and cleared and secured the surrounding area. On the way, they took 20 or so prisoners and captured a wide variety of enemy weapons.

J Company engaged the enemy a couple of times as it moved into its blocking position, and the rear area, where the medics had set up the regimental aid post, came under artillery fire. Nevertheless, the blocking positions were complete by midnight on 21 March. A number of further minor contacts occurred over the next 48 hours, but the block was not penetrated, allowing 40 Commando Group the freedom to secure the rest of Al Faw peninsula and its important oil infrastructure. Several enemy soldiers were killed and some 40 prisoners of war were taken.

The Marines of 3 Troop also managed to seize what they considered a valuable military asset – transport. A Nissan Sunny may not be standard issue in the British Armed Forces, but it proved useful for carrying the kit. However, in Corporal Sheraton's opinion, the owner's taste in music left something to be desired.

Later, they commandeered an Iraqi four-tonne truck to carry the lads, though one of them broke his leg jumping out of it. This was the only casualty Corporal Sheraton's unit were to suffer during their time on the Al Faw peninsula.

Major Harry Taylor of the Royal Marine Reserve (RMR) was also with J Company. In mid-January he had received a phone call from the commanding officer of the Royal Marines in London telling him to pack his bergen and report to Chilwell. He was on his way to Kuwait as part of Operation Telic. He was one of the 130 Royal Marine Reservists to be mobilised. When he arrived in Kuwait on 7 February, he joined 3 Commando Brigade's headquarters, before being appointed commanding officer of psyops with 42 Commando.

Following 40 Commando's initial assault on 20 March and the CH-46 crash, the cancelled US helicopter lift and a sleepless night, Taylor found himself being airlifted into Al Faw on board an RAF Puma with four pairs of snipers, including Colour Sergeant 'Ginge' Davidson of the Manchester Detachment of the RMR.

'Like most, I was somewhat apprehensive at flying into enemy territory in broad daylight, especially in the knowledge that 40 Commando was still involved in firefights,' said Taylor. 'Ginge, as ever, remained focused on the task at hand: "Let's just get on the ground and get on with it" was his sage advice.'

After wading through mud on their route from the landing site and yomping to their vehicles, Taylor and Marine Andy Thompson of the Portsmouth Detachment teamed up with elements of J Company to deploy tactical loudspeakers – or 'battlefield boogie boxes', as the men call them – on the main supply route to the north-west of Al Faw. Given the shortage of interpreters and the Marines' limited knowledge of Arabic, playing tapes through these systems allowed some rudimentary communication with the enemy and civilians alike.

Taylor and Thompson followed J Company through their various firefights and the ineffectual bombardment by the Iraqis until they established their blocking position between 40 Commando and the enemy. The psyops team then spent another sleepless night manning the loudspeakers, with the help of Sergeant Ali MacPherson of the Inverness Detachment, who had dug in along the roadside. That night they were treated to a fireworks display by US Cobra gunships and an A-10, which, having made a kill, barrel-rolled into the night sky popping flares and showboating for the boys on the ground.

Briggs also found the initial yomp over soft ground slow going. The lads in the UMST were carrying bergens weighing over 90 kilos (200 pounds). Inside were weapons, ammunition, food and water – and definitely no luxuries. The rest of the ammunition was carried on quad bikes. A number of times, both men and machines got bogged down in thick mud.

They had the task of blocking two main supply routes and stopping anyone going in or out of Al Faw town. To do this the troop was split in half, one half under Briggs, the other under Sergeant Farimond, who had been sent to the Gulf ostensibly to teach AFV (armoured fighting vehicles).

As they moved to the first blocking point, they dropped a detachment off with one of L Company's machine gun sections to give covering fire for their move. The one-mile yomp into position took an hour and 15 minutes. Then, as they began digging in, they heard the machine gunners engage the enemy.

'This was our first action of the campaign,' said Sergeant Briggs, 'and it gave a tingle down the spine that cannot be easily described.'

The reserve brought their weapons system onto the target and a heavy rate of fire poured down on the enemy. Later, they found out that they had destroyed four D30 former Soviet 122mm field howitzers, one heavy machine gun position, a large ammunition dump and a troop of enemy soldiers. The job was finished off by two USMC Cobra helicopters, which unleashed their full payload onto the target.

The UMST then consolidated their position and, although they were the first line of defence in the blocking position, the presence of USMC aircraft and the armoured vehicles of the Queen's Dragoon Guards meant that they were not troubled any further.

'In many ways this was disappointing,' said Briggs, 'as it only allowed us to use a slack handful of MILAN [anti-tank] missiles, 0.5 and 7.62, which only slightly lightened our bergens.'

Alpha Company of 40 Commando had already established blocking positions, and moved south of the Al Faw. Although they had not originally been tasked with clearing the town, this was what they were now asked to do. Indeed, they were delighted to get on with the job rather than spend another night in a mosquito-infested bog. Their first objective was the Ba'ath Party headquarters, which seemed to be the heart of the resistance that British troops were facing on the Al Faw peninsula. Two Troop began to move though Al Faw itself, while 1 Troop moved down the right flank between the town and the Shatt al-Arab waterway to a holding area.

The friendly smiles that greeted them at first soon disappeared. The situation grew more sinister when they ran into an agitated mob and it came as no surprise when shots rang out as they crossed a patch of waste ground. They found themselves caught in a crude ambush by enemy soldiers who had abandoned their uniforms for plain clothes. There were no conventional bunkers or trenches. Instead, the enemy hid around street corners and in houses.

The Marines flung themselves to the ground and took cover behind the kerbstones, which were all of 15 centimetres (6 inches) high.

Fire was sporadic and it was almost impossible to pin the enemy down as they constantly changed position. But then one bold Iraqi strolled around the street corner and started firing only a couple of metres (6 feet) from the lead section. Corporal Bowgen loosed off a few shots, silencing the man, before his rifle packed up. Another Iraqi took cover behind a horse, which, when hit by a volley, rolled over with its legs in the air. The fate of the hapless animal sent a twinge of guilt through the British troops.

By this time, their fire was suppressing the enemy. A 51mm mortar was brought into play with Marine Weclawak firing several high-explosive rounds into buildings being used as firing points. But the Marines then came under heavy small-arms fire from the left and machine-gun fire from the front. Under the cover of smoke, they began to withdraw, only to come under more fire from an unexpected quarter.

'The last thing we needed or expected was for Iran to open up on us from across the water,' said Lieutenant Buczkiewicz. 'It may only have been pot shots from a bored sentry but it was another problem which had to be dealt with.'

Fifty minutes later, they broke off contact after Corporal Storey had killed a sniper on the roof of a building 600 metres (about 650 yards) away. Then the Marines withdrew 500 metres (about 550 yards) down the road.

Later that night the decision was made to bring in 2 Troop to take the building that seemed to be the centre of the resistance. 2 Troop's attack began with the deafening blast of two AE charges going off. Then they poured in some heavy fire. Several light anti-tank weapons accompanied the assault as lead sections entered the building. Added to the din was the noise of two USMC Cobras circling above. The attack was going well, with room after room being cleared using grenades and small-arms fire. But disaster was waiting around the corner. While clearing the last room, the Marines hit the gas supply. There was an explosion. Several Marines were caught up in the blast and ran from the building with their clothes on fire. Worse, journalists were on hand to witness this.

'We were later to learn that the press thought the pictures of the assault were fantastic,' said Buczkiewicz. 'They were shown over and over again on the news, but the images of casualties caused much consternation among relatives back home who were left wondering whether it was their sons.'

Alpha Company then spent a cold and uncomfortable night in a palatial amphitheatre dedicated to Saddam Hussein. At first light they returned to the job of clearing the town. But that morning the atmosphere was completely different. Within a few minutes, a local man of some standing came to ask for a ceasefire. The enemy, it seemed, had lost seven men in their makeshift ambush and the firepower employed in 2 Troop's assault the previous night had cause them to think better of it. They had turned tail and fled, leaving much of their equipment. As Alpha Company patrolled through the town, they were led to a huge arms cache. With Al Faw now pacified, Alpha Company supported the clearance of the west bank of the Shatt al-Arab waterway, before returning to regroup at the MMS.

Over the next few days, 40 Commando advanced north, encountering and dealing with pockets of Iraqi resistance, including two armoured counter-attacks, until they were ordered to halt at Abu al-Khasib, 14 kilometres (9 miles) from Basra, where an all-arms concentration of Iraqi forces had been located. The Royal Engineers travelled with them, building sangars, setting claymore mines, erecting fences and other obstacles, and setting flare traps to thwart the enemy counter-attacks that came each evening.

Experts from 2 Commando Troop of 49 Squadron, EOD, cleared mines and other ordnance, while sappers from 3 Troop of 59 Independent Command Squadron, RE, helped secure the blocking positions across the Al Faw peninsula. J and L Company Groups, with 2 and 3 Sections of 3 Troop, launched a formidable attack on a series of buildings, either killing the enemy or leaving them under no illusion as to the fate that awaited them, according to Lieutenant Iain Lamont, who was with them. As the companies cleared their areas, sappers destroyed artillery pieces, cordoned mined areas, commandeered Iraqi troop-carrying vehicles and destroyed ordnance, as well as engaging the enemy alongside the Royal Marines.

Embedded with the Commando Engineer Group, 299 Troop, 131 Independent Commando Squadron, RE(V), moved north to establish another crossing point to the Al Faw peninsula near Umm Qasr. This involved the first operational fly-forward of the new seven-bay DS MGB bridge. The bridge allowed the reconnaissance vehicles of the Queen's Dragoon Guards (QDG) under Major Henry Sugden onto the peninsula and provided a hardened recce screen. C Squadron of the QDG joined K Company of 42 Commando to clear the north bank of the Khawz al-Arab, allowing mine-clearing operations in the waterway to begin.

As Sugden led C Squadron north to contact with the

enemy, he found himself in daylight on raised roads crossing exposed salt flats. This left his squadron at a considerable disadvantage when facing ex-Soviet T-55 tanks and armoured personnel carriers (APCs) in prepared positions. So he called down air and artillery strikes which destroyed significant numbers of Iraqi tanks and APCs, preventing enemy attempts to outflank his squadron and the Royal Marines. His mobile column provided vital intelligence over the next few days. Later, he supported their attack on Abu al-Khasib, where two of his vehicles were disabled by enemy fire. C Company remained in continuous contact with the enemy for twelve days and Sugden was subsequently awarded the Military Cross. During the three weeks of the second Gulf War, says the citation, Major Sugden 'displayed leadership, intelligence and courage of the highest order and in the very best traditions of the light cavalry. It is true to say that without his efforts and steadfast support, 3 Commando Brigade could not have achieved its mission.'

The 299 Troop also established a crossing point on the Khwar Az Zubayr, nearer Basra. During one of the worst electrical storms any of them had ever experienced, they battled against time and the elements to grade the banks and lay a trackway to let a squadron of Challenger 2 tanks cross the river and repel the threat from T-55 tanks breaking out of Basra. Of the many jobs 299 Troop undertook when hostilities were over, the most gruesome was to excavate the concrete foundation of a monument to prove to the people of Al Faw that their relatives had not been entombed in a secret chamber there.

The Royal Marine's Communications Squadron also followed the main body in, keen to join in the action.

'Corporal Tucker had us all in a flat spin when he was in

position on the Al Faw peninsula and said he was under artillery attack,' said Warrant Officer Cluetts. 'Luckily there was only one incoming round. The next morning a clearance patrol was sent out to investigate. They found a broken-down Land Rover abandoned by the BRF and a scorched piece of ground where the BRF had destroyed the surplus ammunition they could not carry.'

Running ahead of 40 Commando was a pathfinder unit (callsign A13F), under Corporal of Horse Richard Gallagher. His was the only patrol assigned to watch the American eastern flank in a critical area, deep behind enemy lines. A US elite reconnaissance force had attempted the task, been compromised and hurriedly extracted. But Gallagher's 12-man unit, mounted on four Land Rovers, was inserted by helicopter and remained undetected for eight days in a heavily populated area with little cover. He set up an observation post between an Iraqi infantry battalion and an artillery battery. He also managed to win the support of local people, so much so that they protected the patrol and helped the coalition forces in subsequent operations.

Corporal Steve Brown, another pathfinder unit commander, led four deep reconnaissance missions for 16 Air Assault Brigade. On one occasion, his 12-man unit (callsign A13D) infiltrated 70 kilometres (some 43 miles) behind enemy lines across almost impassable marshland. He also kept his patrol undetected for eight days and, when compromised, reinserted a new observation post, prepared his patrol for immediate action against three armed men tactically approaching their new position, relocated to another place and stayed on task for a further five days, continuing to report vital intelligence.

The Royal Artillery also had their men out in front.

Warrant Officer Second Class Alec Harvey, Battery Sergeant Major of 7 (Sphinx) Commando Battery, led a small force mounted in two Land Rovers and armed with light anti-tank weapons to counter the threat posed by several T-55 tanks to an undefended flank of 3 Commando Brigade, during operations on the Al Faw peninsula. In poor visibility caused by a sandstorm, he set up an ambush 20 kilometres (12 miles) from the nearest friendly forces, engaged the tanks with machine gun fire and called in high-explosive artillery rounds that forced the enemy to withdraw.

Meanwhile, Sergeant Thomas Rutherford of Y Company of the 1st Fusiliers Battle Group led several covert operations and close-target reconnaissance patrols into enemy territory. As commander of the Manoeuvre Support Section, he also provided sniper and heavy-machine-gun fire to protect the Kuwait–Iraq border-crossing sites for the 7th Armoured Brigade. All four men were Mentioned in Dispatches.

As part of the assault on Al Faw there was to be an amphibious landing on the southern shore across the Khawz al-Arab from Kuwait. This was to be undertaken by 539 Assault Squadron of the Royal Marines. For the landings, it was to be reinforced with elements from 4 and 9 Assault Squadrons, 10 Training Squadron and a troop of the Royal Marines Reserve, giving a total of 50 craft and 185 personnel. In addition, Australian landing craft, US Naval Special Warfare riverine craft, and UK and US EOD were to be seconded to it.

The main body of the squadron's craft and personnel had been loaded onto the landing ships RFA *Sir Percivale* and RFA *Sir Galahad*, which left from Marchwood, while the Landing Craft Control and Tasking Detachment and its vehicles had joined HMS *Ark Royal* in Portsmouth. Other elements had been loaded onto heavy-lift ships and shipped out. After training on Cyprus, they sailed through the Suez Canal to Forward Operating Base Freya – formerly a Kuwaiti Coast Guard station – in the Gulf. There, the squadron began intensive engineering and training programmes in preparation for offensive operations. In March they were joined by the US Naval Special Warfare SOC-Rs, or Special Operations Craft-Riverine. FOB Freya was the furthest forward of 3 Commando Brigade's outpost with lines of communications of 60 and 90 kilometres (37 and 56 miles) to Camps Rhino and Gibraltar.

The assignment of 539 Assault Squadron was to the secure Red Beach on Al Faw peninsula, so that combat forces could be built up on shore ready for the push on to Basra. The beach was to be cleared from the landside and waterside simultaneously. On the landside, Royal Engineers and Amphibious Beach Unit (ABU) personnel flew in with 40 Commando. Their first task was to confirm the suitability of the beaches, clear obstacles and dispose of any ordnance. At the same time, air-cushioned landing craft – hovercraft – would cross the Khawz al-Arab waterway from Blue Beach on Bubiyan Island to Red Beach, a distance of nine nautical miles. Again, with them there would be RE, EOD and ABU personnel to clear obstacles or explosives in their way. Once the route was clear, other landing craft were to start shipping vehicles in from Blue Beach and USS *Rushmore*. However, co-ordination between the various UK and US elements proved problematic. They had only two rehearsals using similar beaches and the US Navy's EOD diving team confirmed that it was joining the operation only one day before the off.

After 40 Commando had secured the oil facilities on the Al Faw peninsula, the RE and ABU teams quickly identified the part of the beach to be cleared ready for use. With them were 62 Territorials of 299 Troop of 131 Independent Commando Squadron RE(V), who were to be embedded with the Commando Engineer Group.

'We were rewarded by being involved in a helicopter landing on the Al Faw peninsula on D-Day to open up a landing point to enable the brigade's vehicles to catch up with the troops airlifted in,' said Captain Chris Wilcock.

As anticipated, Red Beach had been mined and was littered with obstacles. Clearance of the landside started immediately, but on the waterside the hovercraft were initially driven back by the obstacles and the high tide. At first light, a landing craft under Sergeant Cochrane, carrying UK and US EOD teams began clearing the seaward obstacles. By 12.00 Zulu they had breached four lines of obstacles and were within 200 metres (218 yards) of the landside EOD teams. It was then that the United States Navy said that it would not commit the heavier, vehicle-laden landing craft to Red Beach, and clearance stopped.

'Despite valiant efforts to clear obstacles and V69 fragmentation mines, the landing point was not opened because the Americans would not let their hovercraft near the mines,' said Wilcock.

Both landside and waterside teams reckoned that it would have taken only another two to four hours to open the beach to the larger craft and, by first light of the second day, the beach would have been cleared completely of its five lines of obstacles and a minefield. As it was, the entire amphibious landing was called off. Without a bridgehead at Red Beach, the commandos on Al Faw had to be supplied by an airlift from ships out to sea. The Assault Supply Team on HMS *Ocean* worked continuously for 72 hours, sending ashore more than 355 loads of ammunition, water, rations and medical supplies slung under helicopters.

The amphibious assault group now had to be redeployed. The men of 299 Troop moved north with the Commando Engineer Group. At the same time, Boat Group 1 moved the 16 kilometres (10 miles) from FOB Freya to FOB Poseidon, the Kuwaiti Naval Base at Bohaith. This lay just south of Warbah Island at the mouth of the Khawr Az Zubayr. It would wait there until 15 Marine Expeditionary Unit had cleared the Umm Qasr and they could move into the port facilities. Its mission would be to dominate the waterway, then identify, establish and operate a crossing point over the Khawr Az Zubayr. The Boat Group had with it four SOC-Rs to provide firepower and protection. However, its advance up the waterway was held back by the slow progress the US Marines made in taking Umm Qasr.

CHAPTER 5

UMM QASR AND BEYOND

J Company of 42 Commando were involved in numerous small engagements as they pushed north along the bank of the Shatt al-Arab waterway. Then, once Al Faw peninsula was secure, they were flown by RAF Chinook back to TAA Viking for a short stand-down period.

'This stand-down was in fact so short that few of us even realised we had had it,' said Corporal Sheraton, 'although it did give us an opportunity to receive some mail, have a shower and backload some kit not needed for the next phase of the operation ... It transpired that the USMC were having trouble cleaning up the means streets of Umm Qasr. Cue 42 Commando.'

The US Marine Corps were supported by British artillery – some of the 500 members of 17/16 Battery, 26 Regiment, Royal Artillery and their supporting elements, who arrived in the Gulf as the 4th Battery of 3 Royal Horse Artillery. The plan had been for the battery to move north in support of 1st Division of the US Marines, through the breach in the Iraqi lines at H-hour plus three in the main thrust on

Baghdad. But then the plans were changed. On 18 March they moved east in their newly received beige kit to join D Battery. Their new mission was to provide fire support for 15 MEU, an American all-arms formation whose first objective was the capture of Umm Qasr. Having been used to training with just six guns, a command post and a few 432 armoured fighting vehicles, they were now going into war in a full battle-ready armoured column.

On 20 March, following Scud and SAM (surface-to-air) missile attacks, they had moved towards their H-hour firing position a few miles south of the Iraq–Kuwait border with eight AS-90s, twelve 432 AFVs, an armoured ambulance, a Royal Electrical and Mechanical Engineers (REME) fitter section with recovery vehicles, and a huge echelon of other support vehicles. At 04.00 on 21 March – H-hour – they began firing high-explosive and smoke shells at observation towers and police posts along the Iraqi border and into Umm Qasr, 2 kilometres (1.25 miles) away. This came as a noisy surprise to Detachment 4 of Y Troop, who were dug in just 15 metres (50 feet) away. 'The guns opened up without warning with their highest charge,' said Marine Jones of the Air Defence Troop, 'giving Marine Spence a valid reason to change his pants for once.' On the other hand, they had a grandstand view of the artillery softening up Umm Qasr and the Al Faw peninsula before 40 and 42 Commando went in.

'It was a bit like playing battleships with AS-90s,' said Staff Sergeant Metherill.

For the next few days, they saw Umm Qasr pummelled by mortars, artillery and air strikes as the Americans tried to take control of Iraq's only deep-water port. But then Y Troop's position was compromised.

'We had unidentified people approaching our position

one night,' said Lance Corporal Harle, 'so we were not best pleased when, after a brief chat with the Kuwaiti border police a few days later, they left our position with a blast of their horn and blue and red lights flashing.'

By then the artillery had moved on. They had remained in position throughout the first day, firing sporadically. Then, at nightfall, they moved through the breach of the defences into Iraq itself. Along the way, they spotted former artillery and tank posts, stacked with abandoned ammunition. Locals emerged from their shacks along the roadside to wave them on their way. As the battery moved into its first position in Iraq, the recce party managed to get itself embroiled in a tank battle. With Union flag flying, it managed to avoid friendly fire, but the rest of the battery had to wait on the sidelines until the battle was won. Then they deployed, through the remnants of Iraqi vehicles left burning after the battle, to their next gun position just south of the town of At Tubah al-Hamra, some 16 kilometres (10 miles) west of Basra. They stayed there for three days, firing in support of the 7th Armoured Brigade as it engaged regular and irregular forces between Az Zubayr and Basra.

After the briefest of stays at Viking, J Company of 42 Commando were rolling across the border with M Company and 3 Troop of 59 Independent Command Squadron, RE, through the formerly demilitarised zone between Iraq and Kuwait. The taking of Umm Qasr had been the task of the USMC, but after four days the town and the port still had not been secured, and US Marines were making almost no progress in the face of continual sniping. As the USMC pulled out, M Company formed up at the old UN compound and advanced rapidly into the town.

'The enemy within, who'd been keen to engage vehicle-borne US troops, were not so keen on tackling the Royal Marines on foot,' said Major Taylor.

M Company began taking out hard targets in the streets, while handing out boiled sweets to kids at the same time. Within hours, 42 Commando dominated the ground and established a patrol routine. This was much to the disappointment of Lance Corporal Alun 'Jonah' Jones of the Cheltenham Detachment, who had hoped that the Iraqis would put up more of a fight of it and dismissed them as 'cowards'. In the days that followed, M and K Companies rounded up numerous Iraqi soldiers and Ba'ath Party members.

There was also plenty of work for the engineers. They had to blow up ordnance, demolish observations towers, force their way into the houses of Ba'ath Party members and try to make the bombed-out UN compound serviceable. On top of that, each Marine patrol needed two sappers for help and advice.

'The two-week operation in Umm Qasr was an important element of the war,' said Lieutenant Green. 'It showed the Iraqi people that we were there to help, not to conquer.'

Over the period, the focus was on continued patrolling, arrest operations, the prevention of looting and water distribution. The town was declared secure at the end of March.

By then J Company were long gone. While M Company had been conducting reassurance and deterrence patrols around town, J Company had quickly settled into the partly destroyed UN compound. In couple of hours, a couple of ex-electricians in the troop had the electricity on and the air conditioning running, and 3 Troop were microwaving their ration-pack meals. They were relaxing in the patio area after their meal when the order came: 'Pack your kit, we're off.'

The Troop were to move north to Crossing Point Anna, a ferry site, which they were to secure alongside 539 Assault Squadron and the Royal Engineers. From there the armour from Kuwait was to move towards Basra.

During the nights of 21–22 March, Boat Group 1 had been ordered to move past Warbah Island and up the Khawr Az Zubayr. At the time, 15 MEU were moving north along both sides of the waterway and it was thought that Umm Qasr would soon be secured. But as the Boat Group neared the town it became clear that 15 MEU had not yet taken Umm Qasr. They could see A-10s and Cobras attacking targets in the town and infantry fighting for both the old and new ports. The Boat Group itself came under sporadic enemy shell and mortar fire. Then it found it had to help out Team Gelman, a recce team of 15 MEU, who had 90 PoWs on the eastern bank of the Khawr Az Zubayr waterway.

The Boat Group identified several possible crossing points. At one they tried offloading CVR(T)s – Combat Vehicle Reconnaissance (Tracked) – and other transport. But several vehicles got bogged down and one CVR(T) and a Humvee got drowned completely. Another was found to be mined. Eventually, Crossing Point Emily was established as the only feasible crossing point south of Umm Qasr. But it could be used only for light vehicles, because of damage to the eastern bank – and it could be used for only two hours either side of high water.

On 22 March, 539 Assault Squadron's command post moved to Landing Point Miller on the west bank of the Khawr Az Zubayr. The command post administered

Crossing Point Emily for 72 hours while the battle was raging in Umm Qasr. This was crucial. With Red Beach closed and fighting still raging in Umm Qasr, Crossing Point Emily was the only place armoured reinforcements could reach 40 Commando, who were now advancing northwards up the Al Faw peninsula. However, on their first night there, the command post found that they were only about 500 metres (550 yards) from a battery of D30 howitzers and, for the next 36 hours, the crossing point was subject to sporadic enemy fire.

The Royal Engineers set about making the jetties suitable for carrying heavy vehicles, but still they could be carried across the waterway only at high tide. However, at low tide, personnel could cross and a large number of Iraqi PoWs were transported over the Khawr Az Zubayr waterway to makeshift camps on the west bank. Crossing Point Emily was also used as a surface medevac route, though the craft crossing there were regularly hit by small-arms fire.

Until this point, Boat Group 2 had been held back at FOB Freya, the Kuwaiti Coast Guard station. With Boat Group 1 holding Crossing Point Emily, it moved up river to conduct a recce of Az Zubayr Port and the naval base there, with a view to its occupation by 539 Squadron and the brigade headquarters. During these patrols, 539 Assault Squadron encountered four enemy patrol boats and destroyed them.

On 24 March, recces and patrols identified another potential crossing point. This was to be Crossing Point Anna 12 kilometres (7.5 miles) north of Az Zubayr Port in the Shatt al-Basra. Being much further upriver, this was less affected by the tides. Then, one large landing craft brought trackway and plant from FOB Freya to improve the crossing at Anna, which was opened on 25 March. This allowed 42 Commando to drive back onto the Al Faw peninsula.

According to Corporal Sheraton, J Company's first night at Crossing Point Anna was uneventful, despite a rather large tank battle to the north. 'That is unless you count an hour spent on sentry duty during a torrential downpour as a major event,' he said. 'I certainly did.'

That night Anna had to be closed due to a counterattack by enemy armour. It was reopened the next day. Meanwhile, the remaining boats were moved up from FOB Freya to Az Zubayr Naval Base, which was renamed FOB Thor.

With Umm Qasr now pacified, 42 Commando's next objective was to take the water-treatment plant at Umm Khayyal, 15 kilometres (9 miles) to the north. Ensuring a good supply of water was a crucial elements in the hearts and minds campaign, so water treatment plants were seen as high-value assets and, as such, needed to be secured quickly.

Early on 27 March, K Company of 42 Commando entered the town of Umm Khayyal. They reported several contacts, but resistance was light. With them were 1 Section of 3 Troop, 59 Independent Command Squadron, RE, under Corporal Banham. They seized a barracks only to find themselves pinned down by snipers and grenades. Under fire, the sappers managed to set claymores, establishing a line of defence. Then the battle began to turn in their favour.

Lance Corporal Slevin's team also came under fire while out on patrol. During a fierce firefight, they came under mortar attack. Lance Corporal Slevin and Sapper Skene ran forward under fire with a mousehole charge and blew an access hole in the building ahead. The Marines then entered and cleared the objective.

K Company were followed into Umm Khayyal by 3 Troop of J Company, who, on their second night, were sent out to secure objectives in the vicinity. They moved cautiously through the streets trying to locate their target building, but by first light they still had not identified it.

'Hardly surprising, as all the houses looked the same,' said Corporal Sheraton. 'As our troop commander, George, confirmed the objective with the observing snipers, I took the opportunity to change my CWS [common weapon sight] for my SUSAT [telescopic sight]. As I did so, I thought to myself, "What a quiet peaceful town." Whereupon there was a storm of firing with red tracer screaming overhead from a rooftop 300 metres [328 yards] away. As the CWS went one way, I went the other over a conveniently nearby bund line. I peered from the relative safety of the sand and a fire-control order followed.'

By the time one section had joined the fight and were putting down fire, Corporal Sheraton was preparing for the assault. He was just 200 metres (about 218 yards) from the target. George told him that he was about to call in mortar fire and asked him to withdraw. The mortar-fire controller (MFC) liked friendly forces to be at least 250 metres (270 yards) from the target for the sake of safety. But, with the enemy – 'Abdul and his friends', as Sheraton put it – firing from the rooftop, Sheraton thought he was just fine where he was.

As soon as the first mortar round landed, Sheraton realised why the MFCs insisted on an exclusion zone of 250 metres (270 yards). George was naturally concerned for Sheraton's welfare.

'Oscar three-three, are you OK?' he asked.

'We were shaken but not stirred,' said Sheraton. 'I recommended a correction of 50 metres [55 yards]. Knowing a good deal when he hears one, George accepted the recommendation and brought the remainder of the rounds crashing down onto Abdul and his cronies.'

Since there was still a chance that a company of Special Republican Guards was hiding in the basement, George ordered another barrage of mortar fire. Then 3 Troop prepared for the assault. They moved along the wall of the power station next door under covering fire from 1 Section. Then they placed an explosive charge on the perimeter wall of the target building. With an entry point established, smoke grenades were thrown in, followed by the first assault pair.

'As we prepared to clear the building, I informed God that, whilst he is probably excellent company at dinner with some cracking dits [tales] to spin, I would prefer to postpone our meeting for the time being,' said Corporal Sheraton. 'At this point, George, having had the benefit of a university education, observed that enemy movement around the building had ceased and we were therefore to enter the place "green", meaning without firing unless fired upon. Having done so, we captured two prisoners, both with gunshot wounds. George, being an officer in the Royal Marines, spoke excellent English, albeit with a slight impediment. The prisoners, being as they were Iraqi, spoke excellent Arabic. Other than being fluent in their own languages, the two had very little else in common, so hand gestures, grunting and a shrug of the shoulders were the order of the day. Tactical questioning proved ineffective. The final section battle drill beckoned, so without further ado we reorg'd.'

With the prisoners processed and dispatched, the triumphant warriors moved back to company tactical headquarters for a new assignment. There, they were told that a crowd was gathering in the centre of town. After dispersing them, they were to liaise with a K Company callsign at Objective Silver, which turned out to an old barracks.

As they went to attend to the crowd, they heard the crack of automatics and the whiz and thump of incoming fire all around them, though they could not identify where it was coming from. Since the crowd were paying little attention to the Marines or to the incoming fire, 3 Troop decided to move on.

'We were given dodgy directions by K Company, but eventually found our way to Objective Silver, only to be fired on once again,' said Sheraton. 'We slammed the truck into reverse and sped back out at maximum speed.'

Then they found another route in and linked up with the other Marines, who engaged the gunmen in the building with all the firepower they could muster.

'Once safely in the compound, the only threat came from grenade-over-the-wall attacks,' said Sheraton, 'or one lunatic who'd seen one too many episodes of The A-Team with an RPG strapped to the top of his car.'

Although there were outbursts of sporadic fire throughout the rest of the morning, it was largely ineffective and the rest of J Company joined 3 Troop, who now considered themselves 'legends', as they always seemed to first into the thick of it. Silver became a patrol base for company operations in Umm Khayyal. The focus was now on cleaning up the town and imposing the rule of law. Ba'ath Party offices and other properties were raided, yielding several important prisoners, a variety of weapons and plenty of ammunition. The next priority was the distribution of water.

'The troop were impressed by the community spirit, manners and good demeanour of the locals – not,' said Sheraton. Nevertheless, within a few days, J Company were engaging the town's football team. Umm Khayyal won 9–3.

Meanwhile, Corporal Livingston took 3 Section of 3 Troop, 59 Independent Command Squadron, RE, north with L Company of 42 Commando to reinforce 40 Commando, who were in contact with the enemy. In the north of the Brigade area, the enemy had launched another armoured attack from Basra. Fourteen T-55s attacked 40 Commando's position. However, Challenger 2s of C Squadron of the Royal Scots Dragoon Guards were on hand and destroyed all 14 enemy tanks without loss, while 42 Commando came under fire from RPGs at the start line, but fought through.

During another encounter with the Iraqi 6th Armour Division, the lightly armoured Scimitar recce vehicles of D Squadron, Household Cavalry Regiment, suffered proportionately the heaviest casualties of any units of 16 Air Assault Brigade as they were subjected to sustained and accurate artillery fire. However, the squadron never faltered and Major Richard Taylor, who was commanding, called in artillery and air support, and orchestrated a complex three-dimensional battle. D Squadron held its ground for two days under ferocious attacks by the T-55-equipped al-Hakem tank battalion of Iraq's 6th Armoured Division, destroying the battalion and silencing a significant part of the enemy's artillery. A quarter of the squadron's Scimitars were also destroyed. For his actions, Major Taylor was awarded the

Distinguished Service Order. The citation says that throughout the extended engagement he was 'inspirational, fearless, calm and clear-sighted'.

American air support is not an unalloyed advantage in these encounters. As the Household Cavalry were pushing around some 40 kilometres (25 miles) north of Basra, scouting for elements of the Iraqi 6th Armoured Division on 28 March, they were attacked by two American A-10 Tankbuster aircraft.

'I was driving a Scimitar on Route Spear next to the Shatt al-Arab waterway 40 kilometres [25 miles] north of Basra,' said 18-year-old Trooper Christopher Finney of the Blues and Royals, who was a driver with 2 Troop of D Squadron of the Household Cavalry. 'We were running parallel to a small village when we were hit on top. I didn't know what had happened – I thought we were under attack from a rocket-propelled grenade.'

In fact, his Scimitar had been hit and set on fire by 30mm cannon shells from the two A-10s. Ammunition began to explode in the turret.

'The commander got out and the gunner, Lance Corporal Al Tudball, was wounded,' said Trooper Finney. 'I started to reverse but backed into the Scimitar behind, which had also been hit.'

Trooper Finney found cover but returned to the burning Scimitar and climbed back into it to rescue the gunner, though Finney had shrapnel wounds himself.

'I could see that Al Tudball was trapped half out of his hatch, so I got him onto the ground and started first aid,' said Finney. 'His headset was hanging off the side of the turret so I used it to send a report.'

Trooper Finney took the wounded gunner to a Royal Engineers Spartan recce vehicle, which moved up to help as the A-10s began another attack. Sergeant Andrew Sindall of the RE, attached as a recce sergeant to 23 Engineer Regiment (Air Assault), provided first aid and threw red smoke to signal to the A-10s that they were attacking friendly vehicles. But he couldn't stop a second attack, during which his Spartan was hit and he was wounded.

Trooper Finney returned to the second Scimitar to see if he could help.

'Lance Corporal Matty Hull, their gunner, was still stuck in the turret,' he said. 'There were engineers already trying to get him out.'

Trooper Finney was beaten back by the heat, smoke and fumes and Hull died of his wounds. Finney then collapsed, but was recovered by the Spartan crew. An Iraqi tank then turned up to threaten the evacuation of the wounded. It was held off by Lance Corporal Mick Flynn in another Scimitar and Corporal Dave Tellings in a Striker. For 30 minutes, Flynn drew both the tank and artillery fire while himself firing 140 30mm rounds. Days later, he was in a four-hour battle with five T-55s. Flynn received the Conspicuous Gallantry Cross and Telling was Mentioned in Dispatches. Sindall received the Queen's Gallantry Medal and Finney was awarded the George Cross. Later, the coroner in Oxfordshire found that Lance Corporal Hull had been unlawfully killed.

Air Chief Marshall Sir Brian Burridge, who was knighted for his role in commanding British Forces in Iraq, said of Trooper Finney, 'This young man, who was only 18 at the time and had been in the army for less than a year, showed outstanding courage.'

The citation speaks of Trooper Finney's 'clear-headed courage and devotion to his comrades, which was out of all proportion to his age and experience'.

Lance Corporal Tudball survived his injuries.

There was another hero of the action that day – WO2 Rupert Banfield of 4 Regiment, Army Air Corps (AAC), who won the Distinguished Flying Cross (DFC). Flying combat missions with 3 AAC, he was just returning from one patrol where his helicopters had been fired on when he heard that two RAF Pumas were evacuating casualties of the 'blue on blue' attack (that is, from friendly forces) on the Household Cavalry Regiment Scimitars. He led his patrol to cover them, flying close to the ground in poor light. As the Pumas took off with their casualties, an enemy armoured vehicle opened fire. Staff Sergeant Banfield ordered one of his aircraft to engage the enemy, resulting in its destruction and the removal of the threat to the evacuation.

Lynx pilot Captain Richard Cuthill was also involved in the engagement. He and two Gazelles flew in to support the Household Cavalry Regiment's Scimitar recce vehicles, which were in contact with Iraqi T-55s on the west bank of the Shatt al-Arab waterway. With visibility obscured by exploding artillery shells, Cuthill positioned his aircraft so that he could home in on a tank by following the path of tracer rounds fired by a Scimitar. He also destroyed a self-propelled artillery piece by aiming a missile at its muzzle flash as it fired at him. This meant he and the Gazelle crews were in direct view of the enemy and constantly exposed to fire. He too was awarded the DFC.

Unfortunately, blue-on-blue incidents were all too common. In one, Corporal Carl Lewin was blown 6 metres (20 feet) off his Challenger tank. Believing that it was an enemy attack, he secured the area and administered first aid, which saved an injured comrade's life. He won the Queen's Commendation for Bravery.

As 40 Commando pushed on across the Al Faw peninsula towards the south of Basra, plans were drawn up to deploy a boat group from 539 Assault Squadron in the Shatt al-Arab waterway. In preparation, a liaison officer was embedded with 40 Commando headquarters. Plans were also made for a boat group to work with 42 Commando in the clearance of the marshes to the east of Shatt al-Basra, north of Az Zubayr Port. Patrols were sent out on 27 and 28 March. No enemy were seen, although several boats abandoned in the marshes showed signs that they had been used recently. However, enemy transmissions identified as coming from two artillery positions in the marshes were picked up. Hovercraft were sent in again, but again there was no sign of the enemy. That night two landing craft were sent in with two inflatable raiding craft and elements of an Amphibious Beach Unit to set up an observation post to watch for further enemy movements.

On 30 March, two LCVP landing craft and two inflatables were sent to search the marshes and reed beds south-east of Az Zubayr, where fresh radio intercepts had been picked up. After a night patrolling the marshes, one Mark 4 Landing Craft was engaged by small-arms fire. On hearing the contact, Corporal Hiscock, Coxswain of LCVP N1, who was one mile to the south, moved to support the Mark 4. But when Hiscock arrived at the location of the initial contact, there was no sign of the enemy or the other landing craft. As N1 moved slowly into the main waterway to assess the situation, she was hit simultaneously by small-arms fire. Then an anti-tank missile crashed into her from astern. The missile exploded on contact with the rear of the wheelhouse, blowing the electrical systems and destroying the radios. All three men in the wheelhouse were injured. Captain Waite and Corporal Murray were both knocked unconscious and Marine Christopher Maddison was fatally wounded. Two crewmen in the well deck were blown into the water by the blast and Corporal Hiscock received extensive cuts to the face by shrapnel.

With the landing craft still under incoming fire and despite his own injuries, Hiscock dragged Waite and Murray from the burning wheelhouse, then regained control of the damaged vessel. He turned the landing craft towards the enemy fire so Marine Baker, who was manning the machine gun, could return fire. He also made an attempt to rescue the two crew members in the water. Two hovercraft carrying a quick-reaction force rode to the rescue and came under small-arms fire when they tried to pick up the two crewmen. When the men made it safely to the bank, Corporal Hiscock decided that the severity of the injuries to Marine Maddison required he return to FOB Thor, 10 kilometres (6 miles) south. After alerting them using a spare radio in his kit, he made sure that the craft remaining in the area were informed of the location of the two men who had been in the water.

Sadly, Maddison died later in the field hospital. A memorial service was held onboard HMS *Ocean* after the squadron's return to the ship, and Landing Craft N1 was renamed 'NM' after Marine Maddison. It turned out that his death was a result of a friendly fire incident. Other Marines, patrolling in the area, had mistakenly fired an anti-tank missile at the landing craft due to 'bad planning, unreliable communications, inadequate equipment and poor leadership', a board of inquiry concluded.

Shortly after this contact, 42 Commando at Crossing Point Anna used MILAN anti-tank missiles to engage two fast-moving enemy boats, destroying one. An aerial patrol above also reported seeing mortar fire land in the water.

Clearly, the marshes were bandit country. Before first light, armoured patrols were sent in to find the enemy. They identified potential areas of interest, which were investigated by airborne elements of Z Company and troops carried on hovercraft and rivercraft. But no more contact was made with the enemy, who were thought to have fled the area immediately after the contact or during the hours of darkness. Further river-borne assaults ensured that the enemy were cleared from the Khawr Az Zubayr waterway. From there, the Marines could move on.

On 1 April, 539 Assault Squadron conducted a recce of a potential FOB location to support operations on the Shatt al-Arab waterway. This was named FOB Neptune and a boat group moved up. It began patrolling the next day, aiming to deny the enemy access to the waterway and look for potential crossing points, so that Basra could be surrounded. Already 40 Commando were in regular contact with the enemy on the outskirts of the city.

US Naval Special Warfare also wanted access to the Shatt al-Arab waterway, and tried to force a passage from seaward on 3 April. However, when they were still in the estuary and not the river proper, their four SOC-Rs were intercepted by Iranian Boghammer patrol craft. The commander of the SOC-Rs decided to withdraw and returned with the craft to Kuwait Naval Base. From there, they were moved by road to Az Zubayr Port, then carried, underslung, by helicopter to FOB Neptune. Based there, they were able to support 539 Assault Squadron's boat group and 40 Commando along the Shatt al-Arab waterway.

At that time, the Boat Group was very busy as Iraqi irregulars were using the Shatt al-Arab waterway to reinforce their formations on the outskirts of Basra. Several times, craft were required to direct fire or call in armoured patrols to engage enemy bunkers and armour. But soon they began to win the hearts and minds of the local fishermen, who passed on valuable intelligence, allowing the boat group to deny the Shatt al-Arab waterway to enemy forces.

CHAPTER 6

WITH THE YANKS AT NARIRIYAH AND RUMAYLAH

Many American soldiers had been killed at Nasiriyah and battle there was still raging when Pathfinder Patrol (callsign A13A) arrived in the war-torn city. Mistakenly told by an American unit that the way ahead was secure, the three Land Rovers moved north as night fell. But soon they attracted rocket, mortar and machine gun fire as Saddam's fervent Fedayeen militia pursued them and blocked their escape.

Sergeant Nathan Bell, commanding the first of the vehicles, took the patrol off the road some 64 kilometres (40 miles) behind enemy lines. He decided to use the cover of night to circle their pursuers and return along the route they had used. He led the convoy back to the road and, manning the front machine gun, fired on enemy positions as they engaged him. The patrol was attacked four times as it sped south, sustaining many hits.

As they neared the US Marine lines, Sergeant Bell turned on his lights and, at huge personal risk, stood up in the front of his vehicle with his hands up to identify himself.

He stayed with the hard-pressed American Marines throughout the following day, passing on information about enemy positions. He was awarded the MC after leading four more dangerous patrols behind enemy lines.

Some of the fiercest resistance encountered by the Coalition forces in Iraq had occurred around Nasiriyah and, as the US 2nd Marine Division tried to secure key bridge crossings over the Euphrates river, G Battery of 7 Parachute Regiment, Royal Horse Artillery, were called in to help. Credited with firing the first round of the land war in Iraq, the long barrels of 7 Parachute Regiment's 105mm guns scarcely had a chance to stop smoking as hostilities continued. After engaging enemy mortar positions on the opening day of the ground war, the air-deployable gunners completed a constant stream of missions. Firing an average of 400 rounds a day during the first two weeks of the campaign, the men of G Battery in particular rarely strayed from the sharp end of the action.

'When we found out from the Americans that they had been contacted the previous night and had lost ten of their guys and had another 50 or so injured, it really brought home that we were now in a very real situation and that this was not just another training exercise,' said G Battery's troop commander Sergeant Dave Thomas. 'Before we started to move forward we all had five minutes alone to collect our thoughts and think of those back home. Personally, I was very apprehensive and would compare the feeling to how I felt before a fight when I used to box years ago. The feeling of apprehension, nervousness and anxiety that you get as you climb into a ring and wait for the opening bell was exactly how I felt on the road to Nasiriyah. I'd been in the Army for 20 years and that was the first time I'd ever felt that way on an operation.'

Luckily, they did not have to enter the town of Nasiriyah itself, where the fighting was fiercest. Instead, they took up positions outside to provide the US Marines with artillery support.

'We were positioned less than one kilometre [0.6 of a mile] from the south of the city and the scene was nothing short of dramatic,' said Thomas. 'It was dark, but fires silhouetted the town. You could hear the F-18s flying above and, although you could not see them, you could see the flash of their bombs as they exploded. It was far removed from any training exercise back on the range at Sennybridge or Larkhill, because you could actually see the destruction with your own eyes.'

Gunner Challoner, who went on to celebrate his 19th birthday in Iraq on 25 May, was on his first tour with the army when he ended up in Nasiriyah.

'In Nasiriyah we saw a lot of American vehicles that had been attacked,' he said. 'The bullet holes through the windows made me think of my own safety and that it could be me next time. When you're put on sentry [duty] on an exercise you feel like falling asleep, but here you don't even think about sleep because you know there are people out there who want to kill you.'

Following the action at Nasiriyah, G Battery went with the rest of the regiment to attack enemy mortar and artillery positions north of the Hammar Canal in Rumaylah. Here, in a bid to slow the advance of the Coalition forces on the northern reaches of Iraq's oilfields and Baghdad itself, the retreating Iraqi forces had blown a 9-metre (30-foot) section of the Rumaylah bridge, sending the roadway crashing into the waters of the Hammar Canal below. But they had counted without the specialist sappers of 16 Air Assault Brigade.

'Hats off to the Iraqis, who did a pretty good job of creating an obstacle for us,' said Warrant Officer First Class Ian Smith of 23 Engineering Regiment. 'We found a large quantity of high explosives attached to the pillar above and below the water line. Fortunately, it hadn't detonated and had to be cleared by our EOD squadron.'

But that was only one of their worries.

'Because of the way the roadway collapsed we had to do a bit of demolition work of our own,' he said. 'Once it had been blown for a second time, it was possible to rebridge the gap using a 34-metre [37-yard] general support bridge for the first time in anger.'

The whole process took a little over eight hours to complete. This reopened the route around Basra to the north. The 23 Engineering Regiment, formed only in January, were also heavily involved in ensuring the safety of the area in and around Rumaylah oilfield's gas-oil-separation plants.

'The GOSPs represent the wealth of the country,' said WO1 Smith. 'If you wanted to set an oilfield alight the GOSPs would be the place to do it. Since arriving in Iraq we'd been working on making them safe. A number of improvised explosive devices had been found and from them you can surmise the Iraqis intended to booby-trap them, but didn't have a chance to do so.'

Bomb Disposal Officer Lieutenant Toby Rider of 33 Engineering Regiment (EOD) was awarded the MC for efforts in clearing the important North Rumaylah Bridge, which had been prepared for demolition by the Iraqi Army. The dangerous 30-hour mission involved removing more than 200 kilos (44 pounds) of explosives and hundreds of detonators in varying states of decay under cover of darkness. Lieutenant Rider carried out his task under enemy fire from the far bank.

Meanwhile, Captain Grant Ingleton replaced his helmet with his maroon beret to encourage his soldiers to return to their guns under heavy Iraqi fire. Battery Captain of F (Sphinx) Parachute Battery, 7 Para RHA (Royal Horse Artillery), he was supporting 3 Para south of the North Rumaylah Bridge when I Parachute Battery (Bull's Troop) came under fire 1,000 metres (1,094 yards) away and were forced to retire. As his battery provided covering fire, they also came under bombardment and the gunners took cover. Realising I Battery was in the open and vulnerable, Ingleton defiantly put on his beret and walked around the gun position, encouraging his men back to the guns. During the war, F Battery fired more than 3,500 rounds of 105mm ammunition. He also won the MC. The citation says his 'infectious sense of humour and selfless leadership drew the men back to the guns, where they maintained their rate of fire and allowed the other battery to withdraw safely without casualties'.

The 155mm AS-90 guns of the 3rd Battalion of the Royal Horse Artillery and 26 Regiment of the Royal Artillery were deployed in support of the 7th Armoured Brigade and the 16 Air Assault Brigade at Rumaylah, Az Zubayr and Basra. The four batteries were capable of firing three 43-kilo (95-pound) rounds every ten seconds.

'With a total of 32 guns in-theatre and the ability to fire day and night and even during a sandstorm, we certainly have the potential to lay down a lot of fire to shock and awe the enemy,' said Battery Captain Tony O'Rourke of 16/17 Battery of 26 Regiment RA. 'However, our fire missions have generally been done at a rate of two rounds a minute – a more considered approach that reduces the risk of collateral damage, but does not make us any less effective. The guns have been firing air-burst bomblets and, believe me, for the Iraqi troops in tanks and bunkers on the receiving end, it will certainly feel like shock and awe.' (This was the term used during that war, and before, to mean gaining rapid dominance using overwhelming decisive force.)

North of Rumaylah, information was fed to them by men from the 1st Battalion of the Parachute Regiment and 7 Parachute Regiment of the RHA manning observation posts around the region's gas-oil-separation plants with American Air Naval Gunfire Liaison Companies, the US Army's indirect-fire specialists. Using binoculars, NVGs and 7 Para's portable surveillance and target-acquisition radar to detect enemy forces, they were capable of calling in overwhelming firepower.

'Information on anything we spotted was passed to both a battery of AS-90s from 3 RHA and to US close air support, so if a target was positively identified it could be destroyed in a matter of minutes,' said Bombardier Richard Toseland of 7 Para, RHA. 'The Americans are very professional and it was great fun working with them. Some of the guys we met have been real characters and invited us to stay with them in California. One of the ANGLCO [Air and Naval Gunfire Liaison Company] sergeants was a Hollywood stuntman and appeared in *We Were Soldiers*, *Men in Black* and *Austin Powers 2*.'

Captain Jock Barclay, Battery Commander of G Battery, 7 Parachute Regiment, RHA, reserved special praise for the courage of his men when they came under 155mm fire as they moved into position along the Hammar Canal.

'We had a lot of young fellows with us who had just joined the army and some who had come here straight from training,' he said. 'When we came under fire just past the Hammar Canal we all climbed into the mudflats to shelter from the bombardment and it struck me them that there were a lot of young, very white faces around me who looked unsure of exactly what was going on. When the order came to get our own guns in action, to a man they all got out from under cover and got on with the task in hand, which impressed me more than anything I have seen in my military career. The discipline to do what they did under that sort of fear – and you could see the pure fear in a lot of their eyes – was nothing short of admirable. I was, and am, immensely proud of the battery. The guys have been outstanding. They have been on some pretty sticky wickets and it is amazing that we've not had anyone injured or killed.'

Among those young faces were Gunner Gwyn Martin, Gunner Paul Challoner, Gunner Steve Simnett and Gunner Matthew Stephenson, who were all in action for the first time.

'War has been a mixture of excitement and fear,' said Martin, who joined the battery just before Christmas 2002. 'When you come under incoming fire you just want to get your own rounds down to stop any further attack.'

Simnett, who joined the regiment two days before it deployed on Operation Telic, said, 'This is the sort of thing I joined the army for, I just never expected something like this to happen so soon in my military career. There have been times when I've felt very nervous here, but that's something you just get used to, and there are other times when it's been a real buzz.'

Stephenson added, 'When the artillery shells landed just short of our position I was scared and after the event wrote letters home saying how I prayed as the fire was coming over. It doesn't take very long to work out that you're not on a training exercise.'

Although the Coalition effectively secured air supremacy on the first day of the second Gulf War, the soldiers of the 16 Air Assault Brigade's Air Defence Battery did not stand down. With no sightings of enemy aircraft, the 55 men of 21 (Gibraltar 1779–83) Air Assault Battery, RA, part of the 47th Regiment, RA, put down their lightweight, multiple-launcher, close air-defence systems and their air-defence alerting devices, picked up their SA80s and took on an infantry role.

'We have provided force protection for the 3rd Regiment, AAC, in the Rumaylah region, manning vehicle checkpoints, patrolling main supply routes and recovering arms caches,' said troop commander Captain Jason Stones. 'We have also taken more than 200 prisoners of war. This sort of role is not alien to us and, after conducting similar operations in Afghanistan, we're quite adept at it.'

Information gathered by the air-defence gunners from Iraqi travellers passing one of their checkpoints led to a precision American air strike on a Ba'ath Party stronghold in the town of Suq al-Shuyukh. Despite their success on the ground, Stones insisted that his men were ready and waiting to revert to their regular job if required.

'We had not completely discounted the threat of an air strike,' he said. 'There was still a fear that Iraqi forces could still use smaller aircraft to drop chemical munitions.'

Also deployed to secure the Rumaylah region were troops from the 3rd Battalion of the Parachute Regiment, who patrolled the skies overhead in Royal Air Force Puma helicopters in an effort to protect the oilfields. They would then swoop in to mount 'eagle' vehicle checkpoints. These 90-minute sorties, used to good effect in Northern Ireland, aimed to shut down all enemy activity in the Rumaylah region and protect Coalition convoys from ambush.

'"Eagle" VCPs are a tried-and-tested way of dominating an area of operation,' said Captain Dan Jarvis. 'They enable us to move quickly, check out areas of suspicious activity and let enemy forces know that we can appear anywhere at any time.'

Meanwhile, out in the desert, British snipers, hunting in packs of three, were protecting Coalition troops from enemy mortar and artillery fire. Under cover of darkness, they hunted down Iraqi forward-observation posts that were attempting to bring down fire on British and American positions in the Rumaylah region. Equipped with .338 bolt-action rifles and capable of killing a man at 1,500 metres (1,640 yards), the snipers deployed in forward areas for 48-hour periods, lying in wait and reporting enemy activity.

'A sniper can be a hindrance to an opposing force without having to pull the trigger,' said sniper commander Sergeant Iain Illidge of 3 Para. 'We are an asset that can be used in various roles. Snipers can be attached to a company as a defensive screen and used as an early-warning system, and can also work as Forward Observation Officers, adjusting the artillery fire as it falls and pinpointing enemy positions for air strikes. In the event of an assault, an accurate, well-trained sniper can be employed before the attack to eliminate the opposing force's hierarchy, targeting officers in the hope that other soldiers may then lay down arms, or to eliminate the crews of machine guns or anti-tank weapons.'

Gradually the situation began to improve. Daily life for the inhabitants of one secluded village nestled between gas-oil-separation plants in the Rumaylah oilfields changed in a week when A Company of the 1st Battalion of the Royal Irish Regiment arrived. After 15 years the call to prayer could be heard again, echoing through its narrow streets, and plans were being drawn up to build a mosque, a thing prohibited under Saddam Hussein. Law and order was provided by 156 Provost Company of the Royal Military Police rather than Ba'ath Party henchmen. The local school was reopened and in the centre of the village the Ba'ath Party headquarters was taken over by a civil-military co-operation team led by Major Mike Parnell. The changes, welcomed by the 2,000 inhabitants, were put into place by A Company in just seven days.

Within hours of moving into the area, the company conducted household raids, displacing militia and arresting senior Ba'ath Party members, one of whom was described by the locals as 'the executioner'.

'We acted quickly on the intelligence information we had and swooped on key personnel,' said A Company's OC, Major Robbie Boyd. 'In one of the houses belonging to a senior Ba'ath Party officer we recovered nearly four million Iraqi dinars and weapons – it was like walking in on a major drugs bust. The operation was a big success and effectively removed Ba'ath Party influence from the village without our having to fire a single shot.

'We were also quick to impose some authority on the local elders, putting in place a weapons amnesty that led to more than a hundred AK-47s and rifles being handed to us. The people have seen the firm but fair way that we conduct our business and realise that we are here with their best interests at heart. They have greeted us accordingly.'

Welcomed on the streets as liberators, not invaders, the men of A Company were soon conducting foot and vehicle patrols through the village wearing their caubeens instead of combat helmets, and were frequently approached by civilians volunteering information on the movements of rogue operatives. Despite the level of co-operation given to the British troops, villagers still refused to be photographed or identified for fear of reprisal. Many were still not convinced that Saddam's long reign of terror was over in Iraq.

'There's still a slight fear that there might be a repeat of the first Gulf War 12 years ago when the Americans arrived in the village only to hand out food and water before leaving just days later,' said Major Boyd. 'It will take a little more time for them to trust us fully, but in this village we are far and away ahead of the rest of Iraq. I truly believe we have liberated a people here and I have no qualms whatsoever about the ethics and morality of this war after seeing the joy on these people's faces.'

Elsewhere, the regime change did not go so smoothly. During an advance on Al Medina and Al Querna, the swift actions and courage of Warrant Officer First Class Douglas Beattie, Regimental Sergeant Major of the 1st Royal Irish Regiment, in the face of angry and brutal mobs, saved the lives of four local people, supporters of the old regime who faced a brutal fate. At great personal risk, WO1 Beattie sent a signal to the town that taking reprisals in such a brutal fashion was not acceptable. He was given the Queen's Commendation for Bravery.

CHAPTER 7

TAKING AZ ZUBAYR

At a little after 04.00 on Tuesday, 25 March 2003, the Black Watch had reached the bridges over the Shatt al-Basra, overlooking Iraq's second city, the main objective of the British forces. But first the Fedayeen militia and Ba'athists had to be flushed out of the small town of Az Zubayr.

It had been three days since the Black Watch had crossed the border from Kuwait, three long days of hard fighting. First, they moved on to the oil-processing plant near Az Zubayr to secure it against sabotage – though, in fact, their biggest problem turned out to be looters, who were stripping the plant. They walked off with computers, desks, ceiling fans – anything they could carry or sling on the back of a pickup truck. Even forklift trucks and ambulances went missing.

The engineers brought in to run the plant were attacked and, when the troops went in to retrieve what was left of their vehicles, they got their first taste of real war.

'We came under heavy attack from the militia and that

woke everybody up,' said Lieutenant Chris Broadbent. 'It was not training any more – people were trying to kill us.'

By then the militia had killed their first Black Watch soldier, Lance Corporal Barry Stephen, in an ambush on the edge of the town. Two other soldiers from the battle group had gone missing. The two Royal Engineers, 36-year-old Staff-Sergeant Simon Cullingworth and 24-year-old Sapper Luke Allsopp, were out on a mine-clearing operation when they had taken a wrong turn and their Land Rover ran into an ambush. The vehicle was hit by a hail of bullets and then an RPG.

Lance Corporal Marcus Clarke, who was in another Land Rover behind, heard Cullingworth shouting over the radio, 'Keep up! Keep up!' But then Clarke was hit in the shoulder.

'The road disappeared in a cloud of smoke,' he said. 'We drove into smoke and I was then facing the front of their Land Rover. They were going up the road backwards, off to the right. I thought I was going to hit them and swerved around. We continued and got fifteen metres [16.5 yards] past the first vehicle when we were also hit by RPGs, which spun us round and we crashed.'

Their attackers, clad in black and shooting with rifles, began to run towards them, and Clarke and his oppo abandoned their vehicles and took cover in a compound. They could hear Cullingworth two to three minutes after the ambush calling out, 'Clarkie, come back and get me.'

A message saying that the engineers had been ambushed was picked up by 28-year-old Sergeant Scott Shaw on the radio in the back of his Warrior armoured personnel carrier. D Company were to go to their assistance. Three Warriors, each with seven soldiers in the back, a driver, and the commander and his gunner in the turret with its 30mm cannon and 7.62mm chain gun, headed off. When they spotted the engineers' Land Rovers ablaze up ahead, they came to a halt and the soldiers poured out. As Shaw and his men took up position on the left, with Sergeant McGill's platoon on the right, the Fedayeen opened up from the rooftops of buildings nearby. This was their first time under fire.

While Sergeant Shaw's men gave covering fire, a corporal from McGill's platoon fought his way across the open ground to the twisted wreckage that was still burning. The engineers' Land Rovers had no armour and the RPG attack had left nothing more than a mass of twisted metal. According to *Soldier* magazine, RPGs could be picked up from street stalls for as little as $10 in the world's trouble spots. They are now the insurgent's weapon of choice alongside the AK-47 assault rifle, and Sergeant Shaw could see the rockets raining down.

'You could see the RPG rockets coming towards you,' he said. 'I'm at the back and you could see them exploding above the boys' heads because they're firing them from a good range and they self-detonate after so long.'

Atop the third Warrior, Sergeant David Corbett found that his chain gun and 30mm cannon failed after sustained RPG and small-arms fire, so he fired his rifle and 9mm pistol from his open hatch to protect dismounted troops returning to the vehicle, still having sustained no casualties despite a huge weight of enemy fire.

Since there was no sign of the two missing engineers, D Company pulled back to await fresh orders. Although Az Zubayr was a hotbed of resistance, many of the townspeople had no love for Saddam and his henchmen. The word went out: the engineers had to be found. As information filtered back, one name came up over and over again. The following afternoon, the Black Watch thought they knew who they were after.

D Company commander Major Douggie Hay received order to arrest the suspect. The plan was simple: they would make a dawn raid and catch the Iraqis off guard. B Company would stage a diversionary attack on the other side of town, while D Company would seal off the area where the suspect lived. Then, while 15 Platoon made the snatch, the rest of the company would guard their backs and prevent them from being outflanked.

That night they drove a little way from the town to rehearse. Sergeant Euan McGilp, aged 33, from Dunedin in New Zealand, took 13 Platoon through their task of manning the outer perimeter during the raid.

'Everyone is nervous and there is an amount of trepidation but you just have to think that you are on the winning team,' he said. 'If you are going to go out there with the mentality "I'm going to die, I'm going to die", then you probably *are* going to die.'

Then, the following morning, as the dawn broke, the Warriors thundered down the narrow streets of Az Zubayr towards a small square. In the back of one of them, his pale face lit by a dull red bulb, was 20-old Private John Mitchell. He was with 15 Platoon and was about to get his first taste of action.

'They told us we were going to see if we could get the engineers,' he said. 'We got in the back of the Warriors and we were driving down the road. It's noisy and hot in there. The vibrations go everywhere, up your feet and your knees and everything.'

Lieutenant Alex Reading, aged 25, was also wondering what he had let himself in for. He had joined the battle group only a couple of hours before the raid.

'I got in with a bunch of soldiers I had never met and we went into Az Zubayr,' he said. 'In the back of the Warrior, you can't hear what's going on. You're just thundering along and everybody's very quiet.'

Major Hay led the way, with the drivers of the Warriors behind straining to see in the half-light and the clouds of dust kicked up by the vehicles in front. Hay's Warrior roared round the corner into the small square, it hurtled across the square and ploughed straight into the perimeter wall of the suspect's house.

'As the back door of one of the wagons opened,' said Sergeant Shaw, 'one of their guys on the top of a roof was practically firing straight in the back of the wagon. We had to get out there and [we] managed to drop him or keep his head down so everyone else could get out.'

That done, Shaw and his men darted through the hole in the wall made by the Warrior. In front of them was the wooden door to the house. Shaw planted his boot firmly against the woodwork.

'From previous experience the doors were flimsy and you could just kick them in,' he said. 'This one was a nightmare. It just wouldn't open and we were kicking and kicking and kicking, and then one of their sentry positions across the way opened up.'

The Iraqi gunners could not see through the wall, but over the top they could see the helmets of the British soldiers behind it and let rip at the metalwork of the gate, hoping to catch them with a ricochet.

'The front door was just in front of it,' said Private Mitchell. 'Sergeant Shaw was trying to kick the door in and then these people started shooting through the gate at him and hit him in the butt.'

Shaw barely noticed the pain.

'It was at that stage that we started breakdancing as metal started flying everywhere and I got hit in the butt,' he said. 'It was just shrapnel because the door shredded. At the time it was just a question of "That's sore", but I just kept on going because there was no question of going back at that stage because there was no cover. The men outside started taking on the sentry positions and we concentrated on getting in.'

Then, with one final kick, the door shattered, and they were in.

Sergeant McGilp's vehicle screeched to a halt some 500 metres (about 550 yards) behind, where they were to set up the outer cordon. The driver pressed a button and the hydraulics pushed open the rear door. Then all hell broke loose.

'When that door opens I liken it to one of the scenes in *Saving Private Ryan*, when the landing-craft door drops open, but instead of red tracer the Iraqis had green tracer,' said McGilp. 'You could see all this and hear it pinging on the sides of the armoured vehicles and you just get out. This is war fighting, this is the real deal. It is you and them and you just have to deal with it.'

McGilp and his men spilled out of their Warriors into a hail of bullets.

'They were giving it some,' he said. 'They had a lot of ammunition and I believe they were trying to mobilise because the vehicle behind me saw them all getting into a vehicle, a minibus or something. It was quite bizarre, all these armed men getting into a minibus and trying to come round and outflank us.'

The Warrior's turret swung round and that was the end of the minibus. But by then they were taking fire on both flanks. Worse, they were parked next to a petrol station. One stray bullet and the whole lot would go up.

'There was a lot more tracer coming at us than we gave them,' said McGilp. 'I remember the green tracer and I was just cursing myself for being so tall, because my head comes up above the Warrior, and we had camouflage nets on the Warriors and the bullets were zipping in amongst them and I was thinking: "This is just unreal." It was personal: they were shooting at *me*.'

Up on the rooftops Iraqi militiamen crouched behind the low parapets, popping up every few seconds to loose off a burst of fire. Below, the men of D Company of the Black Watch were clustered around their vehicles, with open ground on one side and a labyrinth of alleyways on the other. They were sitting ducks. Militia men were everywhere and bullets were bouncing off the ground all around McGilp and his men.

It was then that he felt the tugging on his sleeve.

'Sarge! Sarge!' said Private Scott Henderson insistently.

Ducking to avoid the bullets zipping overhead McGilp ignored the 18-year-old, who had arrived in Iraq only a few days before to join up with the rest of the battalion. This was Henderson's first mission with the Black Watch, the first time he had ever been under fire.

'Sarge! Sarge!' said Henderson again. McGilp reluctantly responded.

'What is it, Hendo?' McGilp snapped. 'You know I'm busy.'

'There's a guy over there keeps firing at us,' said Henderson and he pointed at an alleyway a short distance away where a figure in a shemag (desert scarf) was firing at them with an AK-47.

'Well, shoot him, then,' said McGilp, and turned back to what he was doing. Henderson aimed at the man's chest and squeezed off a burst of five or six rounds. He wasn't sure whether he got him, but the firing stopped.

'I just shot him and there was no firing coming back,' said Henderson. 'I just wanted to get it over and done with properly.'

Not far away, Lieutenant Reading was receiving his own baptism of fire from gunmen crouching behind the low walls surrounding the top of the single-storey buildings on either side of the junction he and his men had been tasked to hold.

'At first all you could hear was shots going off and tracer going off,' he said. 'And then you come to the grim realisation that you are the focus of their attention,' he said.

Inside the house, Sergeant Shaw and his men had grabbed the suspect, who had been identified by two SAS men with them.

'He had baggy trousers on but no top,' Shaw recalled. 'I wouldn't say he came easily, he was resisting, but we grabbed him and restrained him the best way we could, plasticuffed his hands and put a sandbag over his head to disorientate him.'

His wife and kids were screaming as the soldiers bundled him into the back of Major Hay's Warrior.

Blood was pouring from Shaw's leg where a piece of shrapnel had torn through the skin, but there was no time to worry about that. The Warriors backed up as he and his men leaped in.

'Let's get out of here,' cried Shaw.

Outside the perimeter wall, the firing was showing no signs of easing. Private Mitchell crouched against the side of the house, waiting for the Warriors to get them out.

'We could hear the Warriors firing outside,' he said. 'We were all lying against the wall because the Warriors had moved away a bit.'

Then they seized their opportunity.

'We ran to the back of the Warrior and got in,' said Mitchell. 'As the back door was closing, an RPG hit the right-hand side of the Warrior. It rocks the whole thing – you think it's going to tip over. I thought we'd hit a lamppost or something but when we got out the back bin wasn't there. I was just glad to get out of there.'

The whole operation had lasted just half an hour. But it did not help them locate the missing engineers. The following day they raided another couple of houses and ripped them apart. But it was too late, the engineers were already dead. Their killers filmed the lifeless Sapper Allsopp surrounded by a crowd and the footage was shown on Al Jazeera television. Prime Minister Tony Blair described their killing as an 'execution'. The bodies of the two men were found in shallow graves almost a month later. They had been shot by at least two different rifles and a pistol and left for dead. A forensic expert who examined the Al Jazeera footage said that Allsopp was still breathing, alive some four hours after the shooting.

As the Black Watch pushed on further into the town, the fighting became harder and they were harried by mortars and RPGs at every turn.

'I had a direct hit to my turret with an RPG,' said Lieutenant Chris Broadbent. He had been lucky. Had he not followed the advice of his gunner and retreated inside a moment or two earlier, he would have been killed.

'I'd been getting down because the gunner had kept on at me to batten down,' he said, 'and I'd finally decided to listen to him. Afterwards, when I looked, all that was left of my rifle was a melted and twisted bit of metal. We were on fire for quite a while, but, apparently, it was relatively controlled, not too bad. We were battened down, trying to go through the drills. It was interesting to see how we all stayed focused.'

As his crew fought the fire, the Warrior behind him spotted the two teenage boys who had fired the RPG reloading.

'He killed them,' said Broadbent. 'It's not nice, but they were trying to kill me and I feel justified in the decision that was taken. When you reflect on what's happening and realise that people are trying to kill you it's a sobering thought.'

Sniper Lance Corporal Peter Laing of the 1st Battalion of the Black Watch was one of a group of six covering an assault on Az Zubayr who were ordered to engage militia seen leaving a pickup. One was shot at long range and the rest took cover in a building near a mosque. Laing realised he could not clear the building with a grenade because an old man had been taken hostage, so he dived into the house and pulled the hostage out. In Dispatches, it was said that in the next frenetic moments he showed a 'quite extraordinary bravery and lack of concern for his own safety' as a grenade was thrown at him and an RPG fired at him. He managed to push the hostage out of the way and, when fellow sniper Lance Corporal Scott Robertson threw a grenade into the house, moved into position to engage the enemy with sustained automatic fire.

Corporal John Rose was providing mortar-fire support to the Black Watch Battle Group near Az Zubayr when his position came under fire from a village half a mile away. Under sustained attack, he pushed his two teams across open ground towards their objective and led a flanking attack. Corporal Rose threw two grenades into the enemy-occupied house and, with another soldier, cleared it, killing two of the enemy. Immediately afterwards he led an attack on a second building, killing two more enemy soldiers with grenades and small-arms fire. Rose then reorganised his section and swept through the village to ensure it was clear of enemy. He was awarded the MC.

The 1st Battalion of the Light Infantry were also in Az Zubayr with 2 Royal Tank Regiment (RTR) Battle Group. Corporal Phillip Hellick of D Company of 1 Light Infantry was Mentioned in Dispatches after he led a daring four-man pre-dawn patrol into a militia strongpoint in a maze of small streets in northern Az Zubayr. This produced intelligence that led the company to attack later that day. He returned to lead the break-in, clearing four rooms in the initial objective and saving two members of his section from serious injury when a grenade bounced off a wall and landed at their feet. And Sergeant Ashley Curson of A Company was Mentioned in Dispatches after he led an eight-man patrol into Az Zubayr against fierce resistance. The patrol, the first to attempt to dominate the city, was soon in action against larger groups of militia and became involved in a number of firefights. The report says Curson played a significant role in defeating the militia in Az Zubayr.

There were other acts of conspicuous courage in and around Az Zubayr. When a missile misfired while he was engaging a target, MILAN Anti-tank Detachment Commander Corporal Thomas Symon of Z Company of the 1st Fusiliers Battle Group got out of his Warrior, crossed open ground in view of the enemy and reloaded his firing post. He engaged the Iraqi anti-aircraft gun at maximum range and destroyed it. His actions under fire saved his detachment and prevented the effective use of the gun against the remainder of Z Company. He was Mentioned in Dispatches.

Sergeant McGrath, an RMP section commander, was

awarded the Queen's Commendation for Bravery after he calmly dealt with a 'blue on blue' attack on a Challenger 2 tank near Az Zubayr, saving at least one life. He took command of troops of other cap badges to provide first aid for the wounded and secure a landing site for swift medical evacuation. Despite an artillery bombardment and a lack of armour, he recovered two bodies from the burning tank hulk and took them to a field hospital. And Major Andrew Britton was Mentioned in Dispatches when he led Cyclops Squadron of 2 Royal Tank Regiment through several close-quarters battles, destroying pockets of militia and assisting in the rapid securing of Az Zubayr.

Despite the fierce resistance, Az Zubayr fell within 48 hours. The Black Watch then had to wait in position for the last push into Basra. They were kept awake at night by shells flying over their heads and cursed the artillery men. The night sky glowed orange. Smoke drifted across the horizon. Far way there was the sound of gunfire and the distant thud of 40-kilo (90-pound) high-explosive shells. On the radio, they heard that the Americans were advancing – though the Iraqi divisions they said they had routed the day before, they had also said they'd routed the day before that, and the bridges they said they had already taken, were taken again.

Meanwhile, around Basra, the Irish Guards were fighting beyond the bridge over the canal by the devastated transport yard. The Royal Marines were advancing from the south and the Fusiliers had a toehold to the north. Under mortar and rocket fire, Captain Oliver Campbell's light-assault platoon from Y Company of the 1st Battalion of the Royal Regiment of Fusiliers pressed on across a vital motorway bridge over the Shatt al-Basra waterway and gained a foothold on the far side. Over the next 48 hours

Above: Royal Marine troops of 40 Commando relaxing before they disembark from HMS *Ark Royal* to take part in early operations on the al Faw peninsula of Iraq, March 2003.

Left: Marines sweep through a complex cave network previously used by al-Qaeda forces in June 2002, just prior to demolishing the caves.

Top: A Marine from 42 Commando stands guard at the new port in Umm Qasr, Iraq, March 2003. The port town, on the Kuwait-Iraq border, was secured by coalition forces, enabling humanitarian aid to flow into the country.

Above: Chinook helicopters from 18 Squadron, RAF, insert Royal Marines from 40 Commando into the southern Iraqi city of Basra, early April 2003.

Top: A British Puma helicopter lands at the former palace of ousted Iraqi president Saddam Hussein in Basra. His palace was used as headquarters for the British troops in charge of southern Iraq.

Above: British soldiers fire mortars to illuminate the oil pipeline area for surveillance during a patrol on the southern outskirts of Basra in August 2004.

Top: British soldiers return at sunrise to their base after a night patrol in September 2004 in Al-Amarah, 180 km north of Basra in southern Iraq.

Above: Warrior armoured fighting vehicles on the move close to a main road in Basra.

his platoon held their position in the face of near-continuous enemy assaults on the bridgehead. They were under mortar fire for at least 30 hours during that time, and Campbell organised his small force to repel at least three fierce attempts to dislodge them. He also led a fighting patrol that snatched a prisoner from an enemy position. The citation of his MC says his platoon bore the brunt of Y Company's operations in an extremely demanding period of high-intensity war fighting.

In another attack, 10 Platoon of Z Company of the 1st Fusiliers Battle Group charged across a bridge over the Shatt al-Basra waterway, under heavy and accurate fire, in a devastating assault to prevent Iraqi troops trying to blow the bridge up. Led by Lieutenant Christopher Head, they scattered the demolition party, an action that led the enemy to abandon the entire position, including revetted tanks, anti-tank guns and dug-in infantry positions. Over the following 12 hours, Head maintained his toehold at the end of the bridge on the far bank, leading his men against enemy counter-attacks and inspiring them in 'a manner that belied his age and experience', according to the citation of the MC he was awarded.

Staff Sergeant Richard Johnson of the RE also won an MC for removing demolition charges while exposed to enemy fire on a bridge over the Shatt al-Basra waterway. Serving with the 32nd Engineer Regiment, he and his crew were with the 1st Fusiliers Battle Group trying to secure the crossing. Although he had no cover when Iraqi forces attacked, he worked on to remove the explosives and make the bridge safe. The citation says he 'showed considerable courage, putting himself in danger while giving his crew's safety top priority'.

One man found that the wait for the Black Watch to take

their turn in the final assault on Basra was too much, and he asked another to break his fingers for him so he could be sent home. The second man picked up a heavy jerry can full of water and asked the first if he was sure. When he said he was, the second dropped the jerry can on the first's hand, which was outstretched over a box of bottled water. Everyone expected the first soldier to pull his hand away, but he kept it there. His fingers did not break; they were just bruised.

In the meantime, the Black Watch were given the task of cleaning up Az Zubayr. On the eastern edge of the town they found another Ba'ath Party base. Sergeant Shaw was in the thick of it once again. He and his men had been out on what should have been a one-hour patrol, when they spotted RPG cases in the street outside a building, along with nine crates of rockets and a launcher.

'It wasn't planned,' said Shaw. 'We were just out on patrol, but as we were moving between checkpoints one of the guys spotted the boxes.'

They searched the building, found a container out back and cracked it open with a sledgehammer. Inside were mortars, AK-47s and ammunition, all in pristine condition, altogether weighing more than a tonne. This was their biggest find so far. Then they cleared the building.

'It was a meeting place and seemed to be some sort of headquarters for the Ba'ath Party or the militia,' said Shaw. 'It had two storeys with a long dining room and a big meeting room.'

It became clear how important it was when they found a model room upstairs with a plan of the town made in sand, along with maps and other documents.

'They must obviously have been sitting up there planning their operations against us,' said Shaw. 'A guy from the same street said they all left a week ago. Maybe they had gone to Basra, but they could have still be around, hiding out because they knew we were looking for them.'

In the lull before the final push on Basra, the Black Watch busied themselves with foot patrols and distributing aid, trying to win over the people of the town and make them forget the Ba'ath Party, which had dominated their lives for so long. People began to trust them and weapons caches the militia thought secure began falling into their hands one by one.

Captain Campbell Close of D Company said that when the Black Watch first arrived in the town the militia were still in charge and people were nervous, but once the water was back on the people could see that the British wanted to help. The Ba'ath Party had left and the army had deserted, though those who were more hard-line had probably moved on to Basra.

'Everyone else has seen that the bad stories they told haven't happened – the bayoneting of babies and that sort of thing – and we are giving them food and water,' said Close.

Lieutenant Broadbent and his platoon rested up in a former military compound to the east of the town, recovering after days of fighting, trying to acclimatise to the new role of peacekeepers, while remaining conscious that they would soon be asked to fight again. Before the war had started, Broadbent had been nervous of what to expect. He was not sure how he or the young men in his platoon would react once they were in action.

'It was different from how we thought it would be,' he said. 'The original brief had changed completely. Before we came out, we believed that if we were going to do any fighting it was going to be in the open, but they were using guerrilla tactics.'

He and his men were becoming more professional as they got used to it.

'I had in the back of my mind that it would not be a walkover,' he said. 'But it has been harder than I thought.'

Then there was Basra where, he feared, there would be more fighting to do.

'I don't think Basra will be a walk in the park,' he said. 'Look at the resistance we faced here, and Basra is much bigger.'

CHAPTER 8

THE BATTLE OF ABU AL-KHASIB

After the Al Faw peninsula had been secured, 40 Commando's Brigade Reconnaissance Force quickly reconfigured as a squadron with the task of clearing the numerous date plantations and towns and villages that run parallel to the Shatt al-Arab waterway. They conducted mobile clearance patrols with an attached troop from the Queen's Dragoon Guards in Scimitar light armoured vehicles. This type of operation, last used in the Falklands War, proved highly effective. They could cover and sweep an extensive area of ground in a short time, and the enemy's 'shoot and scoot' tactics did not slow down their rate of advance.

'Many of the Iraqi soldiers showed little willingness to fight and were quite content to give themselves up,' said Sergeant Gaz Veacock. 'The Field Humint [Human Intelligence] Team and their interpreters were used extensively during this phase, enabling us to gain and act on tactical intelligence.'

Each day they pushed further up the Al Faw peninsula,

gaining control of more ground until they reached the division's frontline on the outskirts of the suburbs of Abu al-Khasib, 14 kilometres (9 miles) down the Shatt al-Arab waterway from Basra. Intelligence suggested that there was a high concentration of enemy armour in this area.

'As a result, we found ourselves laid up, with MILANs deployed, for numerous days awaiting orders,' said Veacock. 'This period will always be remembered due to the extreme weather we were exposed to. Apparently, Iraq generally receives approximately five centimetres [2 inches] of rain during the month of March. What we didn't expect was for it all to fall in one day!'

Following the BRF were Alpha Company of 40 Commando, who were moved north to set up an anti-armour ambush. They dug positions into the soft clay and settled in comfortably. Then, the following night, a storm blew up. In high winds, the rain lashed down, the shell scrapes filled with water and the Marines took shelter under anything they could find. To keep warm and dry, they donned chemical warfare suits. Then, at the height of the storm, a gust of wind picked up the six-tonne truck carrying their bergens and deposited it on the other side of the road.

As day broke, the Marines were confronted by a scene that could have been out of World War One. Everything was covered in mud. But broad grins broke out on mud-splattered faces when Alpha Company were ordered forward to positions further north, which were easier to defend and largely dry. Although an expected enemy attack did not materialise, a corporal in the Mobile Support Group dubbed Alpha Company's new position 'Custer's Last Stand'. This was because all the other units had vehicles and could have withdrawn easily if attacked. Only A Company were on foot.

With no new armoured assault by the Iraqis forthcoming, the next objective was the enemy stronghold of Abu al-Khasib. It was thought to be held in battalion strength by Iraqi hard-liners armed with machine guns and RPGs, sometimes operating in troop strength and often dressed in civilian clothes. The terrain was difficult too. Date palm groves and small settlements provided good defensive cover, where pockets of resistance could be concealed from air attack. Between them were wide irrigation channels where the incoming troops would be dangerously exposed.

In Operation James, 40 Commando were to take Abu al-Khasib with a squadron of Challenger 2 tanks from the Royal Scots Dragoon Guards and a squadron of Scimitars from the Queen's Dragoons Guards in support. They were to cross the start line just before first light on 30 March and advance north along four axes.

First, the Brigade Reconnaissance Force were to conduct the preliminary operation to seize an important bridge, called Objective Sennen.

'This was the Brigade Recce Force's first opportunity to carry out a live direct-action task since the Mountain and Arctic Warfare Cadre's attack on Top Malo house in the Falklands,' said Veacock.

The BRF group consisted of some 27 vehicles, including two Scimitars of the Queen's Dragoon Guards, the Recce Troop of 40 Commando and a tactical air-control party, with indirect fire support from 148 Battery of 29 Commando, Royal Artillery, and the Mortar Troop of 40 Commando. With them were two detachments of the Recce Troop of 59 Independent Commando Squadron, RE, under Corporals Joe Hogan and Tony Spanner. Their task was to clear the bridge itself. As usual, they found themselves in danger not just from the enemy.

'Our alarm call took the form of a column of Challengers driving past metres from our position and on into the night,' said Captain Pete Lederer.

As the Recce Team pushed westwards towards the bridge, they scanned the area around it with thermal imaging sights. Spotting the enemy, they engaged them with a 7.62mm mounted on a Land Rover. Then Sapper Taff Betty turned night into day with illumination rounds fired from his 51mm mortar. Artillery and mortars preceded the assault, and then Corporal Spamer and Lance Corporal Trev Michael cleared the near bank. They crossed the bridge under fire and reported that no demolition charges had been laid.

As the battle for the bridge began in earnest, Corporal Hogan's team provided suppressing fire. More fire support came from the 30mm cannons of the two QDG Scimitars, one of which was now on the bridge. While medic Lance Corporal Scott 'Bobby' Vessey was treating a badly hurt Iraqi soldier, the injured man's comrades used the cover of nearby buildings to fire an RPG at the Scimitar that was crossing the bridge. It narrowly missed the vehicle, but, in an effort to evade the RPG, the vehicle ended up in a ditch. The troop became very exposed as dawn broke, and the situation worsened when the vehicle shed a track as Lieutenant Farebrother tried to pull it clear. During the 30 minutes it took the crew to replace the track, Farebrother got out of his vehicle with his headset still on to encourage those making the repair and organise the sappers to give cover. The engineers took up a blocking position, with Sapper Nick Ingram putting down 7.62mm covering fire and calling in mortar support to make sure the Iraqis kept their heads down.

Meanwhile, Farebrother gave fire control orders to his

gunner, who was working the 30mm and 7.62mm gun systems single-handedly. The 30mm was used to open up 'mouseholes' in nearby buildings so that Royal Engineers could enter and clear them and then take up fire-support positions on the roof. During a 45-minute firefight, the enemy RPG teams were wiped out and the bridge was secured. Then the advance continued with the Iraqi bunkers on the far side being cleared with grenades and LAWs (Light Anti-tank Weapon), which opened the way for the attack on Abu Al-Khasib proper. Farebrother was awarded the MC.

The bridge taken, Corporal Hogan led a patrol to clear overlooking houses, capturing 19 militiamen and a significant quantity of arms and ammunition. Earlier, he had drawn fire on the bridge to allow engineers to clear it of demolition charges and he was Mentioned in Dispatches.

The following morning, the BRF raided the house of the local sheikh, capturing a local Ba'ath Party official and a colonel from a mechanised division, along with substantial amounts of weapons and cash.

'The sheikh's house made a comfortable patrol base for the Recce Troop callsigns,' said Captain Lederer. In separate actions, 611 and 612 Tactical Air Control Parties were busy engaging targets to the north and west. Sennen Bridge was later renamed 'Welly' in memory of Lance Bombardier Llewellyn Evans, who had died in the fatal Sea Knight helicopter crash on the first night of invasion.

'The raid was a great success and an indicator of things to come,' said Sergeant Veacock. 'The Brigade Recce Force now became the Brigade Raiding Force.'

Despite a long build-up, the final timings for Operation James took everyone by surprise as the orders were rushed through. Alpha Company's One and Two

Troops were to advance behind four tanks of the Royal Scots Dragoon Guards.

'I couldn't help but conjure up the scene from [the film] *Full Metal Jacket* [Stanley Kubrick, 1987],' said Lieutenant Buczkiewicz, 'and when I spoke to the tank commander later on it turned out that this was exactly what he had in mind.'

Alpha Company moved to the start line under cover of darkness. Things did not go smoothly, as an accident with a four-tonner left Three Troop without a troop sergeant, a sniper, a mortar man and a Minimi machine gunner. As the Marines yomped up to the start line, a message was passed through the troop that a recce element had spotted numerous enemy upfront. In fact, there were no enemy in the area but, according to Lieutenant Buczkiewicz, the rumour 'added a little spice to the move'.

As they crossed the start line, a tank round flattened a building 50 metres (55 yards) ahead. The sudden ferocity of this action came as a shock to the point section, but gave everyone a timely reminder of what a Challenger 2 could do to the enemy. Indeed, during the 3-kilometre (2-mile) advance into the town, the Challenger 2s destroyed several enemy tanks, APCs and other vehicles.

'Working alongside the tanks was fraught with its own dangers,' said Buczkiewicz. 'If you weren't having to double to keep up with them, you were avoiding being crushed as they manoeuvred around or dodging rounds as they cooked off in the burning hulks strewn along the road.'

While One Troop advanced with the tanks, the other two troops were rounding up prisoners. Two Troop even picked up a Major and a Lieutenant Colonel. At the entrance to the town, Buczkiewicz ordered engineers to collapse the roof of a sentry post with AEs. Overenthusiastic, they levelled it and, as One Troop entered the town, nothing was left except smoking rubble.

Once the Marines were inside Abu al-Khasib, the RPG attacks became more numerous. One pair of Iraqis foolishly staged their assault from a donkey cart. However, when they made their getaway, they found that the poor donkey could not outrun the tank that set off after them.

The lead tanks then saw a large contingent of armed men leaving a military barracks near the centre of town and fleeing to the west. The Marines would meet no more organised resistance. But, although Alpha Company quickly dominated the area, they continued to come under sporadic small-arms fire.

Over the next few weeks, Alpha Company remained in Abu al-Khasib in an attempt to pacify it. Acting on intelligence from informers, One Troop took a tank to snatch a local who was suspected of plotting an attack on their positions. The plan was to surround his home and threaten to blast it off the face of the earth if he did not surrender. However, when they got there, they found the suspect sitting outside his house with his wife and children. The man, it turned out, was friendly and helpful. He may have been harmless, but others posed a genuine threat. One Troop stopped a car travelling through town at night and seized ten assorted weapons, and Two Troop raided a house and found a weapon and British DPMs (Disruptive Pattern Material camouflage).

During Alpha Company's stay in Abu al-Khasib their positions came under attack. One night a terrorist bomb was thrown into One Troop's compound. It was small, and at first it looked like a fag butt to Marine Kay who was on sentry duty, but the ensuing explosion blew all the windows out. On another occasion, a would-be suicide bomber turned himself in with grenades still strapped to his body after a last-minute change of heart. Meanwhile, with the Ba'athists gone, the town successfully restructured itself. By the time the Marines left on 22 May and headed back to Britain, Abu al-Khasib had elected a new council and a new police force.

Bravo Company followed Alpha Company into Abu al-Khasib and suffered one of the war's worst friendly-fire incidents on the way. A stand-off company, it comprised one close-combat troop, Four Troop, and the Fire Support Troop. Four Troop was an old rifle troop, while the Fire Support Troop was more flexible. It could either be two separate troops – an anti-tank troop and a heavy machine gun troop – or it could be split into three combat teams, each team equipped with two MILAN anti-tank posts and two 0.5-calibre heavy machine-guns. This was the way it was deployed throughout the second Gulf War and, for Operation James, Five Troop of C Company was attached to the Commando Group.

The build-up to the tragedy began just before nightfall on 30 March, when B Company had just relieved UMST 42 Commando at Objective Blenheim, where they set up the MILAN and heavy machine gun positions. Like the rest of the battalion, B Company were surprised by how quickly battle orders were issued.

'There were no maps, only traces, and no vehicles,' complained two Marines. 'And we had to move in an hour.'

Like A Company, the 122 men of B Company had a 14-kilometre (9-mile) yomp to the start line. They were to arrive there for the 02.00 H-hour. This turned out to be something of a feat. To carry 13,600 kilos (30,000 pounds) of kit, they had only six quad bikes, one four-tonner and a tracked BV Swedish all-terrain transport vehicle. The quads could just about take the load on a normal road, but they were hardly suitable for an unmetalled track where mud came up to the men's knees. For the 36 hours of the attack, each man had to carry more than 40 kilos (90 pounds) of kit.

On the way to the start line, B Company stopped to put on their body armour and helmets. This proved fortuitous. They were just 100 metres (110 yards) from the kick-off when artillery rounds from their own 105mms came raining down. The aim was to clear the ways for the Scots Dragoon's Challengers that were supporting the advance. Luckily, Marine Marsh's quad had broken down, holding the Fire Support Troop back. But Four and Five Troops found themselves directly under airburst and high-explosive rounds from two batteries of eight guns. They were pummelled by 16 barrels for the next two minutes.

Calls for stretchers quickly echoed down the line. Medical Assistant Sumner ran forward to assess the situation. Among the eight casualties, he found some life-threatening injuries. A hasty triage was made, then Sumner quickly stabilised the two worst cases. Corporal Wall had a punctured lung and Marine Leverrit's left had had its triceps torn out. They had survived only because they had stopped to put their helmets and body armour on.

The uninjured Four Troop men helped treat the wounded. But the friendly fire had left nerves strained and the situation confused, and Marine 'Homer' Fell managed accidentally to administer morphine to his own thumb.

'He seemed to have more of a bounce to him after that,' colleagues observed. They also commiserated with Corporal Wall, since no one had time to grab his camera and take his 'wounded in action' picture.

'Sorry, mate. Maybe next time, eh?' said Marines Moore

and Howarth of B Company. They also observed that it was ironic that artillery's Forward Observation Team, who were at the front of the advance, were almost wiped out by their own guns.

After all the men were treated and evacuated by ambulance, B Company regrouped. Despite the casualties, the attack was still going ahead. Four Troop's first objective was Dalmatian, the first main bridge on the outskirts of Abu al-Khasib. But, since they had no maps, they did not fully appreciate the size of the area they had to cover.

As the men of B Company moved down the road towards the outskirts of Abu al-Khasib, the cry went up: 'Mines!' The wasteland to the west of the road was littered with them. There were also anti-tank mines along the edge of the road, so the men had to stick to the hardstanding.

A short distance down the road, Four Troop and Fire Support Troop Combat Team Two came across a building they found suspect. The presence of the enemy was confirmed and a 94mm anti-tank rocket went crashing into it, followed by 0.5 rounds from Marine Wheldon's gun. That threat dealt with, the advance continued. Four Troop and Combat Team Two quickly secured the bridge, while Corporal Beswick took his gun up onto a rooftop to cover the next objectives. Five Troop with Combat Team Three joined them from the west, while Combat Team One came in from the east. As they regrouped, they could hear not far away the ringing of 120mm Challenger shells as they shook up Iraqi tank crews. The whole company then moved forward together.

A little way down the road, Corporal Green's point section found barbed wire stretched across the road. The word was passed down the line that there was 'something a bit iffy here' and, after they passed over it, they came under fire from a building to the front. The Marines returned fire with rifles and machine guns. While One Section laid down suppressing fire, Two Section, under Corporal Adams, moved across the road and cleared a nearby building, then occupied its roof to lend additional fire support. Then Marine Craig, with One Section, fired a 94mm LAW rocket into the side of the enemy-held building and the assault began.

Three Section under Corporal 'Taff' Pearce ran in from the bridge. At a full sprint, Pearce slung his rifle, seized a grenade and lobbed it into a top-floor window. With suppressing fire still coming in, he and his men vaulted the perimeter wall. Marine Laycock heard voices inside the building. He threw two grenades in, followed by a burst of machine gun fire. Then Pearce and his section stormed in.

The sound of women and children screaming could be heard from nearby buildings, but there was no sign of the enemy. The non-combatants were taken to safety and no civilians were injured during the action. Three Section then pulled back and the troop regrouped.

Corporal Taylor's MILAN detachment then moved forward from the bridge to cover the advance. At this point, Marine McGregor spotted an Iraqi soldier on a bike with his AK-47 slung over his shoulder. The man was oblivious to the advancing British troops. Corporal Green shouted to him to stop – to no avail. The Iraqi went for his gun. It was a fatal error.

B Company then split in two. Four Troop and Combat Team Three crossed a bridge and moved over to the adjacent road. Then the advance continued on two fronts, with Five Troop heading down the main road with Combat Teams One and Two following.

After they moved off, Sergeant Donaghey of Combat Team Two spotted two men who seemed to be observing the company advance. Somehow, Five Troop had passed them without spotting them. As Sergeant Donaghey drew closer he saw that one had an AK-47; the other an RPG with eight rounds. Yelling a target indication, Sergeant Donaghey engaged them. Seconds later the 'crack bang' of 0.5 fire from Corporal Beswick's gun, fired by Marine Moran, hammered down on them. Corporal Wood and a section of Five Troop then swept through the area, collecting the AK-47, the RPG and its eight rounds.

Five Troop set off again, covering all arcs. Then, as the Charlie team of the point section crossed another bridge, they came under fire from buildings on the other side of the river, partly obscured by date palms. This isolated them from their Delta team, who swung their weapons around, hit the deck and gave covering fire.

'It was like something out of the movies,' said Corporal Taylor of Combat Team Two, some way to the rear.

D team laid down a heavy weight of fire, while C team popped smoke and peeled back over the bridge to rejoin the rest of the section. A false target indication was given that almost resulted in Four Troop and Combat Team Three on the next road, being taken out in another 'blue on blue' incident. But the potential friendly-fire was averted by the quick thinking of the comms team.

Enemy fire began coming in from further up the river, so the heavy machine gun was brought from the back of the BV. Under fire, with no cover, Marines Wheldon and Brennan set up the gun with Marines Forman and Cameron acting as resupply. As the 0.5 kicked in, Marine Cullen sprinted forward with his .338 sniper rifle – a so-called 'one shot, one kill' asset. Marine Scorah acted as his spotter. Five Troop's commander, Second Lieutenant Coryton, made a quick heads-up to assess the situation and directed the pair to a position across the road behind a tree under enemy fire. Their aim was to take out a bunch of three to five people at a range of 285–300 metres (312–28 yards). Marine Cullen set his scope and sent a shot in the enemy's direction. But the heavy weight of the returned fire made him keep his head down and he was unable to see the fall of shot, so he fired again. This time he just missed the enemy, but he was close enough to set them on their toes. Three ran left and one ran back across the bridge. By the time the Iraqis had decided which way to turn, the .338 had been cocked again and was sending another 'lead hello' in their direction. There was no missing this time. The right-hand soldier fell to the ground with a bullet through the chest.

Marine Cullen then indicated to the rest of Five Troop that three of the other enemy soldiers had fled into the date palms. Immediately, Marine Grant brought his underslung grenade launcher into play, lobbing round after round into the date palms. Plumes of mud and debris flew up into the air. With no enemy response, it was time to clear the area and move on to the next bridge. Not knowing the deployment of the enemy, Five Troop sent a LAW rocket flying into the bunker previously occupied by the Iraqis, while the 0.5 hammered away at the building next to it.

When Combat Team Two reached the bridge, they headed east for about 200 metres (218 yards) and 'went firm', that is, they took up a strong defensive position. Combat Team One then passed through and headed towards the eastern edge of the town to link up with the Brigade Recce Force, who, with C Squadron of the Queen's Dragoon Guards, would provide a screening force ahead of the Brigade's breakout towards Basra. As B Company headed down the road, the locals came out of their houses to welcome the advancing British troops. Then things turned nasty. An RPG round had just missed one Scimitar but its 30mm cannon quickly cleared the enemy's position, which was later discovered to be the house of a high-ranking officer. B Company secured this as the company's patrol base. This marked the end of a 36-hour operation and a 13-hour contact with the enemy, which left no friendly casualties from enemy fire.

Following the early morning pounding of enemy positions by the artillery of 29 Commando, Delta Company move forward towards Objective Blofeld, a sprawling complex that had once housed a university. As they moved in, the enemy were spotted moving to the rear of the buildings. The silence was broken by the sound of 0.50-calibre machine guns and, as tracer fire from Eight Troop poured down on the enemy, Corporal Hines and his engineers formed up to assault the position.

Second Lieutenant Eldridge led Combat Team Two off to clear Objective Dalton, a small village that, he said, reminded him of the movie *Black Hawk Down* (Ridley Scott, 2001). Naturally, his men were apprehensive, but then they heard that three Challenger 2s of the Scots Dragoon Guards were on their way to assist. Corporal Roe, a combat clerk, assumed the role of Anti-tank Section Commander and found himself escorting a tank. He had his ear protectors ready when it opened up with its main armament. This was deafening but effective. The village was cleared with no further enemy contact, though they made a good haul of AK-47s.

The Scots Dragoon Guards then set off on another task, leaving Delta Company to clear a number of small villages.

One of them was Al Yahudiyah. Approaching it, the four-vehicle convoy was caught in an ambush and hit by RPGs and machine-gun fire. Although they were under heavy and effective attack from three sides, Marine Gareth Thomas – with scant regard for his own safety – remounted the nearest vehicle and engaged the enemy positions for some considerable time with a heavy machine gun, even though he had not been trained to use it. Finding himself with two other Marines, isolated from the rest of his company, he then attempted to identify a route back to the frontline. While making their way through difficult terrain and, despite the inevitability of detection, the three identified and successfully engaged a small pocket of enemy at close range before continuing on their way to friendly lines. However, they found their way obstructed by a wide canal. Removing his assault equipment, Marine Thomas swam across to get a boat, which he then used to transport his colleagues and their equipment to safety. He was awarded the MC.

Eight Troop had an especially hard time of it, because they were on foot. Laden with ammunition, water and NBC kit, they had to push on in the searing heat through a tangled patch of date palms.

'This was not what we pictured when we entered Iraq,' said Second Lieutenant Elridge. 'It was more like a jungle than a desert.'

Delta Company reached their final objective with no further contact with the enemy. They then got a call to assist the MSG, who were having a difficult time of taking Objective Galore.

The General Purpose Machine Gun (GPMG) section under Lance Corporal Justin Thomas came under sustained attack from the enemy in a previously undetected location, which left many of his comrades exposed. Moving from the comparative safety of his position, Thomas climbed onto his open-topped vehicle to man a pintle mounted GPMG. Despite small-arms fire and rocket-propelled grenades landing around him, he returned fire for 15 minutes, enabling 20 other members of his troop to move safely to cover and regroup. This act of bravery ensured that the troop were able to extract themselves without loss of life from enemy fire, and launch a successful counter-attack. He was awarded the Conspicuous Gallantry Cross.

Hearing of the contact, Combat Team One under Sergeant Capewell rode to the rescue, pushing west. Meanwhile, the rest of Delta Company conducted vehicle checks while waiting for the order to move off. Then, a radio message came through. Combat Team One had been ambushed.

As they headed towards Objective Galore, a volley of RPGs hit their Pinzgauer all-terrain vehicles. Although two of the vehicles had been hit repeatedly, everyone managed to get out before the RPGs went off. But it was a close-run thing. Corporal Blackman reckoned that he could list the contents of his day sack as the tattered remnants of them came flying past his head.

Combat Team Two moved forward when they heard of the contact and Combat Team One pulled back to their new position. On the way, they were harassed by more RPGs and Fedayeen machine guns. Despite the intense fire, Combat Team One suffered not a single casualty, though they had lost two Pinzgauers.

Delta Company were now eager to hit back. Corporal Willis and his forward observation team called artillery support from 148 Battery under Sergeant Godley. This kept the enemy busy while Delta Company regrouped. Their first task was to destroy all kit that they could not recover.

But they soon found that the enemy were trying to encircle them. Just in time, Eight Troop arrived to help beat off the attack.

The Combat Teams then pushed forward to recover their equipment, with Eight Troop remaining behind to give covering fire from the rooftops and prevent the enemy trying to surround the men on the ground again. Combat Team Two moved off first to the left, clearing buildings on their way. Scaling the perimeter walls was made all the more difficult with a respirator strapped to the thigh.

Eventually, they reached the first Pinzgauer. Lance Corporal Thompson volunteered to drive it, but they were under enemy fire, which was quickly suppressed with a couple of LAWs and heavy covering fire from Corporal Attard's section on the rooftops. With the enemy reeling from the LAW blasts, Thompson ran forward, leaped into the Pinzgauer, started her up and drove to what he thought would be the relative safety of the company tactical headquarters, only to find that it was under fire from enemy soldiers, who were carrying not only the white flag but machine guns too.

The combat teams then pulled back to the company tactical headquarters, only to find that the contact there had been repelled. Then they were ordered back to rendezvous with Lima Company from 42 Commando to 'go firm' for the night.

'They were a most welcome sight for our weary eyes,' said Lieutenant Eldridge. 'When all was said and done, we had only lost two Pinzgauers and a quad, and the company had given a good account of itself against a large number of enemy. Someone was definitely watching our back that day, and a few lives may have been taken away from the nine.'

L Company had been seconded into 40 Commando Group for three days to support offensive operations in the area of Abu al-Khasib. They came up against stiff resistance from militia loyal to Saddam Hussein. On 31 March, they found themselves against armour and fanatical Fedayeen forces. Several major engagements occurred throughout the day, as they were attacked repeatedly with rocket-propelled grenades, heavy machine gun fire and small arms. In the final battle, a section under Corporal David Beresford's section was called upon to support a Challenger tank, which had been disabled by enemy fire about 5 kilometres (3 miles) ahead of friendly lines. The commander of the armoured repair and recovery vehicle, Corporal James Garrett, led a dangerous mission to rescue the stricken tank. In a difficult operation lasting six hours, in near-total darkness and in the face of enemy attacks, Garrett co-ordinated the task on the ground while providing cover with machine gun fire from the turret. During this time, he was exposed from the waist up and at considerable risk. With him was recovery mechanic Corporal Justin Smith, who worked for several hours in darkness and under attack to fix the damaged Challenger 2. Both were Mentioned in Dispatches. Captain Paul Lynch, who moved the MSG forward to provide close protection for the recovery crew, subsequently won the MC.

Corporal Beresford also directed his section to provide covering fire, allowing the regrouping of Coalition troops. At this point, and with complete disregard for his own safety, Beresford moved out of cover to dash forward 20 metres (65 feet) into a chest-deep lagoon of water and mud to rescue two machine gunners weighed down by their equipment. He was awarded the MC. On 2 April, L

Company returned to 42 Commando Group, having suffered no casualties, but with the best dits – stories – of the campaign, according to Lieutenant Roger Green.

UK Landing Force Command Support Group had move off Bubiyan Island and crossed the border into southern Iraq, where their detachments were spread out in various locations, from the edges of the Shatt al-Arab, where they came under sporadic fire with 40 Commando, to the salt marshes, where they suffered the mud and mosquitoes with 29 Commando, RA. Detachment Three found themselves at 40 Commando headquarters in Abu al-Khasib when it came under RPG and small-arms fire.

'Unluckily for us, we were positioned outside between the protection of the main building and the outer wall,' said Marine Jones with the Air Defence Troop, 'which, for some reason, had a five-foot [1.5-metre] gap between the bottom of the wall and the floor.'

The whole of 40 Commando headquarters then proceeded to line up on the roof of their building, assisted by some eager Coalition partners, and returned fire in the direction of the enemy. Little did they know that a few of their rounds were low, hitting the wall and bouncing their way – 'giving everyone else a reason to change their pants instead of just Marine Spence', Jones quipped.

Marine Rowe was with the Recce Troop, which joined BRF and MSG in a joint two-day clearance north of the east side of the Al Faw peninsula. After several mobile clearance operations with D Company in support, the troop went static for a couple of days in a forward position with BRF, 15 kilometres (9 miles) short of Basra. From there, they had made several daring night raids on possible enemy positions along the edge of the date palms with armed Land Rovers blazing, softening up the objectives for Operation James.

At 23.59 Zulu on the night of the attack on Abu al-Khasib, the troop moved into a facility to the east of the Iraqi naval base. Sergeant Trev Houghton's team took over the cranes there. This allowed Corporal Jack Broughton to position the troop's sniper section on the top of a crane, perched precariously 18 metres (60 feet) up and just 950 metres (about 1,000 yards) from the enemy naval base. Over three hours, well co-ordinated sniper shots wreaked havoc below with three confirmed dead and many more injured. Meanwhile, Corporal Twycross acted as a forward observer and pounded the compound with mortars. And, in the waterway that ran alongside, Sergeant Houghton's team engaged an enemy patrol boat which was being used to carry weapons. It was blasted out of the water when Captain Paul Boschi put two Lynx TOW missiles in its side.

After clearing Objective Galore, where D Company had been ambushed the day before, Eight Troop moved on to Objective Pussy. This was a Y-shaped road junction 7 kilometres (4.5 miles) short of Saddam Hussein's palace in Basra. As they arrived at the junction, Three Section of Eight Troop engaged an approaching saloon carrying Fedayeen with AK-47s. The car turned tail and disappeared in the opposite direction. As Eight Troop made their final approach on the objective, a funeral procession passed by, the result of the Marines' handiwork the previous day. Eight Troop then established a blocking position and a patrol base at the junction and settled in for a long wait.

'As far as we knew Basra was to be left until Baghdad had fallen, which could have been weeks rather than days,' said the officer commanding Eight Troop, Second Lieutenant Archer.

The position was easier to secure than they had first anticipated. Three of the their .50 calibre machine guns had arcs down the main routes, the other down a track to the south. They also had a sniper section from Recce Troop attached and, to improve their arcs of fire, Corporal Hines's engineers removed a tree using plastic explosives.

'In such a close environment, MIRA [the thermal imagine sight for MILAN anti-tank weapons] would not have been effective,' said Lieutenant Archer, 'so claymores and trip flares were deployed to the south and west along likely approaches.'

The Anti-tank Troop and Eight Troop were then able to perform close security and patrol tasks. This was made all the easier because they were near the Shatt al-Arab waterway. Numerous large irrigation canals ran off it, which closed off various approach routes.

Over the next few days, things fell into a routine. During the day, the Marines saw only local residents who wanted to return to their homes. Delta Troop did not allow this because, in the background, they noticed furtive movements by Fedayeen who waited for darkness in order to attack. On the first night, the enemy fired RPGs and small arms aimed, at best, in Delta Company's general direction. In response, the Marines' mortar team put illumination rounds in the sky, which set off fresh bursts of fire.

'Although the enemy seemed keen on making a lot of noise,' said Lieutenant Archer, 'they showed no signs of wanting to test the Marines' resolve.'

Earlier in the evening, a dog had set off a trip and received the benefit of two claymore mines. This had clearly sent a message to the enemy that it was best not to tangle with Delta Company.

They did, however, go through the motions. For Delta Company's remaining days at Objective Pussy, the Fedayeen maintained a distant threat, occasionally firing RPGs or mortars at the Marines' position. However, reports came through that more substantial enemy formations were approaching. This meant that the Marines spent most of the night standing to or in a 50–50 routine – and certainly nowhere near their beloved sleeping bags.

Even though they were maintaining a static position, their resupply was interrupted at one point. This proved to be a blessing in disguise. The company managed to get rice, potatoes, onions, cabbages, garlic, chickens, a duck and even some freshly-baked bread from the locals.

'If that had been us,' said a USMC staff sergeant, 'we'd just have starved, man.'

In all, Delta Company spent four relatively edgy days in the forward line. Although one night 2,500 enemy troops appeared just a few miles away, the threat never materialised. But the Iraqis never allowed them to relax. Even on the last night before they were relieved by B Company, an RPG went off within 50 metres (55 yards) of one of their vehicle checkpoints.

'In the face of our willingness to engage them when we had identified them, and when they probed during darkness, the Fedayeen certainly seemed to lack the will to put a more concentrated effort into the fight,' said Lieutenant Archer. 'It never pays to be half-hearted, and I'm certain that no Bootneck will ever be accused of that.'

In its two weeks in-country up to this point, 40 Commando had secured key oil infrastructure, cleared a large expanse of enemy-held terrain and taken the major enemy stronghold of Abu al-Khasib, killing more than 150 Iraqi soldiers and taking 440 prisoners in the process.

CHAPTER 9

INTO BASRA

In an RPG-ridden 24 hours as they steamed across the Al Faw peninsula, 40 Commando had secured a number of objectives, while the Recce Troop pushed westwards to protect the unit's flank. The troop then began a six-day period of aggressive mobile patrolling to find enemy dispositions and to take the fight to them enemy on the outskirts of Basra. And, when Sergeant Houghton's team located an enemy position protecting a bridge, a three-hour firefight ensued.

'Reacting quickly, Sergeant Houghton gained the initiative by using accurate indirect fire and deploying the mobile quick-reaction force,' said Marine Rowe, who was with them.

Within an hour, the whole troop had arrived at the battle and were aggressively pursuing the enemy at the western edge of their area of operations. The action was not halted till nightfall. Three enemy were confirmed dead and six Iraqi prisoners were taken to Commando headquarters for interrogation. There, two of them were confirmed as Category A prisoners – the most wanted. During the three-hour contact, Marine Dave Atkinson was injured in the leg by shrapnel from friendly-force mortar fire. But he continued firing his machine gun and manning his radio throughout the battle before eventually being evacuated to the regimental aid post.

For A Squadron of the Royal Scots Dragoon Guards, the morning of 29 March began under heavy mortar fire and saw a daring dawn raid into Iraq's second city. Having previously encountered only minor resistance in and around the town of Az Zubayr, the soldiers of Scotland's cavalry were left in no doubt that they were engaging a determined enemy when militia attacked their position on the outskirts of Basra with mortars shortly before midnight, destroying a truck and leaving two British soldiers in need of medical attention. Less than six hours later, A Squadron, supported by two infantry companies from 1st Battalion of the Black Watch, switched from defensive to offensive operations in response to an Iraqi attack and stormed into the centre of Basra.

Trooper Callum Hope was asleep on top of a Land Rover when the first mortar rounds exploded around him.

'I sat up in my sleeping bag and remember thinking to myself that some poor bugger was taking a pounding, but as I lay down again there was an explosion 30 feet [9 metres] away, and a further three close by after that,' he said. 'Everyone was racing to get their body armour and helmets on and dived into the nearest tank ditch. Then we had to sit and wait, which was the worst bit. Sitting there listening to the thuds was terrifying. When I joined the army I never actually thought that I would be at war and that attack was certainly a rude awakening to me where I was. For now I just want to get home without losing any of our guys.'

Sergeant Stewart Watson also found himself under fire.

'On a fear factor of one to ten, being mortared definitely warrants an extreme ten,' he said. 'In all honesty, we just never expected anything like that would happen to us. We knew that they had mortars and artillery. We knew they were capable of using them. But we never imagined we would be on the end of them. The Iraqis could not have caught us at a worse time – we were all curled up sleeping in our beds. Some of the rounds were less than twenty metres [22 yards] away from me and God only knows how someone was not seriously injured or killed. God willing, the two guys who were hurt will be OK and that we all get to go home in one piece.'

Within Twenty minutes, A Squadron counter-attacked. Its 11 Challenger 2 main battle tanks toppled a monument to Saddam Hussein, destroyed a television and radio transmitter and levelled a suspected Ba'ath Party headquarters with some accurate gunnery.

'Just as light was coming up we crossed the bridge and headed straight to Basra on the main dual carriageway,' said Major Tim Brown, leader of A Squadron.

'It is impossible to explain the feeling in my stomach as we waited on the bridge before rolling into Basra,' said Trooper Stuart Herkes. 'We were told to expect incoming fire and my nerves were building as we got closer to the off. As a driver I could not really see much of what was going on around us as we charged into the city, but I could see rockets flying across in front of us and the tank in front taking a lot of incoming.'

But A Squadron were soon giving as good as they got.

'As soon as we were moving the adrenalin just took over,' said Herkes, 'but I was glad that we had the guys in the turrets doing their thing and doing it well. This sort of thing is definitely what I joined the army to do – the feeling of elation as we hit our targets and pulled back was a real buzz. It's hard not to feel a bit low when it's all over – you've been on the biggest rollercoaster ride of your life and all of a sudden you have to get off and the adrenalin stops flowing.'

It was adrenalin all round.

'During the raid itself I experience an almighty adrenalin rush and my training just took over completely,' said Sergeant Watson. 'All I was focused on was doing my job – loading as many rounds as I possibly could. Fortunately, as the operator, I couldn't see all the incoming fire, but I could hear it over the net and hear the small-arms fire and RPG shells whooshing as they came past.'

The early-morning bombardment had made A Squadron eager for the off.

'After being attacked I really wanted to get into Basra and get on with things,' said Corporal Craig Brown. 'There was a lot of incoming fire and our tank was hit by an RPG round. I felt a thud inside the tank, but was too busy concentrating on doing my job to worry about it. It was not until after the raid that we discovered the round had mangled the bottom of the track.'

They expected resistance.

'The targets we had been tasked with engaging were by far and away the farthest into Basra any British forces had been, and following the mortar attack we suspected that we would come under fire,' said Major Brown. 'Sure enough, 2 to 3 kilometres [1.25–1.9 miles] from the bridge, the RPG and sniper fire began and remained fairly constant throughout. A couple of our tanks did take hits, but, fortunately, the round struck the side armour and caused only minimal damage. It was pretty scary stuff, but we woke up to it – it was a miracle that no one was killed.'

But they were oblivious of the dangers at the time.

'Hearing the rockets whizzing past was a wee bit frightening, especially because as an operator I couldn't really see what was going on for myself,' said Lance Corporal Paul Musson. 'Being involved in the raid was a major buzz, but you experience a massive comedown when you get back and realise that you could have been killed. At the time you don't think about the dangers because you're so focused on your job, but you have plenty of time to contemplate what might have been after the event.'

Challenger 2 gunner Trooper Vince McLeod was credited with being the crack shot who felled the television transmitter.

'All of the tanks were putting fire on the mast's base,' he said, 'but it was having no real effect at all, so I decided to aim for its four stanchions. My first round hit one of them, and, although the tower stayed up, I could see that I had blown a bit chunk of metalwork away. Two more shots and the whole thing came tumbling down. The whole crew were buzzing when it fell and it was such a great feeling – talk about job satisfaction!'

After this initial skirmish, the main attack was held back for a week. Meanwhile, 42 Commando continued its sweep northwards from the Al Faw peninsula. Then, on 5 April, 42 Commando Group deployed by road and helicopter to a forward assembly area to the east of Basra, on the edge of the date-palm-fringed Shatt al-Arab waterway. J Company moved up by RAF Chinook, after making more arrests and weapons finds in Umm Khayyal. After working in and around Abu al-Khasib in support of 40 Commando, the BRF was moved up and attached to 42 Commando for the final push into Basra.

'It was clear to many in the Commando Group that this

was likely to be a decisive moment in the campaign,' said Lieutenant Roger Green, who was with them. 'As the second city of Iraq, and with its extensive suburbs, the move on Basra could entail intense street-to-street fighting with its attendant risk of casualties.'

At 12.30 Zulu on 6 April, after 24 hours of preparation, 42 Commando Group – with C Squadron of the Queen's Dragoon Guards with F Squadron of the Royal Tank Regiment under its command – moved in to secure key bridges in the eastern part of the Basra suburbs, along with a water treatment plant and the presidential palace, both of which were on the banks of the Shatt al-Arab waterway. In a bold and decisive move, 42 Commando Group entered Basra from the south and east. Their swift advance encountered little resistance. It appeared that the enemy had recently fled and only M Company Group made any contact. They had spent a little over a week in Umm Qasr and Umm Khayyal before moving north to begin the historic charge into Basra.

'Once again, it was M Company who led the way,' said Major Harry Taylor, who was attached to them. 'BVs rolling through the streets alongside the Challenger 2s of the 7th Armoured Brigade. Although there were some contacts that first night, our entry was better remembered by the hundreds of locals who turned out to cheer us in.'

'The local people were overjoyed at their liberation,' said Lieutenant Green, 'although some were rightly apprehensive of our presence.'

Lieutenant David Pinkstone, leader of Nine Troop of Egypt Squadron of Two Royal Tank Regiment, told a different story. He said that, as they were going into Basra, his tanks encountered a minefield, a lorry across the road which was also mined, two bunkers and a T-55 tank.

'Our squadron, after destroying these enemy positions, advanced into Basra, destroying the Ba'ath HQ before securing various military compounds,' he said. 'The remainder of the Black Watch Battle Group followed up to clear the compounds. Only then did elements of the Royal Scots Dragoon Guards and Fusiliers enter the city. They did not lead the operation, as the *Daily Telegraph* reported.'

He felt strongly that a number of times during the war, the contribution of E Squadron of 2 RTR was ignored by the media.

'It performed with such measured professionalism on 6 April that it is very disheartening to see others receive the praise, although I obviously don't want to take anything away from the Scots Dragoon Guards, who were also involved,' he said. 'I hope I don't come across as a whinger, but, having sat on the road into Basra being hit by RPGs and small arms and having experienced the emotions we did on entering the city first, I hope you understand my position.'

Credit should also go to the 3rd Regiment of the Royal Horse Artillery, supporting the 7th Armoured Brigade, who had softened up the defences with their 45-tonne AS-90 guns. These could put down 4,500 kilos (10,000 pounds) of high explosives and steel splinters across an area the size of a football pitch in 15 seconds, and were greatly in demand as artillery support. Formed just seven weeks before the start of hostilities, the battery had charged across the Kuwaiti border and through the southern Iraqi desert on the first day. Their forward observers had called in artillery and air strikes while themselves under fire, and were much in demand by the US forces as well as the Paras, the Commandos and the Desert Rats.

Also in support was 17/16 Battery of 26 Regiment, RA,

who were operating in the Gulf as the 4th Battery of 3 RHA. From At Tubah al Hamra, they had moved up to the former military air base at Shaibah, 19 kilometres (12 miles) south-west of Basra. The Brigade HQ was housed in a huge stone bunker there. They also shared the airfield with Challenger tanks, armoured infantry, engineers and a battery of Phoenix Unmanned Aerial Vehicles from 32 Regiment, RA.

From this position, they fired a large amount of high explosive and bomblets into Basra and the surrounding area. Battle damage assessments indicated that their use of the L20 bomblet round was highly effective, destroying dozens of tanks, mortars and enemy positions as well as aiding numerous allied advances and forays. However, great care had to be taken to ensure that 'collateral damage' was kept to a minimum.

Captain Paul Whitbread of the RHA, a forward-observation officer with the Black Watch, was instrumental in co-ordinating several dismounted artillery and helicopter attacks, to assist the 7th Armoured Brigade's entry into Basra. In the urban battle that followed, he was Mentioned in Dispatches for 'his professional expertise [which] helped reduce collateral damage to the city'.

The use of bomblets also caused problems for friendly forces. A Royal Logistic Corps Bomb Disposal Officer was awarded the Queen's Gallantry Medal after he removed by hand unstable M-42 bomblets from beneath the body of a mortally injured colleague. Captain Timothy Gould, a member of the Joint EOD Group, cleared a safe route to Staff Sergeant Chris Muir RLC, but realised that he could not be moved because he was lying on a number of unexploded bomblets. Time was critical if Muir was to get treatment, so Gould took the considerable risk of dealing with the M-42 bomblets by hand – a dangerous practice carried out only as a last resort. Despite his efforts, Muir died at the scene of his horrific injuries. Gould later removed for demolition a container of more than 80 bomblets in Muir's vehicle.

Later, 17/16 Battery saw with their own eyes the damage they had wreaked. As they advanced, they saw burned-out tanks, devastated Iraqi positions, shattered artillery pieces and rubble littering the area. At night, they made gun raids towards Basra to attack targets that would otherwise have been out of range. During these forays, they were vulnerable to attack by RPGs, which were fast becoming the Iraqis' weapon of choice. Although the battery quickly won the respect of the tank and infantry men, their commanders found them noisy and the battery was ordered to relocate, with J Battery, to a factory compound nearby so that headquarters staff could get a good night's sleep. There, the artillery men found they had to share their quarters with news teams from the BBC, Sky and GMTV. Then, drums of chlorine were found on the site and the guns were relocated again to an abandoned military detention centre on marshy ground about 5 kilometres (3 miles) outside Basra. From there, they fired more bomblets and illuminating shells while the 7th Armoured Brigade secured Basra, meeting little more resistance.

The key to taking Basra was the capture of the four bridges that span the broad Shatt al-Basra to the south of the city. They provided direct routes into the southern suburbs, which the 7th Armoured Brigade used to mount incursions against targeted pockets of resistance before the final capture of the city. The strategic importance of these solid concrete structures was not lost on Saddam's supporters in the city, who refused to let the Coalition take them unchallenged. Soldiers from the 1st Battalion of the Royal Regiment of Fusiliers (RRF) and the 1st Battalion of the Irish Guards (IG) were among the armoured infantry battalions charged with taking and holding the causeways under the threat of tank, mortar and small-arms fire. For many of them it would be their first time in action.

'Even though it was my first firefight, it's hard to remember any details because everything seemed to happen so quickly,' said Corporal Jason Thomas of Y Company, 1 RRF. 'It was a real buzz and, to be honest, fear didn't play a big part because, like a lot of the lads, I was just relieved to actually be doing something.'

Lance Corporal Maddar of 1 IG was another who felt no fear. 'I didn't fear for my own safety because I had complete faith in our equipment and the support that we had, especially from the tankies,' he said. 'All my skills and drills came to the fore and I just got on with the job in hand.'

With him was Guardsman Gavin Meers of 1 IG. 'Being on the bridge was different from anything else I have experienced,' he said. 'The training kicks in and you just get on with it. I've enjoyed being out there and it's exactly what I joined the army for.'

Others also felt that all their training now paid off. 'When it was happening I fell back on my training and automatically did what I needed to do,' said Lance Sergeant Mick Welch of 1 IG. 'The main difference between war fighting and training is that you have a fear inside you, but that's not a bad thing. Fear makes you sharper in everything you do.'

'It was a hairy time and it made us realise we were at war and that this was where the fighting was going to start,' said Guardsman Ricky Banner of 1 IG. 'I kept asking to have a Challenger 2 by our side. Being in an APC was bit nerve-racking and it was a case of 72 hours of wanting someone there next to us.'

But Challenger 2s did not necessarily guarantee protection. Corporal Craig Comber of the REME, an armoured recovery mechanic attached to the Queen's Royal Lancers (QRL), recovered damaged Challenger 2 tanks and their crews in great danger on at least three occasions. One rescue was carried out under fire, another from the middle of an unmarked minefield. On another occasion, he used the dozer blade on his vehicle to plough a safe route through a minefield to allow the 1st Fusiliers Battle Group to maintain the momentum of its advances into Basra. He was awarded the MC and later promoted to sergeant.

Staff Sergeant John Southam, a troop leader with B Squadron of the QRL, was Mentioned in Dispatches for protecting an isolated Challenger 2 tank from enemy RPG teams. He pushed the enemy back – engaging them closely for ten hours under fire – before eventually advancing within sight of the Iraqi Naval Academy, then co-ordinated artillery fire on it.

But the young men in the Warriors were naturally full of trepidation as they rode into Basra.

'There was certainly a lot of excitement, but it was tempered with nerves,' said Sergeant Stu Wickham of Z Company, 1 RRF. 'There were a lot of young lads in my wagon and I was impressed and proud with the way they handled themselves under pressure.'

For most, sitting in the back of the APC was the worst part. 'Initially, it was quite scary being in the back of the wagon, but once we were on the ground it all came together,' said Fusilier Dan Moran of Z Company, 1 RRF. 'I found it exciting and it's certainly the sort of thing I joined up for.'

'We were expecting trouble when we went up there and were prepared for it,' said Corporal Farrier of Z Company, 1 RRF. 'The worst bit was not when we got out of the wagon, but as we were *waiting* to get out, not knowing what was going on outside. Once we hit the ground it felt like seconds, but we were probably on the ground for 20 minutes.'

For others getting out of the APC was the nerve-racking bit. 'It was my first experience of a firefight and I was quite scared when we debussed on the bridge,' said another Fusilier, 'but after a short while adrenalin just took over. You can't compare it to training – nobody shoots back at you on an exercise.'

Then there were the mortars. 'When the mortar rounds came in I have never been so scared in all my life,' said Fusilier Lee Wines of Y Company, 1 RRF. 'I'm glad we can look back and laugh about it now.'

Drummer Andrew Carr of Y Company, 1 RRF, also felt that a surge of adrenalin helped him through. 'Being in a live situation is totally different from training – it is one hell of an experience and a complete adrenalin rush,' he said. 'Your personal safety is always at the back of your mind but you just crack on with your job.'

Lance Corporal Lee Morris of Y Company, 1 RRF, felt the same. 'I was nervous at the time and have never experienced anything like being mortared,' he said. 'Training takes over and you don't really think about what you're doing. You just do it instinctively. It's not till you sit back afterwards that you begin to analyse things in more detail.'

The way had been cleared by the Royal Engineers. Armoured Vehicle Commander Corporal Peter Brown of the RE was Mentioned in Dispatches when cleared a route

---

though an obstacle laced with anti-tank mines in a daylight attack on Basra, despite sustaining a direct hit to his vehicle.

During the Irish Guards' advance into Basra, Lieutenant Daniel O'Connell commanded a platoon of Warriors, part of One Company of One IG, attached to the Scots Dragoon Guards Battle Group. When One Company was ordered to assault an objective centred on the Basra College of Literature, O'Connell's platoon was first into position to assault the most heavily defended area of the complex. He manoeuvred his platoon into position, engaging several enemy bunkers, before dismounting and breaking into the first building. The speed of his attack reduced the chances of his platoon being engaged by dug-in troops. After supporting the next assault platoon, O'Connell remounted and cleared five more buildings, driving his men on and leading each clearance himself, placing himself in great personal danger.

As the light faded, his section – now in a defensive perimeter around the complex – was attacked, with two men killed and two wounded. O'Connell calmed and steadied his troops, organising the swift extraction of casualties. He was awarded the MC, while senior medical officer Major Kevin Burgess was Mentioned in Dispatches when he and his team administered the treatment – while under enemy fire – that saved the life of an Irish Guardsman who had been hit in the chest.

During the fierce and protracted battle for the College of Literature, a Warrior turret gunner, Lance Sergeant Alan Hanger of Three Company Commando – 1 IG – spotted an enemy soldier, who had pretended to be dead, picking up an RPG and aiming at a fellow Warrior. Realising that he risked hitting friendly vehicles and civilians in the area if he used his Warrior armaments, he opened his turret, exposing himself to enemy fire, picked up his rifle and shot the man with the RPG. In a separate incident, Sergeant Hanger used his Warrior to shield a soldier shot on foot patrol – again exposing himself to enemy fire – to give first aid and get the casualty into the back of the armoured fighting vehicle. He was Mentioned in Dispatches.

As commander of a Warrior platoon of Two Company 1 IG Second Lieutenant Thomas Orde-Powlett was directed to clear an enemy position north of Basra. He carried out a successful night attack on two bunkers before killing a group of enemy soldiers who attacked with RPGs and small arms. In a subsequent action in Basra, he cleared an enemy position despite his Warrior coming under sustained attack and being hit twice by RPG rounds.

'His sole concern was the completion of his military task, during which he showed a total disregard for his own safety,' says the citation with his MC.

On three occasions, an Armoured Vehicle Commander, Corporal Peter Chilton of the RE, played a leading role during the Scots Dragoon Guards' advance into Basra city. His efforts included leading a raid to clear an enemy barricade from a main route into the city and extinguishing an enemy oil trench fire obscuring visibility of enemy positions. He was Mentioned in Dispatches.

Later, a dismounted section of Irish Guardsmen from 2 Company 1 IG approached a previously cleared bunker in Basra, when they were engaged by machine-gun fire from the position. Then the Iraqi machine-gunner ran out with a grenade. Everyone dived for cover except 19-year-old Guardsman Anton Branchflower, who hit the Iraqi soldier as he attempted to throw the grenade, which detonated, killing the man. Branchflower, who had completed recruit training just days before deploying to the Gulf, was awarded the MC.

During the advance, Lance Sergeant Rodney Holland's Warrior was attacked by gunmen. Two of his section were killed and he and a colleague injured. Despite a shoulder wound, Holland returned fire until he ran out of ammunition, then remounted into the Platoon Commander's vehicle and returned to his section to assist with the security of the area and the evacuation of casualties. He was Mentioned in Dispatches.

Two soldiers who were killed in action during the assault on Basra received posthumous Mentions in Dispatches. Lance Corporal Barry Stephen of the 1st Battalion of the Black Watch was killed after he left the safety of an armoured vehicle to provide covering fire for comrades. And Fusilier Keith Turrington, of 1 RRF, fell during an assault on an enemy trench to the north of Basra.

'They and others made the ultimate sacrifice for their country. We must not forget them, their friends and their families,' said Air Chief Marshal Sir Brian Burridge.

Once in Basra, M Company spent a busy 24 hours manning vehicle checkpoints and endeavouring to keep law and order as looters moved into abandoned regime houses. This kept them extremely busy.

'"Jonah" Jones finally broke into a smile after shooting up a suspected suicide bomber who crashed through the gates of Basra's hospital in a stolen car,' said Major Harry Taylor of M Company. 'Meanwhile, a section under Corporal Ritchie Mockle of the London Royal Marine Reserves was controlling a key bridge and engaging armed looters who were running riot along the riverbank.'

While M Company were on the streets of Basra, J Company had been given the job of taking of Saddam

Hussein's presidential palace, just to the east of the city, with the support of the tanks of the 7th Armoured Brigade. They cleared the building room by room, noting on their way the gold taps, marble floors and porcelain toilets. Photographs of Marines on Saddam's lavatory abounded.

The presidential palace was surprisingly free of Iraqi troops, although there were some intransigent civilians living there. Marine Lewis Stallar of Bristol Royal Marine Reserves, serving with J Company, was among those tasked with sorting out the situation. This he duly did, frightening one man so much that he passed out at his feet.

With the world's media only a couple of hours behind them, J Company of 42 Commando figured prominently in the international press for the next few days.

'However, the glory was short-lived for Three Troop, as the numerous guard towers dotted around the palace beckoned,' said Sheraton.

The BRF also arrived at the presidential palace, but were less impressed.

'The presidential palace was a unique experience,' said Sergeant Gaz Veacock. 'However, it was not the Aladdin's Cave that most were expecting.'

After Umm Khayyal, Three Troop of 59 Independent Commando Squadron of the RE also headed to Basra, where they were to clear the water treatment plant and Saddam's palace in ordnance.

'The air conditioning, double beds, power and plumbing provided a welcome break,' said Lieutenant Lamont.

However, it was not to be theirs for long. The Headquarters Company of 42 Commando had taken up residence by the time M Company moved in, and Taylor found himself greeted by WO2 Al Starr and Sergeant Steve Boland, of the Isle of Man and Mersey Detachments of the

RMR respectively, who were manning the checkpoint when he arrived. By the time M Company had settled in, they heard on the BBC World Service that Baghdad had fallen.

'Over 40 Reservists served with 42 Commando on Operation Telic and no doubt every one of them has a different story to tell,' said Major Taylor. 'But one thing we all have in common is that there is no place we would rather have been. It was a privilege to be apart of 3 Commando Brigade and I would like to thank our regular counterparts for making the Royal Marine Reserve so welcome and utilising us so effectively.'

Soon, J Company were on the move again. This time they were sent to Rumaylah to guard the oilfields that 16 Air Assault Brigade had secured. Three Troop of 59 Independent Commando Squadron, RE also moved on to Rumaylah to take over a crossing on the Hammar Canal from 9 Parachute Squadron and secure the gas–oil-separation plants there.

The BRF remained in Basra, where they quickly switched to a peacekeeping role, supporting 42 Commando, who were trying to maintain law and order in the eastern part of the city.

'Joy had quickly turned into criminal activity,' said Lieutenant Green. 'With Saddam Hussein's forces gone, law and order had broken down and there was an orgy of mass looting. K and M Companies quickly deployed throughout the area of operations to deter looters and stabilise the situation in the suburbs. Meanwhile, L Company started to conduct river patrols along the Shatt al-Arab waterway.'

The Commando Group had no chance to get used to a life of luxury living in Saddam Hussein's palace. Within a few days, it was handed over to the headquarters of the 7th Armoured Brigade and 42 Commando Group's area of operations was handed over to C Company of 40 Commando.

'At this point, we had to bid a fond farewell to F Squadron of the Royal Tank Regiment and 29 Commando Regiment Tactical Parties, who had been with them since January,' said Lieutenant Green. '29 Commando Regiment Tactical Parties included a detachment from the US Marine Group we had built up a particularly strong relationship with.'

At midday on 12 April, the rest of 42 Commando Group left the presidential palace to relieve elements of 16 Air Assault Brigade at the key gas-oil-separation plants in the Rumaylah oilfields 50 kilometres (31 miles) to the west of Basra. L Company patrolled the town of Rumaylah, while the other companies secured the GOSPs to deter sabotage.

The BRF's final area of operations was in the town of Az Zubayr in support of the Duke of Wellington Regiment, working with the Field Humint Team. This area, previously untouched, provided a rich source of intelligence that led to numerous house searches and the arrests of suspects. They continued to exploit this intelligence with some success until the end of operations was announced.

'Operation Telic was an emotional roller coaster from start to finish for the BRC,' said Sergeant Veacock at the end of it. 'We've experience initial devastation, followed by elation for a job well done. We've been successful in all that we'd been involved in, but, most of all, the BRF has become a very strong organisation as a result.'

There was other mopping up to be done. Throughout the main assault on Basra, 40 Commando's Recce Troop had been patrolling out to the west of the city. But that did not mean they missed out on the action. Several days after they had made their initial contact with the enemy on the outskirts of Basra, Sergeant Dave Cockcroft's team were probing west in vehicles, clearing the area. As they approached a village he thought might be occupied by the enemy, he noticed several suspicious-looking characters observing his patrol. So he dismounted his team and they moved cautiously on foot towards what they took to be an enemy-occupied building.

Suddenly, Marine Leo King threw himself to the ground as an RPG round flew by only a few centimetres from his chest. Marine Sam McCormick returned fire with a heavy barrage of machine gun fire, allowing the forward men to retreat. Then the armed Land Rovers moved up. Cockcroft extracted his patrol, allowing accurate air-burst artillery fire to destroy the enemy.

'After that the enemy disappeared from Recce Troop's area of operations,' said Marine Rowe. 'Nevertheless, we continued patrolling, though they allowed one team to rotate through B echelon to shower, get some fresh food and sleep in cot beds for the first time in four weeks. The troop subsequently supported 539 Assault Squadron RM's boat patrols and D Company's foot patrols, before being pulled out to HMS *Ocean* to the welcome sound of beer cans popping.'

The Royal Marines Boat Group was already patrolling the Shatt al-Arab waterway with 40 Commando and eventually made contact with 42 Commando at the presidential palace. They undertook further recce work on the Khawr Az Zubayr, clearing the waterway and port. They also sent one landing craft to prevent local fishermen interfering with mine clearing work. When this task was complete on 15 April, 40 Commando Recce Troop used hovercraft and inflatables to insert observations posts in the marshes and conduct clearance patrols. By then, 539 Assault Squadron, with the exception of the Amphibious Ready Boat Group, was being pulled out. Their craft were loaded onto the MV *Smit Enterprise* and RFA *Sir Bedivere* to return to the UK.

With Basra secure, 17/16 Battery moved out of their swampy home and into Basra International Airport. From there they were sent to a position 70 kilometres (about 43 miles) north of Basra to work with 7 Para, RHA, in support of the 16 Air Assault Brigade. But there the resistance soon melted away and they found themselves headed south again to rejoin 3 RHA, who were preparing for peacekeeping operations.

In 17-days of continuous firing, 3 RHA had expended 9,513 shells, while logging 250 kilometres (155 miles) of operational movements. Then they switched effortlessly to an infantry role, picking up the SA80s and patrolling the streets of a city where every house had an AK-47. Their job was to ensure humanitarian aid got through. Lieutenant Helena Bevan and Second Lieutenant Ben Watson said that they found 17/16 Battery's entrance into Basra humbling, as the crowds waved and cheered while taking time off to attack images of Saddam Hussein with sticks and rocks. By mid-April, they were occupying an area of Basra University and conducting heavy maintenance on their guns. Soon after, they were returned to their base at Gütersloh, Germany.

During 21 days of hostilities up until the fall of Baghdad, there was only one day when Sergeant Mark Heley, Patrol Commander in the Recce Troop of 23 Engineer Regiment (Air Assault) and his team of six were not dangerously close to the enemy. Mounted in unarmoured, stripped-down Land Rovers, they were time and again tasked to accompany fresh infantry patrols to provide engineer-based intelligence for 16 Air Assault Brigade. On a joint patrol with Sergeant Nathan Bell's Pathfinders, Heley won the MC for his leadership during a constant running night battle, and for maintaining a constant rate of machine-gun fire to suppress an enemy intent on killing them. He carried on fighting after being struck in the chest by a round, which deflected off his pistol and lodged in his notebook. The citation says, 'Sergeant Heley is one of a very rare breed, able to overcome his own fears in spite of the threats around him and yet lead by personal example.'

CHAPTER 10

RED CAPS AT AL-MAJARR AL-KABIR

Just as British forces in southern Iraq appeared to be adjusting to their post-conflict peacekeeping role, the British Army suffered its heaviest loss of life in a single incident since the start of the war. Six Royal Military Police soldiers were killed and eight other military personnel were wounded on 24 June in the town of al-Majarr al-Kabir, 160 kilometres (100 miles) north of Basra.

The incident occurred when the Red Caps were searching homes in the town for heavy weapons. Tensions had been running high and Salah Mohammed, a local community leader appointed by British soldiers, said that the military police had ignored a written agreement, signed by both sides, that they would give adequate notice before they searched people's homes for illegal weapons. Locals were also angered because, they said, the British soldiers had used dogs during their searches. This is unacceptable in a Muslim country. British authorities denied this, saying that they had always tried to observe Muslim customs while carrying out their searches.

Whatever the case, there was a demonstration and

shooting broke out. It is unclear who started firing first. A sniper may have been at work, or the Red Caps may have fired warning shots or used rubber bullets to quell the crowd who were loyal to Saddam Hussein. But the word soon passed that four demonstrators had been killed.

The military police were then forced to retreat to the abandoned police station before the angry crowd stormed the building. In a frenzied attack, the six policemen were killed and the building was set on fire. There have been allegations that the men surrendered after running out of ammunition, but were killed anyway. It has also been said that radio communications in the area were poor and relationships between the 1 Para Battle Group, who controlled the sector, and the RMP platoon were confused.

There had been trouble in the town before. Locals in al-Majarr al-Kabir routinely carried machine guns and small arms, and resisted British attempts to disarm them. Earlier that day, while on patrol in the town, troops from the 1 Para came under attack from RPGs, machine guns and rifles wielded by a large number of Iraqi gunmen.

A quick-reaction force, including a troop of Scimitar armoured vehicles and a Chinook helicopter, were called in to help, but they also came under fire. Seven men in the helicopter and one man on the ground were injured in the fighting.

According to Captain Dennis Abbot of 19 Mechanised Brigade Media Ops, the death toll at al-Majarr al-Kabir might have been higher but for the prompt actions and professionalism of the tri-service accident and emergency team at 1 Close Support Medical Regiment dressing station in Al Amarah. After the helicopter came under fire as it attempted to land in the town, the quick-thinking pilot flew to 1 Para Battle Group headquarters, 15 minutes to the north at Al Amarah, and landed beside the dressing station. The 35-strong A&E team split into groups so that all the injured could receive treatment simultaneously. They then worked furiously. The whole process, from the arrival of the injured at the dressing station to their evacuation to 202 Field Hospital at Shaibah, was completed in less than 40 minutes, a critical period that almost certainly made the difference between life and death for the two most badly injured.

The bodies of the six RMP men were returned to the UK for burial with military honours. Those who died were: Sergeant Simon Alexander Hamilton-Jewell (aged 41); Corporal Russell Aston (30); Corporal Paul Graham Long (24); Corporal Simon Miller (21); Lance Corporal Benjamin John McGowan Hyde (23); and Lance Corporal Thomas Richard Keys (20). All from 156 Provost Company.

CHAPTER 11

ACTIONS IN AL AMARAH

So far, operations in Iraq have yielded only one Victoria Cross. It was awarded to Private Johnson Beharry of C Company, the 1st Battalion of the Princess of Wales's Royal Regiment (PWRR). He was the first person since 1965 to be awarded Britain's highest award for gallantry while still alive.

Born on the Caribbean island of Grenada, he was just 24 when he won the VC. He emigrated to Britain in 1999 and joined the British Army in 2001. Within 15 minutes of being deployed to active duty, the compound he was assigned to came under rocket fire.

On 1 May 2004, he was at the British Army base at Abu Naji, just south of the Iraqi city of Al Amarah. About 160 kilometres (100 miles) north of Basra, it was a centre of activity of the Iranian-backed Mahdi Army, loyal to rogue Shiite cleric Muqtada al-Sadr. Just after lunch that day, he was with one of the five 30-tonne Warrior armoured vehicles of Eight Platoon that were lined up facing the gate, ready to go. He was driving Whisky Two Zero, the platoon commander's vehicle, which always leads the patrols.

It was a hot afternoon and Beharry and his best friend, Jamaican-born Private Troy 'Sammy' Samuels, Whisky Two Zero's gunner, headed for the Quick Response Force Room, a small brick building close to where the Warriors are parked. It was 47°C (117°F) and they were hoping to catch a precious few minutes' sleep in the shade before they were summoned to deploy. But the place was crowded and there was no chance to get settled. Just then, Woody, another of Whisky Two Zero's crew, came to the door and said, 'Looks like party time.'

Another armoured patrol had come under fire from RPGs and Eight Platoon were going to the rescue. Privates Beharry and Samuels picked up their helmets and body armour and headed out of the door. By the time they got outside, the platoon commander, Second Lieutenant Richard Deane, was already lowering himself into the commander's hatch of Whisky Two Zero. Beharry pulled on his body armour, leaped up on the hull and slid into his seat. Once his helmet was on, he ran a quick intercom check.

'Boss, Sammy, can you hear me?'

'Roger,' said Deane.

'Loud and clear,' said Sammy.

He checked that his SA80 combat rifle was in the footwell next to his knee, then pressed the starter button. Once the diesel engine roared into life, he put the vehicle into drive and moved out of the compound.

The road in Al Amarah was rough. The water main was broken and water bubbled up through the asphalt. Private Beharry drove with the hatch open, otherwise his vision would have been badly restricted. But the sewers were broken too and the smell of excrement in the hot sun made him gag. Behind him, he heard Deane open his hatch, too.

The street was busy. A man selling watermelons from a

cart at the side of the road waved. A motorcycle overtook then. The man on the pillion had an AK-47 slung over his shoulder. Youths on the street corners also brandished AKs. Beharry checked in the mirror that the four other Warriors were following in convoy. Whisky Two Two was 50 metres (55 yards) behind. The rest were spaced out evenly behind him. Whisky Two Two's turret was traversing from right to left, with the gun angled towards the rooftops. Apart from Deane and Beharry, everybody else had his hatch closed.

At the junction ahead, Beharry slowed.

'Bee, what is it?' Deane asked. 'Why are you slowing?'

Beharry said that he felt that something was not right. The junction was clear of people. When he checked in his mirror again, he saw that the behind road was empty of other traffic. Just a few minutes before, it had been busy. The Warriors were now bunched up and vulnerable. The street was narrow and the houses either side were high. The soldiers nervously looked around them, expecting an ambush, but seeing nothing.

Then Sammy came on the intercom.

'Left-hand side,' he shouted. 'There's a kid across the street. Eleven, maybe 12 years old. He's holding what looks like an RPG.'

Before Beharry got a chance to turn and look, the rocket-propelled grenade hit the Warrior. There was a massive explosion and the vehicle shook violently. Beharry grabbed the cross that he wore around his neck and began to pray.

Looking out of the open hatch, Beharry could see nothing. Al Amarah was still like a ghost town. Still dazed from the explosion, he got on the intercom.

'Boss, what was that?' he said, trying to keep the fear from his voice.

But the headphones were dead. There was not even the crackle of static.

'Boss, what's happened?' he asked again.

He tried to crane his neck around to see Lieutenant Deane, but his view was blocked by the turret. But he could smell burning and heard a scream. Then his training kicked in. Where there is one RPG, there are likely to be more. He jammed his foot hard down on the accelerator, but before the power kicked in a second explosion knocked the back end of the vehicle 2 metres (6 feet) across the road.

The engine spluttered and Beharry feared it was going to die on him. But the revs picked up and he turned the Warrior towards the open road, determined to make a run for it. He saw a barricade of hastily erected breeze-blocks too late. But, before he hit it, there was another explosion, bigger than the last. Beharry felt a pressure wave, filled with noise and heat, tearing past him and out of the open hatch. The Warrior was on fire and filling rapidly with thick, noxious smoke. He braced himself for another explosion, but then he felt a more reassuring movement. The Warrior was slowly forcing its way through the makeshift barricade.

From the back of the vehicle, he could hear more screaming. Then the bullets came down like hailstones, pinging off the Warrior's hull. Gunmen were shooting at them from the rooftops. Then he heard answering fire from the Warrior. However, it was not the rat-a-tat-tat of the chain gun on the turret, but Samuels with his SA80 on single shot.

'Drive, Paki!' Samuels shouted to Beharry. 'For Christ's sake, drive! There's more of them lining up with RPGs.'

Beharry stamped down on the accelerator, but the engine barely responded.

'Move, Beharry! Move, move, move!' yelled Woody from the back.

Then Beharry called out to the boss.

'Stop calling the boss,' Samuels shouted. 'The boss is dead. He got hit by the first RPG. He's lying on the floor of the turret. He's a mess.'

As Beharry sped down the street, a man in Arab dress ran out into the road and started firing an AK-47. The bullets ricocheted off the Warrior's front armour. Beharry shouted up at Samuels to use the chain gun. But it was jammed. All Sammy had was Lieutenant Deane's rifle.

The man with the AK-47 was now 50 metres (55 yards) away, firing from the hip. A bullet slammed into Beharry's helmet and his head was thrown back against the hatch. But Beharry drove on and, at the last possible moment, the man with the AK-47 leaped back into an alleyway while the Warrior thundered off down the road.

Further down the street, the houses were decked with the Black Flag of Islam. Beharry feared that the black flags foretold their deaths. Then, out of the corner of his eyes, he saw a movement in the shadows. A man stepped out, heaved a tube over his shoulder and fired. Beharry should have yelled 'RPG', but was mesmerised by the shell as it headed towards the Warrior. Then he suddenly realised that he was coming straight for him. He ducked and pulled down his hatch, before an explosion tore it from his hand. There was a scream behind and Beharry realised that Samuels has been caught by the blast.

Now with no hatch to protect him, Beharry made off down the road. Checking in his mirror, he could still see the other vehicles. Plainly they were following because they thought that Lieutenant Deane was alive and in charge. They did not know that Deane was out of action and that, effectively, Private Beharry was now in command of the convoy.

Beharry suddenly realised that the responsibility for getting his muckers out of this mess now fell to him. The Warrior's crew were depending on him. The platoon following were in his hands, too. And the situation was not looking good. Whisky Two Zero had already been hit by up to three RPGs. It could not take another. Fortunately, all they were taking then was small-arms fire, though this was little comfort to Beharry, because his hatch had been blown away and there was nothing to protect him.

A mile away, at the end of the street, Beharry saw another Warrior. When he reached it, he pulled up alongside and the head of his commanding officer, Major Coote, appeared. Coote touched the top of his head, signalling Beharry to follow him to the walled compound of Cimic House. But this afforded little safety. As soon as Coote's Warrior came to a halt, bullets were ricocheting off it.

As Beharry began to pull himself out of the hatch, four or five rounds hit the front of the Warrior and he dropped back into his seat. He had a choice now. He could jump out, sprint through the bullets and throw himself behind one of the galvanised steel and polypropylene barriers nearby, where he would be safe. On the other hand, he could try to help rest of his injured crewmates.

As he pulled himself out of the hatch again, a bullet whined through the air above his head. Then he rolled onto the turret and a bullet ricocheted off it 30 centimetres (a foot) from his face. Leaning over the hatch, he saw Lieutenant Deane slumped on the floor. There was blood on his seat, along with the shredded remains of his body armour.

Beharry leaned inside the turret and tapped the back of

Deane's helmet. Deane did not move. But Samuels, hunched up next to him, did. He was clutching his sides. The explosion has ripped the clothes from his torso and his chest was covered with burns.

'Sammy, man, it's me,' said Beharry.

Samuels looked up. He face was badly burned and his eyes bloodshot.

'Paki?' he said.

Beharry grabbed Samuels by the waist and tried to pull him out. But, at that moment, a bullet hit the hatch. Beharry let go and Samuels fell back, prompting a groan from Lieutenant Deane. It was only then that they realised he was alive.

By this time, smoke was pouring into the turret from deep inside the vehicle. The heat was building up and it was plain that the vehicle was getting ready to blow. Beharry and Samuels then tried to pull Deane out, while bullets pinged from the armour all around them.

Despite the constant fire, they manage to manoeuvre Deane out of the hatch. Beharry then slung the lieutenant over his shoulders and carried him to Major Coote's Warrior. Once he was safely inside, Beharry went back to get Samuels.

Sammy was already halfway out of the hatch. His face was covered with so much blood that Beharry was not sure that he could see. The sniper opened up again and Beharry grabbed Samuels and pulled him down behind the turret. They slid down the Warrior's hull. Once they were down on the ground Beharry dragged Samuels over to Coote's Warrior, and then went back to Whisky Two Zero. Smoke was now pouring from the turret. He ran around to the back and opened the door – to be confronted by Big Erv, the radio operator, who was pointing his SA80 at Beharry's chest. His face was covered in blood and there was wild look in his eyes. At any minute, Beharry thought, he might pull the trigger.

'Erv, it's Beharry!' said Woody, appearing through the smoke behind him. Erv lowered his rifle.

Woody's face was covered in cuts. His helmet had been blown off and he had lost most of his hair. There was blood on the floor and the walls, and there was a hole through the hull where an RPG had hit.

A sergeant came running up and told them to get out. The vehicle was on fire. Together they got Big Erv and Woody to safety. The sixth crew man, Clifton, though wounded by shrapnel, was safe.

Once he knew that all his crewmates had been taken care of, Beharry asked Major Coote what they should do next.

'Follow me,' shouted the major through the noise of gunfire. 'We're going to drive out of the contact area.'

Beharry was halfway back to Whisky Two Zero when he realised that he had not told Coote how badly damaged the Warrior was. But it was too late. He could already hear Coote's Warrior moving off. Whisky Two Zero's engine was still running and he managed to follow Coote a little way. Then the Major realised that he was in trouble and stopped. He told Beharry to take the Warrior back to the walled compound. He was fired on most of the way, but, when he got there, he saw the other Warriors from Eight Platoon and realised that, if he parked there and Whisky Two Zero blew up, it would take them with her. So he risked his life again to manoeuvre the Warrior behind a blast wall. Then he switched off the engine and pulled the handle that discharged the built-in fire extinguisher, which disabled the vehicle.

He grabbed his rifle and clambered out of the vehicle, then climbed up onto the turret to disabled the main armaments. The last thing his platoon needed was the Mahdi army turning the Warrior's weapons on them. Then he grabbed Lieutenant Deane's rifle and his own, Deane's and Samuel's rucksacks and ran back to Coote's Warrior. Once in the back, he collapsed.

When he came round, he was in hospital. He asked the doctor about the rest of the crew. They had all survived. Beharry himself was suffering from heat exhaustion, but later his sergeant major showed him his helmet. It had a hole in the top of it where it had been hit by a bullet from an AK-47. Beharry was lucky to be alive.

After spending a night in an Army Medical Centre, Beharry was returned to active duty on 3 May, driving a replacement Whisky Two Zero. It was once again to be commanded by Lieutenant Deane, who, after recovering from shrapnel wounds, returned to active duty a week later. On the night of 11 June 2004, they were called out as part of a rapid-reaction force tasked with cutting off a mortar team that had attacked the Coalition forces in Al Amarah. Moving through the dark streets at night, they drove straight into another ambush.

Beharry spotted a flash to his left. Deane shouted a warning. Samuels called out his name. Then he saw the RPG with its fins flipped out, followed by a plume of smoke, less than the length of the vehicle away. It hit the frontal armour just 15 centimetres (6 inches) above Beharry's head. For a moment, he was stunned. Then Lieutenant Deane's persistent calling got through to him.

'Bee, can you hear me?' he asked

'I hear you,' said Beharry, still groggy.

'Get us out of here!' yelled the lieutenant. 'Go, go, go!'

Barely conscious of where he was and with blood from his head injury obscuring his vision, Beharry slipped the Warrior into reverse and hit the accelerator. It shot backwards.

'Go, Paki, go!' yelled Samuels. 'There's more of 'em out there. They're lining up for another shot!'

More RPGs pounded into Whisky Two Zero, incapacitating Deane and wounding several of the crew. Nevertheless, despite his extensive injuries, Beharry held firm. The Warrior raced backwards across 200 metres (218 yards) of open ground. Then, through the darkness, they saw another Warrior.

'Follow him, Bee,' said Deane.

'OK,' said Beharry. But he could not move his foot. He could drive no further but they were, at least, out of the danger zone. Beharry was still conscious when Sergeant Chris Broome – aka 'Broomstick' – from the other Warrior opened the hatch and pulled him out.

'Stick, am I dying?' asked Beharry.

'Nah, mate, you're not dying,' said Broome.

However, he had severe head wounds that doctors feared he would not survive. Extensive brain surgery was needed. His skull had been smashed like an eggshell and had to be reconstructed.

After weeks in a coma, Private Johnson Beharry woke to find himself back in Britain, where the newspapers were saying he should be awarded the Victoria Cross. After extensive reconstructive surgery, he recovered and received his award on 18 March 2005.

Private Sammy Samuels was award the Military Cross for his actions and Sergeant Chris Broome, who was wounded in the action, was awarded the Conspicuous Gallantry Cross, second only to the VC for bravery in the face of the enemy.

Although Beharry was too badly injured to return to Iraq, action continued in Al Amarah. In August 2004, a hundred of his comrades from the PWRR's Battle Group fought for 23 days to hold Cimic House, where he had sought refuge. During that time, the 70 men of Y Company, supplemented with a platoon of 24 from the regiment's A Company and 12 soldiers on loan from the Royal Welch Fusiliers, were attacked 85 times by a 500-strong militia in an action that has been compared to Rorke's Drift, where a handful of redcoats held off 5,000 Zulus in South Africa in 1879, during the Anglo-Zulu War.

Mortars, rockets and bullets rained down on the squaddies day and night, but they repulsed every charge and killed 200 enemy fighters in the longest continuous action fought by the British Army since the Korean War 50 years before.

Corporal Chris Mulrine, a 33-year-old marksman from Y Company's six-man sniper team, said, 'They kept coming, day after day. But the more they gave us, the more we gave them back. It just made us more determined and morale was awesome.'

The building sits by the River Tigris and was once the residence of the governor of Maysan Province. It had been the home to Y Company since April. In August, Muqtada al Sadr's Mahdi Army set out to take it. The garrison there was the UK's fragile foothold in the hostile city of Al Amarah. The rest of the Battle Group were based at an old Iraqi army camp 32 kilometres (20 miles) to the south. In some ways, the Coalition presence at Cimic House was merely symbolic, but its loss would have been devastating. Nevertheless, Major Justin Featherstone, the 33-year-old officer who led the heroic defence, was told by his commanding officer that he could withdraw at any time. He refused.

'It was our turf,' he said. 'It was our home. We had never left it and we just decided we were not going to be pushed out of it. None of the lads wanted to leave and would have been furious if I ordered them to. Pulling out would have set us back months in this part of Iraq. It would also have meant defeat and our pride wouldn't let us do that.'

During the 23-day battle that began on 5 August, the Mahdi Army fired 595 mortar rounds at Cimic House. They scored direct hits with 59 rocket-propelled grenades and six 107mm rockets. Black-clad fighters of the Mahdi Army once got within 27 metres (30 yards) of Cimic House's gates before being driven back, leaving bullet and shrapnel holes peppering every wall. Fences that surrounded the site were shredded and the outbuildings were gutted by bomb blasts and fire. The site was also littered with the burned-out wrecks of five of the company's vehicles that had been destroyed.

In all, Y Company fired 33,000 rounds from Minimi machine guns, general-purpose machine guns and SA80 rifles. They also fired 81mm mortars and underslung grenade launchers at the enemy. Even so, the troops believed that only a miracle had prevented them from losing at least a dozen men.

In fact, they had six seriously wounded, and 22-year-old Private Chris Rayment from London was killed in an accident when a road barrier fell on his head. The enemy was thought to have suffered more than two hundred dead.

Tweny-Four-year-old Lance Corporal Jonathan Rush's life was saved by his body armour. A 7.62mm bullet from an AK-47 rifle smashed into the bottom right-hand corner of the ceramic plate as he ran across the rooftop. He was knocked backwards but suffered only superficial bruising.

'If the bullet had been one inch lower it would have made a horrible mess,' he said. 'I am a very lucky boy.'

The second-in-command, 25-year-old Captain Steve Brooks from Sandwich in Kent, said his men would often only reluctantly leave their battle positions to rest when given a direct order.

'The men's dedication was just extraordinary,' he said. 'They would refuse to be relieved and say, "No, I'm OK here, sir", when they were falling asleep where they crouched. It's a testament to character and commitment.'

The defenders had to be resupplied by armoured columns of Warriors, led by Challenger 2 tanks from the Queen's Royal Lancers. They would have to fight their way through Mahdi Army ambushes and, for ten days between 15 and 25 August, it was considered too dangerous to go through the convoys, and the garrison stood alone.

Despite the action on the frontline, the men of Y Company insisted that the real heroes of the siege were Royal Logistic Corps cooks Corporals Lewis Dodds and Debbie Kaye – the only woman at the outpost. In an ill-equipped field kitchen, they produced a hot meal every day, even though they were exposed to mortar fire as they ran back and forth from stores tents. During one such dash, Dodds was hit in the right leg by a piece of shrapnel that almost sliced it off.

The 1 PWRR commanding officer, Lieutenant Colonel Matt Maer, said, 'Many of the soldiers were just 18 and 19. But what they did was extraordinary. Their dogged determination is an example to all of us.'

During their seven-month tour of duty, Maer's one thousand men were attacked 863 times, and lost two dead and 43 wounded.

CHAPTER 12
INTO THE TRIANGLE OF DEATH

In 2004, 40 Commando were back in Iraq and in late October they found themselves in Az Zubayr Port, where they were responsible for guarding movement across the Basra area. They maintained the capability to deploy CH-47s for interdiction operations at four hours' notice. Personnel were also sent to Baghdad, providing close protection to the British diplomatic community in the International Green Zone. Moving VIPs to and from Baghdad International Airport involved almost daily running the gauntlet on Route Irish, a 10-kilometre (6-mile) drag then reputed to be as the most dangerous stretch of road in the world.

'It was as much by luck as judgement that none of our convoys were hit with IEDs [improvised explosive devices] or targeted by the seemingly never-ending supply of suicide bombers,' said route planner Marine Matty Taylor. 'Several contacts with small arms had taken place but good drills always won the day – that and the fact that our drivers could navigate the route at speeds that would cause Jensen

Button to black out at the wheel. Obviously, some rescheduling of moves was in order to keep the movement on Irish down to a minimum. This proved to be a slight inconvenience but, since an alarming number of crazed, freshly shaven, heavily sweating dissidents seemed more than happy to drive a Vauxhall Astra packed with 82mm mortar rounds into a coalition convoy, most people were willing to accommodate this. We preferred to be messed around a little bit, rather than risk being blown 500 feet into the air – which would put a dent in even the most robust V8 snatch wagon, and scatter the occupants along several kilometres of main supply route.'

The situation in the Iraqi capital came as a shock to Matty Taylor, who had travelled to Baghdad after an uncomfortable night at Basra Air Station, lying in a ridiculously hot room while the locals peddled cold drinks at inflated prices. When he arrived he was promptly bundled into the back of a snatch wagon and driven at breakneck speed to the Green Zone – though he said that this made a nice change from yomping 3 kilometres (nearly 2 miles) to work three times a day as he had in Basra. It was dangerous, though.

'Attacks in Basra account for only 3.8 per cent of the attacks aimed at coalition forces throughout the country, averaging about three per day,' said Taylor. 'By contrast, Baghdad, sees about 30 per cent of the country's total and attacks were up to around 50 a day during the assault on Fallujah, including indirect fire attacks in the International Zone (IZ) itself. As a result, evenings were spent wearing body armour and carrying your helmet, but, again, complaints about this minor inconvenience were kept to a minimum when, in the twilight hours, large Russian-made mortars started landing dubiously close to your bed.'

But it was not all bad.

'As long as the myriad of ordnance scattered on the roadsides can be avoided,' he said, 'and you can stay clear of the Chinese rockets that drop into the IZ occasionally, it's a pleasant and worthwhile tasking. Not as pleasant and worthwhile as Christmas at home, but I don't like turkey, anyway.'

C Company were deployed under tactical command of the Danish Battalion to conduct interdiction operations on the supply routes being used by the 4th Armoured Brigade that were routinely targeted by insurgents. The recce troops set up covert observation posts and the arrival of 845 Naval Air Squadron allowed them to swamp the area through 'eagle' VCPs, resulting in significant arrests.

D Company were sent to Basra Palace, where they were to spend Christmas and New Year. They were to be a quick-reaction force and, having purloined boats from 4th Armoured Brigade, they made nightly river patrols on the Shatt al-Arab waterway.

'In the palace you could see just how selfish Saddam was,' said Marine Llewellyn. 'His life was spent in luxury, yet his people allowed to live in squalor... Outside the camp, the general consensus is that British Forces are welcome and people are able to see that our presence is not for our benefit, but for the stabilisation and rebuilding of Iraq.'

For the most part, things were relatively peaceful and quiet. However, during the January elections, there was an upsurge in mortar and other attacks. From their sangars, they kept a special eye on the island in the Shatt al-Arab, which was a haven for RPGs and mortars. Then there were the day and night patrols to gather intelligence.

'Patrolling offered a sense of adventure and anxiety,' said

Llewellyn, 'since you never know what's out there. Around any comer, down any alleyway, there could be an RPG waiting for you, or one of the million rabid, flee-ridden dogs that run wild, day and night.'

D Company also provided convoy protection for Prime Minister Tony Blair during his visit to Basra.

In October 2004, there were rumours that British troops were going to be deployed to support US forces in the infamous 'Triangle of Death' – the hostile area between Baghdad, Fallujah and Karbala to the south – while the Americans undertook Operation Phantom Fury, a second attempt to pacify the city of Fallujah. Armoured Infantry were required, so the 1st Battalion of the Black Watch, who were based at Shaibah Logistics Base, were given the job. Operation Bracken was to last 30 days, so the Battalion would be home for Christmas. They would be supported by a 24-man rifle troop from A Company of 40 Commando and four barrels from 40 Commando's Mortar Troop. The Marines packed their kit and made their way to the Black Watch camp at Shaibah, where they were greeted by a media circus.

The Mortar Troop had re-formed after performing various other roles within the unit and needed a refresher course and a trip to the range at Shaibah.

'With the lads' drills, skills and confidence up to scratch, we were off,' said Corporal Richie Westwood of 40 Commando's Mortar Troop.

On the morning of 27 October, they drove out of Shaibah Logistics Base to the sound of bagpipes played for the benefit of the TV cameras. The convoy was escorted by the US Army. The 500-kilometre (310-mile) journey went smoothly enough, but during a temporary halt, one of the Humvee escort vehicles smashed into the passenger door of a stationary Pinzgauer, which was being held open by a passenger's leg.

'The Yanks stopped and debussed while their top cover gobbed off about leaving the door open,' said Westwood. 'They were then confronted by the passenger, one very angry Colour Sergeant Steve 'Vinney' Reed. The Yanks took one look, begged for forgiveness, didn't make eye contact, stepped back to the vehicle and drove away – quickly.'

Then there was the weather.

'Other top-cover convoy experiences from the warmer months have been likened to standing in front of a hairdryer for eight hours,' said Second Lieutenant Simpson of A Company. 'This one was probably more like being in a dishwasher for 24 hours. After having experienced an emotionally lengthy drive through a thunderstorm, the convoy was halted due to a breakdown; the storm then caught up and had to be negotiated again, much to the delight of the WMIK [armed Land Rover] crews.'

Arriving at the US base Camp Dogwood on Al Iskandaryah Air Base 48 kilometres (30 miles) south of Baghdad, the British troops found they were to be accommodated in some derelict buildings within a broken-down power plant and chemical storage facility in open desert.

'"In the field" is what we were told and "in the field" is was what it was,' said Richie Westwood.

The Marines moved off to one flank of the camp, 'away from the chaos of arriving Jocks', and set up. Immediately they lost their Commanding Officer, Captain Murphy, who was admitted to the regimental aid post with a bad case of D&V – diarrhoea and vomiting. The troop were then left in the capable hands of the second-in-command and the section commanders.

A Troop of 40 Commando was attached to B Company of the 1st Battalion of the Black Watch and took up residence in the old chemical-weapons compound – in 'bunkers in the desert resembling bat caves', according to Lieutenant Simpson.

That evening, as they settled in, the 'insurgent welcoming committee' gave them a demonstration of firepower, launching rockets and mortars into the centre of the camp.

'Fortunately, no one was injured,' said Westwood. 'Nonetheless, the demonstration left us with an idea of their accuracy and, knowing that Sky News had succeeded in telling the world where we were, there was an obvious need for us to dig in a little deeper.'

The following morning the Commandos moved forward, out of the killing zone in the centre of the camp. This also gave Mortar Troop better range for denying the insurgents freedom of movement to set up indirect fire attacks and plant improvised explosive devices.

By day, the mortar men went out on patrols with Alpha Company. At night, they fired illumination rounds, while the armed Land Rovers laid down defensive fire. The artillery's acoustic sensors also gave them target information so they could quickly bombard any enemy firing point within range. They had a measure of success as the number of indirect fire attacks quickly dropped off. However, one target continued to cause trouble. On the north bank of the Euphrates, there was a huge tower inside an industrial compound, which dominated the area. This provided an obvious observation post and there was a good firing point for the insurgents' 81mm mortar at its base. The problem was that the area around the tower was home to a large civilian population. Nevertheless, something had to be done.

'While out on patrol with a Warrior callsign, John Hawkshaw and I debussed and moved off, a couple of hundred metres [218 yards] to a flank, to get eyes on a target area,' said Westwood.

They called in a mortar on the first target. Then, as they were inside the safety distance of the second, they moved back to the cover of the Warriors before calling in the next round. They stayed outside the Warrior, where Westwood told the commander how close he could expect the round to land. As they heard it whistle outbound towards the target, they heard a simultaneous whistle come over their heads from the target direction.

'Feeling that it sounded closer than the first whistling round, I suggested that the Warrior crew close down their hatches,' said Westwood. 'I checked my watch for time of flight and looked into the target area. Then, a feeling of dread washed over me as a round exploded 200 metres [218 yards] to my rear.'

The fear at this stage was not that it was an enemy mortar, but that their own had dropped short.

'I turned to look back at the target area only to see the remains of the "splash-down" of our round,' said Westwood. 'Then the penny dropped. The rounds had literally crossed in the air above us with an impact time difference of a couple of seconds.'

They quickly moved out of the killing zone and headed off to set up a new OP – observation post – to engage the mortar position that had fired at them. Unfortunately, the new position was out of range of the British mortars, and the enemy knew it.

'The speed and accuracy of these insurgents should not be underestimated,' said Westwood. 'They had put that "shoot" together in 30 minutes and were "on for line" with their first round and only out by 200 metres [218 yards] for range.'

A gaunt Captain Murphy returned to the helm. This gave the Mortar Troop a voice at the top table in the Battle Group. Their next major task would be to support operations across the Euphrates to an old munitions compound that had been the scene of many executions, judging by the number of corpses found there. It was during this operation that two suicide car bombers killed four Black Watch soldiers. However, mortars firing both high-explosive and illumination rounds successfully denied the insurgents freedom of movement.

'Two barrels were tasked under the command of Sergeant Si Mayo with the "Geordie Duo" Pegster and Digger as the Alpha-Bravo,' said Westwood. 'We also fired-in DFs [direct fire] from air OPs, where Corporal Spud Murphy proved that timing is everything and that, if there is an Allah up there, he was smiling down on one lucky Iraqi driver.'

The night of 21 November became the Mortar Troop's unofficial bonfire night when a chacon (a wooden container developed at Chatham Dockyards) and tent containing their spare kit, equipment, spare mortars, small-arms ammunition and grenades went up in smoke. As the fire raged, one army SNCO, unaware that the tent contained ammunition, tried to fight the fire. Risking life and limb 'Big Vinney' – Colour Sergeant Reed – raced in and dragged him to safety as a fusillade of rounds cooked off. An administrative nightmare followed for the troop as they tried to get replacements.

'The Troop Sergeant was emotional,' said Westwood, 'but not as emotional as we were at not having our cold-weather kit when the frost set in.'

While the Black Watch were conducting patrols, A Company provided protection for the 40 Commando mortars at Forward Operating Base Springfield and manned a sentry position. They went out on patrol the local area both on foot and in WMIKs, augmenting the dismounted Warrior crews. They also set up quick-reaction operations and ambushes after two Warriors were hit by improvised explosive devices on consecutive days. No one was killed, but the rules of engagement were changed and, from then on, all movement was by Warrior. Soon after, a 05.30 stand-to became a part of the daily routine in anticipation of a dawn attack.

'Marine Postlethwaite mastered the art of "dripping" [moaning] about this time,' said Lieutenant Simpson. 'Other tasks included "eagle" VCPs, and Troop Sergeant "Ginge" Anderson developed a very effective set of SOPs for this task and put them to good use, especially when the TV cameras were rolling.'

Between mortar attacks, time was taken up by various tasks such as the budgeting of the 9 litres (16 pints UK, 19 pints US) of water issued per man per day, which had to serve for cooking, drinking, clothes washing and a dhobi.

'This was a bit of an issue for Royal as he was trying to make a point to the "gopping pongos" [smelly soldiers] by field-showering as often as he could,' said Simpson. 'The rest of the time was spent discussing and perfecting the many variations to a meal that can be achieved using the contents of Menu A.'

The highlight of A Company's time in Dogwood was Operation Tobruk. This was a Black Watch-led cordon and search operation. It was a Battle Group task and the Marines were to be attached to 1 Black Watch's A Company for most of it. After getting the warning order, they had time to conduct thorough day and night rehearsals, assaulting and clearing buildings as well as practising a complex company move that included a river crossing led by armoured engineers.

'Vehicle commander Corporal Danny Veale was particularly delighted when, during rehearsals, his driver Marine Garbutt managed to write off one of the snatch vehicles by parking it on top of a highly obvious rock mountain, snapping the steering only hours before the H-hour,' said Simpson.

At 02.00, the Marines set off across country in snatch vehicles – Corporal Veale's freshly fixed vehicle included – as part of the company convoy of 40 Warriors. They arrived in position at H-hour with Spectre gunships, Harriers and a Cobra on station, and 81mm mortars that had marked their targets in support.

The first target was a compound of nine buildings on 'Millionaires' Row'. All buildings were considered hostile. This area had been identified as a hotbed of insurgency. Consequently, they would enter with a 'hard knock'. Every male was to be detained for further investigation and houses searched thoroughly.

It was still dark when the assault started and the dawn silence was broken by thunder flashes and sledgehammers. The next five hours were taken up with intense action – cut-offs, room entry and clearance, arrests, searches, back-loading detainees, protecting the interpreter, fighting off savage animals and keeping a grip on embedded Sky reporters.

'There was one other job that Marine Rob Wilmot made his own,' said Lieutenant Simpson, 'the close and personal protection of the female RMP attached to the troop.'

A large number of men were detained and a lot of

valuable intelligence was acquired. The experience gained was invaluable – and unforgettable.

'For instance,' said Lieutenant Simpson, 'Marines Hawkins and Bailey will no doubt never forget the day they stacked up outside a door, weapons made ready and safety catch off, threw in a thunder flash and stormed in only to be confronted by an incredibly startled-looking cow, although they will tell you it was a half-crazed bull.'

There were other operations during their remaining time in Dogwood. One involved the clearance of a 6-kilometre (3.7-mile) stretch of rural homesteads and plantations, which A Company of 40 Commando noted was remarkably similar to the pre-deployment training area at Thetford.

With the US operation in Fallujah winding down, Operation Bracken ended. The insurgents gave the Black Watch Battle Group a going-away present in the form of a rocket attack, but otherwise the recovery passed without incident. The convoy left under the cover of darkness, though it failed to escape the media spotlight. On its way south, it made scheduled stops at various US bases along to refuel both vehicles and men.

'I concluded that an American galley is definitely the place to make a Bootneck happy after a month in the field,' said Lieutenant Simpson.

The Marines went back to Shaibah with the Black Watch, then on to Az Zubayr Port.

'We parked up and were ushered through to what we thought was the usual pusser's brief about camp dos and don'ts,' said Corporal Westwood, 'not exactly what you look forward to after a long drive. To our surprise, we arrived in the officers' and seniors' mess tent to a large buffet and crates of beer. To greet us were the new

Commanding Officer, Lieutenant Colonel King, and our various Company OCs and CSMs. After a short welcome-back speech from the CO we tucked into the much-needed fresh scran [food] and got on it.'

CHAPTER 13
DEATH IN BASRA

By early 2006, the situation in southern Iraq was deteriorating. The local government refused to speak to the Coalition forces and the deployment of the 20th Armoured Brigade began in May with the downing of a Lynx helicopter, killing five.

The Lynx Mark 7 was flying low over central Basra on a sortie to familiarise Wing Commander John Coxen, who was about to take command of the British helicopter fleet in southern Iraq, with the dangers that his pilots might face. At first, it was said that the helicopter had been brought down by a 'lucky hit' from a rocket-propelled grenade, but discarded parts of a sophisticated Russian-made SAM were found by British troops. A military observation post had also reported an unusual level of activity in the building where they were found, during the previous two days, suggesting that the Iraqi terrorists had been planning an ambush of British aircraft for some time. The missile was of a type that could be concealed easily, assembled quickly and fired by one person with minimal training.

Among the dead was 32-year-old Flight Lieutenant Sarah-Jayne Mulvihill, who was the first British servicewoman to be killed in overseas combat since World War Two. The other three men killed were the pilot, Lieutenant Commander Darren Chapman (40), his co-pilot, Captain David Dobson (27) and the door gunner, Marine Paul Collins (21).

Then, on 16 June, Corporal John Cosby of the 1st Battalion of the Devonshire and Dorset Light Infantry died in Basra. He was on an operation led by the 2nd Battalion of the Royal Anglian Regiment.

In temperatures that never dipped much below 40°C (104°F), wearing full body armour and facing an unpredictable situation, the men of the 20th Armoured Brigade moved into position. Under cover of nightfall, they closed in on a location in a north-eastern suburb of Basra. It quickly became obvious that they were not welcome. As the 2 RAR approached the target building, they were greeted with a barrage of small-arms fire, RPGs and mortar rounds. In the darkness, it was impossible to tell how many terrorists were there, but the troops returned fire, shooting dead up to five of them.

Having ousted the enemy, the task force entered the building and unearthed an Aladdin's cave of terror – two tonnes of bomb-making kit and other weapons. This was the largest cache seized in the three years the British had been in Iraq. Despite having a company of Warrior armoured vehicles at their disposal, the soldiers struggled to take it all away in one move. During the raid, three terrorist suspects were also detained.

However, while the premises were being searched, Cosby's team was ambushed by gunmen and, in the ensuing firefight, 27-year-old Corporal Cosby from Belfast was fatally wounded.

Although the military authorities claimed that they were regularly seizing weapons caches and neutralising terror cells, Coalition soldiers continued to come under attack in their bases in Basra. A mortar attack at the centre of the city in August claimed the life of 29-year-old Corporal Matthew Cornish of the 1st Battalion of the Light Infantry. Badly wounded, he was evacuated by helicopter to the Field Hospital at Shaibah Logistics Base, where he died from his injuries.

On 16 August, the British base at the Old State Building in Basra came under attack. Private Daniel Jones was in a sangar there. He had been in the army just a year and this was his first tour in Iraq.

'I fired off 2,000 rounds in about 30 minutes and the whole thing was pretty scary,' he said. 'The RPG attacks were a bit of shock, too. I didn't expect, as we were on Op Telic 8, that the terrorists would be able to get so close to us.'

It was also Private Moore's first tour with 1 LI.

'I came straight out to Iraq from the depot – I did my OPTAG [Operational Training and Advisory Group] training and deployed,' he said. 'During the tour we were involved in a few contacts and had some RPG attacks.'

He was in a sangar in front of the Old State Building in Basra when it came under attack, too.

'Two gunmen opened fire and I exchanged around 30 rounds with them,' he said. 'Nothing can really prepare you for how you feel when you're in a firefight for the first time – it's something you have to experience. Other than hostile fire, dealing with the summer heat was hard, especially when you have to wear body armour all the time.

But, on the upside of the tour, I made a lot of new friends. I was out in Iraq with a load of really good lads.'

Another first-timer with the 1 LI was Sergeant James Mason. 'It was my first Op Telic tour and I managed to get blown up and injured twice,' he said 'Both occasions were obviously quite a low point of the tour for me. In the first incident, my Warrior armoured vehicle got hit. I got shrapnel in my head, arm and neck and was evacuated back to Germany. One other soldier was also injured. I was flown back to Iraq after I'd been treated. But then, two weeks later, an improvised explosive device went off and I was hit by shrapnel again. However, on both occasions I have to say that the medical chain was superb. Other than those two low points, I have had a couple of RPGs fired at me and some small-arms contacts. But there have been plenty of high points on tour, including successful arrest operations.'

Sergeant Roy Steel had done 19 years in the army and five tours of Northern Ireland before he found himself in Iraq for the first time. He remained uninjured, but others around him were not so lucky.

'Everybody's been in a few contacts,' he said. 'I was in one in which a lad from the 2nd Battalion, the Royal Anglian Regiment, was seriously injured. We stopped outside a police station while our soldiers were doing some liaison work, when somebody fired an RPG at us. They were aiming at a Snatch Land Rover but missed. The round didn't explode but bounced off a wall and hit one of our troops in the shin. His leg was splintered and we had to apply a tourniquet and get him out. The whole thing happened very quickly.'

Sergeant James Rock was with the Adjutant General's Corps (Staff and Personnel Support). He was on his third tour in 2006 and had had some pretty close calls.

'Generally, we were dealing with attacks on our bases several times a week,' he said. 'I was based at the Shatt al-Arab Hotel and, on one occasion, we had the AGC personnel doing their PT when enemy mortar rounds started falling all around us. We all ran for some hard cover and were very lucky that nobody was injured.'

There was another near miss when a patrol of TA soldiers cheated death after a new and lethal type of roadside bomb sent their shattered Snatch Land Rover skidding out of control. The Lancastrian and Cumbrian Volunteers, who were responsible for protecting Basra air station, saw the engine of their vehicle hurled 75 metres (82 yards) across the road when the blast from the explosively formed projectile (EFP) detonated without warning immediately in front of them. Their Land Rover, one of a three-vehicle convoy, was set on fire in the bomb attack.

The crew's body armour shattered as the vehicle careered out of control. But all instinctively carried out their drills to secure the area and were prepared for a firefight with the insurgents. Lieutenant John Eastham, a solicitor in civilian life, recalled how the Snatch had skidded as the bomb detonated about 20 metres (65 feet) in front of the vehicle.

'I was in the front passenger seat,' he said. 'There was a massive explosion and the Land Rover skidded across the road. I threw myself out of the vehicle and took up a firing position in case we were engaged by the enemy.'

Lieutenant Eastham escaped from the wreckage with shock, cuts and bruising, while top cover sentry Rifleman Rob Allen had his helmet and goggles blown off by the explosion. He sustained a broken jaw and injured eye socket, and was later sent home.

Private Christopher Addis, who had been a student at the University of Central Lancashire before he was sent to Iraq in March 2006, was knocked unconscious by the blast.

'I came to on the floor,' he said. 'I kicked the vehicle doors open, saw Lieutenant Eastham on the ground and thought he was dead. Then I cocked my rifle and peered around the side of the vehicle, expecting to be shot at. I had a bump on my head, bruised ribs and was in shock. We were extremely lucky.'

The driver, Private Dave Forshaw, a painter and decorator from London, said he saw a flash and heard the explosion before the vehicle went out of control. When detonated, EFPs fire a football-size chunk of metal that can punch a hole in a Snatch Land Rover.

'I was rocked around all over the place and the vehicle skidded to a halt,' he said. 'There was smoke and dust everywhere. I got out and went to my right, expecting to come under fire.'

Nineteen-year-old Private Alex James was in the back of the vehicle and saw his body armour shatter.

'Your training kicks in and you do exactly what you've been taught,' he said. 'You go down into cover and you protect everyone.'

Meanwhile, in Maysan Province, newly qualified medic Private Michelle Norris of the RAMC risked her life to save a wounded Warrior commander. She climbed on top of the armoured vehicle to reach the wounded man as bullets flew around her. One round narrowly missed her leg. The 19-year-old – nicknamed 'Chuck' after the action hero – was attached to C Company of the 1st Battalion of the Princess of Wales's Royal Regiment when her team were called to recover a Warrior stuck in a ditch in the town of Al Amarah. Arriving at the scene, they stopped and she heard 'dings' on the Warrior's armour.

'I thought it was stones,' she said. 'Then I heard the

turret getting hit, so I got on the intercom and asked, "Is anybody hit, then?" '

The driver, Private Nani Ratawake, shouted down to her that the commander had been wounded.

'I didn't know how bad it was at this stage,' she said. 'So I jumped out of the back, climbed on top of the turret and saw the extent of his injuries.'

Norris then found herself exposed as sniper fire ricocheted around her. 'Private Ratawake pulled me down head first into the turret,' she said. 'A round went over and hit the battery, which was at my knee height, so, if he hadn't pulled me down at that point, my knee or my leg would have been shot.'

They managed to cross the turret under sniper fire from five different positions. One bullet from an AK-47 ripped through her rucksack, but she refused to let go of the injured Colour Sergeant Ian Page, dragging him to safety in the back, where one of the lads put a 'sweat rag' over him. Jokingly referring to him as 'Dad', she administered first aid and checked for vital signs. Meanwhile, Ratawake drove the Warrior to a helicopter pad. From there, the wounded NCO was taken to a field hospital.

Norris, who was based at Paderborn in Germany, later admitted that she found dealing with a seriously injured soldier daunting. 'It was my first casualty since training, which was pretty scary,' she said.

Her Commanding Officer, Lieutenant Colonel David Labouchere, commended her conduct and bravery.

'Private Norris acted completely selflessly and, in the face of great danger, concentrated on her job and saved someone else's life,' he said. 'She was part of a larger team, all of whom are acquitting themselves admirably in the face of danger.' She became the first woman to be awarded the MC.

By December 2006, the situation in southern Iraq had improved somewhat with politicians and community leaders re-engaging with the troops and two provinces – Dhi Qar and Al Muthanna – returned to Iraqi control. The Iraqi Army and the police were giving more autonomy in matters of security, and the British turned their attention to stopping smuggling across the Iraqi border from Iran. The Queen's Royal Hussars Battle Group were delighted to leave Camp Abu Naji, near Maysan's volatile provincial capital Al Amarah, and make their home in sand dunes along the frontier. There, the soldiers set about shoring up security and compiling intelligence from local people on illegal smuggling activity. Armed with stripped-down weapons-mounted Land Rovers, they then adopted the tactics of the long-range desert patrols used in North Africa during World War Two, the forerunners of the SAS. The idea was to stay in the area for longer that the two-week patrols that had been tried before, so the troops were supplied by air as they moved through the hostile desert and marshland. In those conditions, each soldier got through 12 litres (21 pints UK, 25 pints US) of water a day.

'The heat certainly took a little getting used to,' said Battle Group Logistics Officer Major Dave Sparks.

The Queen's Royal Hussars were supported by troops from B Squadron of the Queen's Dragoon Guards. Major Dominic Roberts of the QDG said that his squadron coped well with the conditions and that his troops' expertise in recce operations and their 'natural inquisitiveness' made them a perfect counter to the smugglers.

Private Adam Sale, a Royal Logistic Corps driver attached to the Hussars, said he quickly adapted to desert life. 'It was hard work, but a very good experience,' he said. 'The sand got everywhere but you soon got used to it.'

Fellow RLC driver Private Stephen Dogbey said the desert operations were a welcome change to the routine tasks in and around the British base at Shaibah.

'I preferred it out there,' he said. 'We were doing real soldiering and it's the sort of thing you join up to do.'

Captain Tom Lilleyman of 35 Engineer Regiment positively enjoyed himself in the desert after being at Camp Abu Naji, where you got shot at. 'The best part of the tour for me was conducting patrols and living in the desert – it was by far the best stuff we did,' he said. 'I was out there 26 days and it was brilliant. I don't adapt well to hot weather, and initially trying to get away from the heat was awful. The water got so hot that you couldn't take a solar shower in the afternoon. However, just two weeks after we deployed, I needed a sleeping bag instead of the sheet I had with me because it was so cold at night.'

Even this was welcome since, at Abu Naji, the British did not enjoy the benefits of air conditioning.

As well as visiting border forts and venturing far out into inhospitable areas, the 20th Armoured Brigade troops conducted hearts and minds operations in border communities. In one of the highest-profile visits, soldiers from the 4th Troop of the QDG called in on the village of Al Muddarah, a few miles from the Iranian frontier. The British patrol took with it a doctor to set up a basic clinic for the villages, who had neither reliable water nor continuous electricity supplies. Medical officer Captain Matt Reeves of the 12th Regiment of the Royal Artillery said most of the villagers' complaints, such as dehydration, could be solved by basic infrastructure improvements.

'The main thing for us was that the villagers didn't begin to rely on us,' he said. 'We purposely travelled light, as my role was to support the Battle Group, so we had to be quite thrifty with medical supplies.'

Desert operations were a safe alternative to patrolling the Shatt al-Arab waterway. Sergeant Kev Cameron of 35 Engineer Regiment was on board a patrol boat when the convoy was ambushed from a bridge. Six gunmen opened fire. In the ferocious gun battle that followed, the soldiers were thought to have shot at least one of their attackers dead. But the troops reckoned that their four-boat convoy was lucky to have escaped unscathed from the contact where hundreds of rounds were exchanged.

Sergeant Cameron, normally based in Paderborn in Germany, said the cool reaction of the soldiers had undoubtedly saved their lives.

'We were approaching the Qarmat Ali Bridge on the Shatt al-Arab,' he said. 'It's a big bridge on a motorway running east to west over it. The gunmen were about 30 metres [33 yards] above us and must have fired between 200 and 400 rounds at the boats. We returned a 105 back at them. But all of the guys on board reacted exactly has they should – three to the four boats pushed on through the killing area and the others remained out of range. It was my first experience of a firefight and the first time for everybody else. It helped that we had done a lot of training before we went on tour.'

Fellow Royal Engineer Corporal Jimmy Collins, who was cox on one of two rigid raiding craft in the convoy, said he had remained focused on escaping the incoming fire.

'There were ricochets coming off the boat and tracer fire going over our heads, but the soldiers managed to get rounds back at the terrorists. My role was to get the boat out of the killing zone, but how none of us were hit or killed I cannot tell you – there was fire coming in all around.'

There were also fears that the terrorists had been trying to plant a bomb.

'It may have been that we managed to scare them,' he said. 'But, whatever they were doing, we all did our jobs correctly and as a result are still here to tell the story.'

The streets of Basra were no safer – for the insurgents at least. Having ambushed troops from the 1st Battalion of the Staffordshire Regiment and the 1st Battalion of the Royal Green Jackets, three gunmen crumpled under hail of bullets in the city's Al-Jumhuriyah district. The skirmish began when the British soldiers, who had only recently arrived in the theatre, came under attack from insurgents. Spotting the enemy's muzzle flashes down an unlit street, troops dismounted from their three Warriors, supported by a rain of fire from the armoured vehicles' lethal 30mm Rarden cannons and 7.62mm chain guns. The gunmen sought cover before attacking again, but found themselves facing a fresh onslaught when Lance Corporal Daniel Hargreaves of the Staffords blasted their position with his 40mm underslung grenade launcher.

Having shot three terrorists dead, the soldiers attempted to give chase but were cut off by a canal. The troops then regrouped to continue their patrol. While the Al-Jumhuriyah area was normally friendly during the day, after dark it attracted terrorist groups who aimed to set up mortars and hit coalition bases.

The troops were with 19 Light Brigade, who tried to lock down Basra in Operation Troy, which began on 15 February 2007. Permanent vehicle checkpoints were set up on major thoroughfares and 539 Assault Squadron of the

Royal Marines were deployed to patrol the Shatt al-Arab waterway. It was during Operation Troy that 15 Royal Navy personnel and their boat were seized by the Iranians.

CHAPTER 14
HELMAND

Meanwhile in Afghanistan, the situation was no better. In the southern province of Helmand, that borders on Pakistan, the Taliban began staging a comeback. On 13 June 2006, they attacked a ten-vehicle US supply convoy. With some of their vehicles disabled, the Americans were cut off near the town of Sangin.

A hundred British troops from A Company of the 3rd Battalion of the Parachute Regiment went to the rescue. Acting as a quick-reaction force, they deployed outside the contact zone by helicopter and formed a defensive cordon around the American vehicles. But, as darkness fell, they came under fire from Taliban heavy machine guns and RPGs. A missile hit a Humvee, wounding two American soldiers from the logistics unit, but then the Paras moved on the Taliban positions. The battle lasted around six hours and it was thought that ten insurgents were killed.

Of the many heroes that night, one singled out for his 'massive display of bravery' was 21-year-old Private Peter McKinley, the trained first-aider of his eight-man section.

When he heard one of the American soldiers screaming, 'Medic, medic!' He sprinted across open ground to the stricken vehicle, despite the ferocious firefight that was under way.

He found the Americans covered in blood and the sergeant's face shredded by shrapnel. One eye was dislodged, his scalp was torn back, and he had a broken arm, an injury to his neck and fragments in his legs. As heavy machine gun fire and tracer flew overhead, McKinley dragged the Sergeant to safety.

'The Sergeant was in a pretty bad way,' said McKinley, 'but my training just kicked in and I spent about 15 minutes looking after his wounds, stemming the flow of blood and keeping his airway clear.'

This emergency treatment saved the man's life. A medical officer later confirmed that the injured soldier was a 'P1 Casualty' – the highest priority for evacuation and treatment – and he was evacuated to Camp Bastion, the British Army's heavily fortified base in the desert near the city of Lashkar Gah.

In the encounter, one US soldier was killed and two others were wounded. There were no British casualties and the Paras remained on the scene for 36 hours. Then, low on food and water, they were relieved by US troops.

The 2,000-strong 3 Para Battle Group had been in Helmand for two months and, for the previous two weeks, they had been forward in the north of the province. Just two days before the attack on the American convoy, the first British soldier had been killed in Helmand. Twenty-nine-year-old Captain Jim Philippson of the 7th Parachute Regiment, Royal Horse Artillery, was with the Afghan National Army when his patrol was ambushed by the Taliban. Two other soldiers were also injured.

Then in late June, under pressure from President Hamid Karzai to ensure the Afghan flag flew in the remote district centres of northern Helmand, British commanders sent A Company back into Sangin to defend the mud-walled government compound. The government representative and his police guard were under constant attack from the Taliban, who threatened to overrun the town. Sangin was the centre of the opium trade in Helmand and was hardly likely to welcome representatives of a Kabul government that was bent on eradicating Afghanistan's poppy crop.

A Company staged an air assault, landing by helicopter 2.5 kilometres (1.5 miles) outside the town. Much to their surprise, they made it into the government compound without incident and evacuated the wounded Afghans. Then they set up sangars and other makeshift fortifications, and made themselves as comfortable as they could. For a week, nothing happened. Then, one night, without warning, the sky was full of Chinese-made 107mm rockets and rocket-propelled grenades. AK-47s set on automatic peppered the Paras' machine gun posts from the houses that overlooked the British base. The Paras, many of whom were wearing only shorts because of the heat, ran for their body armour and responded with heavy machine gun fire, eventually silencing the Taliban. From then on there were daily firefights, with large numbers of Taliban launching near-suicidal assaults on the compound.

On 27 June, two members of the Special Forces, Captain David Patten of the Special Reconnaissance Regiment and Sergeant Paul Bartlett of the Special Boat Service (SBS), were killed during covert operations in the town. Four days later, a Taliban rocket hit the tower where Corporal Peter Thorpe of the Royal Signals and Lance Corporal Jabron Hashmi of the Intelligence Corps were listening in on

Taliban communications, killing them instantly. Then A Company lost one of its number on the day it was being pulled out. Private Damien Jackson was fatally wounded when his platoon were trying to secure the helicopter landing site for the RAF Chinooks that were ferrying in B Company to mount an 'RIP' – relief in place. Six British soldiers had now died in action in Helmand; all six had been killed in Sangin.

B Company had been stuck in Camp Bastion for six weeks and there were many who were happy to be sent forward to Sangin to escape the boredom. But, within hours of arriving, they came under sustained enemy fire. For their entire month-long stay in Sangin, they were under unremitting attack from the insurgents, who were hell-bent on pushing them out of the town. To hold their position, the Paras had to call in repeated air attacks from British Apache helicopter gunships, RAF Harriers and US A-10 Tankbusters. B Company suffered no losses, but were constantly harassed by incoming fire. As if that was not bad enough, they had to sleep on the floor in mud-brick huts that were riddled with large bullet holes. The daytime temperature soared to over 50°C (122°F). There were limited supplies of bottled water. They had to wash in a muddy stream running through the compound. The makeshift latrines comprised of oil drums sawn in half and filled with petrol; when they were full, they were set on fire.

The RAF C-130 Hercules that were supposed to keep them supplied kept breaking down. Worse, one night a Hercules missed the compound and dropped their supplies in the compound of a mosque controlled by the Taliban. While the Paras' ammunition and rations dwindled, the RAF found they were unable to mount a second operation, so a flight of US helicopters flew in enough temporary rations to keep them going. Then a Canadian relief convoy forced its way through, finding a scene one officer described as something out of the 'Wild West'.

'When we arrived in Sangin the locals began throwing rocks and anything they could at us,' he said. 'During the last few hundred metres we began receiving mortar fire.'

The Canadians found themselves stranded for four days alongside the Paras, who were fighting off several mortar, rocket and machine-gun attacks a day.

'I still can't believe that the Brits spent over a month living there under those conditions,' the Canadian officer said. 'It was impressive to watch them. They are unbelievable soldiers.'

When A Company returned to Sangin on 27 July, the situation appeared to be improving, so Lieutenant Hugo Farmer and One Platoon undertook the first patrol into the town. But, as they returned to the compound, they spotted signs of an imminent Taliban attack. They were moving back along a dried-up river bed when they noticed that the merchants in the bazaar were hurriedly shutting up shop, and women in their blue and black burkas were nervously shepherding children back into their houses. Suddenly, the usually busy streets were deserted. Soon, Private McKinley found himself in the thick of it once again. Over to his right, he spotted two Taliban gunmen running half-crouched across the roof of a mud-brick building. He shouted out a warning, swung his rifle over and let off a burst of fire. The response was a hail of AK-47 bullets and RPGs that arched towards the patrol from two other enemy positions. McKinley and Private Neil Edwards fell wounded in open ground as 7.62mm bullets kicked up the earth around them.

Corporal Bryan Budd, who was with them, realised that

he needed to regain the initiative and that the enemy needed to be driven back, so that the casualties could be evacuated. His section engaged the gunmen on the roof. Budd led an assault where the enemy fire was heaviest. Then, without regard for his own safety, he single-handedly stormed the building using hand grenades and his rifle to kill the enemy.

'He pushed forward to drive the enemy back, and personally dispatched some enemy taking cover "in the public shitters" with a couple of grenades and some rifle fire,' said his commander, Major Jamie Loden.

This allowed men from the Household Cavalry in a Scimitar light tank and a Spartan armoured reconnaissance vehicle to move forward to McKinley and Edwards. The only thing stopping their evacuation was McKinley's insistence on taking a continuing part in the action, despite a shrapnel wound. Budd's action forced the remaining fighters to flee across an open field where they were successfully engaged once again.

Three days later, One Platoon were out on patrol again when they made another contact. This time it was Lieutenant Farmer who led the assault on a Taliban hideout, forcing them to flee. However, the Afghan police, whom the Paras had originally gone into Sangin to defend, began defecting to the enemy. This gave the Taliban detailed intelligence about the Paras' disposition inside the compound and they came under repeated mortar and rocket attacks. But engineers from 51 Para Squadron got to work to build up the fortifications. They had only second-rate body armour, and the noise of their equipment was often so loud that they did not even realise they were being shot at. However, work in such temperatures was so exhausting that they had to be rotated out every two weeks. When the first party returned to Camp Bastion on 10 August, everyone was shocked by their gaunt condition.

When the Chinook returned with fresh engineers, it also brought back McKinley, who had insisted on returning to his comrades, despite the medics' recommendation that he spend more time recuperating. Two days later, Sangin claimed another casualty, when Lance Corporal Sean Tansey of the Life Guards was crushed by a Scimitar.

Within days of his return, McKinley and the men of One Platoon were in the thick of it once more. On 17 August, supported by a Scimitar and a Spartan, Lieutenant Farmer led an operation to flush the Taliban out of the drainage ditches and maize fields near the helicopter landing zone. As they were arresting two insurgents, caught reporting their activities by radio, the Paras came under heavy fire. A running firefight ensued. Eventually the Paras managed to force the Taliban into an ambush, calling down air and artillery attacks on them, which inflicted such heavy casualties on the enemy that they were forced to flee. But they soon returned

On 20 August, Budd was leading his section on the right forward flank of a platoon clearance patrol when, again, the Paras came under heavy fire. He and his men were ordered to hold a small, isolated Coalition outpost – dubbed a platoon house – against a vicious daily onslaught by the Taliban that had been going on for months.

'We were sent out to protect some engineers who were blowing holes in a compound 500 metres [546 yards] away from the platoon house,' said one of Budd's men. 'That was so we could cut through the compound quickly and avoid enemy fire when we were out on patrol. There were three sections of us out, a total of 24 guys, all spread out in a head-high cornfield around the compound. Bryan was the first to spot about four Taliban approaching, really close to us, only about 50 metres [55 yards] away.'

Using hand signals, Budd led his section in a flanking manoeuvre round to the cornfield's outskirts to try to cut them off. Another section was advancing, with a Land Rover fitted with a .50-calibre heavy machine gun on the patrol's left flank. The enemy spotted the Land Rover and the element of surprise was lost. The Taliban opened fire. Then a further contingent of insurgents hidden behind a wall further away also opened up on Budd's section.

'The guys were taking heavy fire from two positions,' said Budd's comrade. 'The enemy were just blasting away, their AK-47s above their heads, and rounds were coming in from all over the shop.'

One soldier got a bullet in the shoulder. Another was shot in the nose.

'Everyone was kneeling or lying down, trying to take cover. It was mayhem.'

Bryan Budd could see that his men were in mortal danger and knew that he had to do something about it.

'That's when Bryan made his move,' said his comrade. 'He knew how dangerous it was but he obviously decided it was his responsibility to destroy the threat, because the enemy were cutting us to pieces.'

Budd got up and rushed straight through the corn in the direction of the Taliban just 20 metres (65 feet) away.

'We heard Bryan's rifle open up on them on fully automatic mode,' said his comrade-in-arms, 'but that was the last anyone heard of him. All contact was lost with Bryan. Straight afterwards, the enemy's fire lessened and allowed the rest of his section to withdraw back to safety so the casualties could be treated.'

Inspired by Corporal Budd's example, the rest of the

platoon reorganised and pushed forward with their attack, eliminating more of the enemy and eventually forcing their withdrawal. Budd was listed missing in action and the whole company were then sent back to try to find him. They were accompanied by Lieutenant Farmer, even though he was wounded by shrapnel.

Lance Corporal Carse, who helped recover his friend's body, said, 'A patrol had been ambushed with machine guns and there was a Para missing. We formed a quick-reaction force and, with a Para sniper, we went out to find him. We ran out through the gates of the platoon house under fire. We took a lot of fire as we got into a cornfield where the soldier was and then we had to fight our way back to the platoon house with Corporal Budd. He was one of the best and bravest soldiers I had met – he had taken on the Taliban virtually on his own.'

'We went into the cornfield to fight our way forward,' said another comrade. 'Apache and Harrier air support was called in, and after a long fight we beat the Taliban back. About an hour later, some of the lads found Bryan's body beside two dead Taliban. It was obvious he was the one who had wasted them but he was obviously hit at the same time – by either them or the fighters behind the wall. He was badly wounded and he had no pulse.'

The Company Sergeant Major rushed forward on a quad bike to collect him and carried him back to the platoon house. But, by then, there was nothing anyone could do for him, and he was declared dead.

'What Bryan did was amazing,' his comrade added. 'He made the ultimate sacrifice for his men.'

It was later established that Corporal Budd had been shot in the back and was probably a victim of friendly fire. A pathologist established that his wounds had been inflicted by British bullets. Nevertheless, no one doubted his gallantry and he was awarded the Victoria Cross, posthumously. Private McKinley received the MC and Lieutenant Farmer the Distinguished Gallantry Cross.

But they were by no means the only heroes of the action. Major Loden had been forced to use anyone at hand to recover Budd and the other casualties, including two military policemen who had been flown in to investigate Lance Corporal Tansey's death.

'There were many people on that day who will go unrecognised, but simply volunteered immediately to go out as part of the reinforcements regardless of rank or experience,' he said.

A Company were pulled out of Sangin again on 29 August and replaced by C Company, in a major 36-hour operation that saw both B and C Companies mount an airborne assault on Sangin, while a supply convoy moved in by road. There was an eight-hour firefight as B Company provided a defensive shield during company handover. Air attacks on the main enemy position did not quell the Taliban, who responded by making full-scale assaults on two houses where the Paras had set up their positions, over-running one of them completely. Loss of British life was prevented only by an artillery assault. This gave the Paras the cover they needed to get back to their compound and inflict heavy casualties on the Taliban.

C Company remained in place until they were relieved by the Royal Marines five weeks later. By then, the Taliban were reluctant to make direct attacks and concentrated on rocket and mortar attacks. However, one of these took the life of Lance Corporal Luke McCulloch of the Royal Irish Regiment, a week into the deployment. He was the eighth British soldier to die in Sangin. On withdrawing, Lance

Corporal Thomas Gray of 3 Para said, 'It was a very intense experience but we did our job well. Being in the platoon house at Sangin was the toughest. We were getting contacted up to four times every day. Sometimes they would fire for an hour and a half at a time; other times they would shoot and scoot. At the time you don't think about it, but this is the most difficult thing I have done by far and will probably be the toughest thing I'll ever do.'

Private Martin Smith agreed. 'It's been a really steep learning curve,' he said. 'I came straight out of training, had a month off and then went straight out there. It was really intense: we were stood to every day because we were always under threat. We spent a month in a platoon house in Sangin, which was pretty hardcore. We had five or six contacts a day, then it died down to one in the morning and one in the evening. The first time it happened I wasn't really sure what was going on – I actually saw a mortar coming out of the sky. One of my mates got shrapnelled. But we gave as good as we got.'

While 3 Paras were under siege in Sangin, elite troops from 16 Air Assault Brigade began storming key areas controlled by the Taliban in a UK-led offensive, codenamed Operation Snakebite. In temperatures close to 47°C (116°F), more than 500 British and Afghan National Army troops boarded Chinook helicopters, and flew under the protection of attack helicopters and RAF Harriers to the north of the province, where they planned to intercept the enemy's command-and-control network and supply network around the village of Musa Qaleh. Situated in the Sangin valley, 25 miles north of the town, Musa Qaleh had suffered almost constant attacks from the Taliban.

During the operation, which lasted more than ten hours, Coalition forces came under heavy fire. The assault group responded with overwhelming firepower in a deliberate action to dislocate and disrupt the enemy. Then 3 Para Pathfinders went in on what was supposed to have been a week-long mission. Instead, they spent 52 days in and around Musa Qaleh, with 26 days spent in intense fighting with insurgents.

Sergeant Rhys Matthews went in with 16 Close-Support Medical Regiment to support the Paras and reported that such a long stay brought with it logistical problems.

'I was in Musa Qaleh for six weeks and at one stage we ran out of rations,' he said. 'We had to get the local Afghan police to go downtown and buy us food with what money we had until resupplies came in. Living conditions weren't brilliant – the place was riddled with old needles and syringes and there was excrement, rubbish and rats everywhere. I slept on a stretcher I had pulled off the side of our wagon, and we built our own toilets using 50-gallon [227-litre UK, 190-litre US] oil drums cut in half and burned the contents every day. We had a limited amount of water, so we didn't really wash, just cleaned our teeth, and, rather than shaving, all of us grew beards. It's the toughest tour I have ever done but I enjoyed it and would be quite happy to go back out again. It is what I joined the army for. The main thing I kept thinking when I got back was, "Where have I left my weapon?" Out there your weapon is with you all the time.'

Two REME mechanics actually got involved in the fighting. 'We had a call from the Pathfinders in Musa Qaleh, who said they had a problem with one of their WMIKs,' said Staff Sergeant Craig Midgley, who had been at Camp Bastion. 'It needed a new clutch, so we sent up two guys in a helicopter to help them out. They got it repaired but, when the Chinook came to extract them, it couldn't land because there was a lot of dust in the air and it had to fly off. The Pathfinders can't just sit around – they had to carry on with their operation – so the two REME blokes were embedded with the patrol and were engaged in a seven-hour firefight with the Taliban. They loved it. It's not what the average REME soldier expects to be doing.'

One of the engineers was injured when a hot shell case landed on his neck.

The fighting was intense. By the time the Paras had finished their tour, they had expended 45,000 rifle and machine-gun rounds, 7,500 mortar rounds, 4,300 high-explosive artillery shells, 1,050 grenades and 85 anti-tank missiles.

That autumn, there were problems elsewhere in Helmand. Army Air Corps Apache helicopter crews had rained down fire on the Taliban, pinning them down for over two hours, when friendly forces came under attack in the town of Garmsir, 120 kilometres (75 miles) south of Sangin. Garmsir was formerly known as the breadbasket of Afghanistan, due to the fertile flood plains of the Helmand River, which form an elongated oasis in the southern Afghan desert. It was also known to be a Taliban stronghold and rumour had it that many foreign Jihadists visit this area to train and get blooded. On that occasion, the gunships did their job, allowing soldiers from the Afghan National Army to wrest the town's central district from enemy control. British commanders reckoned that around 20 Taliban fighters were killed during this combined operation.

The men of A Company Group of the 2nd Battalion of the Royal Regiment of Fusiliers nicknamed the war-torn town of Nowzad, 48 kilometres (30 miles) from Sangin, 'Apocalypse Now-zad'. This dangerous desert outpost became the scene of one of the most prolonged and intense periods of fighting involving British troops in Helmand Province. The Fusiliers defended it against ferocious Taliban attacks no fewer than 149 times during their 107-day deployment.

A Company Group had moved to Nowzad on 16 July 2006 to defend the town's district compound. This contained the local police station, which had come under repeated insurgent attacks. The Fusiliers also occupied ANP (Afghan National Police) Hill, a strategic position which overlooked the troubled town. Nicknamed the Dragon's Lair, this well-defended fortification was built by the Afghans during the Russian invasion.

'The Taliban gave us a few days' grace when we first arrived,' said Major Jon Swift, Officer Commanding, A Company of 2 RRF. 'Then they started hitting us with all they had: mortars, rockets, rocket-propelled grenades and AK-47s, machine gun and sniper fire. Contacts could last up to three hours and we had a number of very close shaves. On one occasion a 107mm rocket bounced off the peak of ANP Hill. Had it detonated it could have caused significant casualties.'

Reinforcements were called for and, just before dawn on 30 July, 16 Air Assault Brigade struck in force. Elements of 3 Para Battle Group, including Ghurkhas, engineers and the Household Cavalry Regiment's light armour, supported by 7 Regiment Royal Horse Artillery as well as attack and transport helicopters, swept through the town of Nowzad in Operation Mutay. The mission's objective was to secure and search a suspected Taliban leader's compound, which was built like a maze and provided near-perfect cover for the enemy to open fire from all directions.

In the operation, the Royal Air Force dropped 71 225-

kilo (500-pound) bombs and fired 1,400 rockets. In such close-combat work, skilled, ground-based Forward Air Controllers (FACs) were vital. They had to co-ordinate the firepower of jets covering just over a kilometre and a half (a mile) every eight seconds, with bombers and Apache attack helicopters that support the troops fighting on the ground, while preventing 'blue on blue' and civilian casualties. In Afghanistan, FACs were in such demand that, during his time in-country, Captain Barry de Goede, an FAC from the Household Cavalry Regiment, spent fewer than five days in a row at Camp Bastion.

During the three-pronged assault on Nowzad, de Goede was attached to a platoon from the 2nd Battalion of the Royal Ghurkha Rifles, attacking from the northeast. The main airborne thrust into the target compound was made by a company of paratroopers, accompanied by Staff Corporal Shaun Fry, another FAC from the Life Guards, who won the Military Cross for his bravery on Operation Mutay and two subsequent actions while on his 2006 tour.

'You must know the mission,' he said, 'because, if it's winning hearts and minds, putting a rocket into the side of a house is not going to help.'

As they entered Nowzad, the Taliban hit de Goede's Gurkha platoon before it could get close to its objectives. This meant that the Chinooks delivering Fry and his Paras to the target compound had to set down in a hot landing zone.

'As soon as we hit the deck the whole place erupted,' said Fry. 'It was as if the world and his wife had opened fire on us. We secured the compound with the support of Apache helicopters but then got reports of people gathered in a nearby orchard. I went with my platoon to see who it was and we immediately came under heavy fire – we all got it, nobody was left out.'

They ended up being pinned down for about two hours by Taliban attacking at close range from behind the orchard wall. De Goede sent over a B-1 bomber as a show of force, but it did not discourage the Taliban.

'Eventually, we were given the order to get out,' said Fry. 'We had taken the Taliban's flank and taken out some snipers but we were still under attack, so I stayed with my Fire Support Team commander to cover the withdrawal.'

He had a line to a couple of A-10s to support the troops pulling out, but he had to hold off calling the pilots onto the targets.

'One platoon, also engaged in the fighting, was too close and I couldn't risk hitting them,' he said. 'Once everyone had got out, I confirmed the target to the A-10 pilot and then ran as fast as I could through enemy bullets and hid behind the wall just 250 metres [270 yards] away... I had the opportunity to dump a 500-pound 225-kilo] bomb but refused to do so because of the risk of "friendlies" close to the target area. But at the back of my mind I also knew that I was the platoon's FAC and the troops were relying on me to support them. If I didn't call in the air support, it would be like having a rifleman who couldn't fire his weapon.'

While the Paras pulled out, the Fusiliers were left in place for a 15-week onslaught. They operated out of trenches and fortified sangars that overlooked no man's land – a 500-metre (550-yard) stretch of uninhabited town between their position to the west and Taliban forces to the east. The conditions were reminiscent of World War One.

'There were two battles going on,' explained Company Sergeant Major 'Jimmy' Greaves. 'One was against the Taliban; the other was against the elements. It was a harsh environment in which to live and fight.'

Despite the intensity of the fighting, no Fusiliers were

killed. However, three were wounded – two when an RPG exploded after hitting their sangar, and one who lost a leg in a minefield.

'It is amazing that the casualty count isn't higher,' said Major Swift. 'If I was a religious man, I would say that someone was smiling on us. But I think the fact that we escaped relatively unscathed is a result of good luck, good battle discipline and the fact that we were wearing all the right kit at the right times. The Taliban were tenacious, fanatical and knew how to use the ground. They kept coming at us despite the casualties we were inflicting on them.'

By the time A Company of 2 RRF passed responsibility for Nowzad to K Company of 42 Commando of the RM in November 2006, the Fusiliers estimated they had fired 89,000 GPMG rounds, 10,000 light-machine-gun and rifle rounds, and 1,500 mortar rounds. They had also called in more than 30 air strikes.

'We must have had just about every airframe in the theatre supporting us at some point,' said Major Swift. 'French Mirage aircraft, Dutch F-16s, American F-14s, F-15s, F-16s, F-18s and B-1 bombers, RAF GR7s and Army Air Corps Apaches.'

CHAPTER 15

THE RETURN OF THE MARINES

On Monday 10 July 2006, Defence Secretary Des Browne announced plans for elements of 3 Commando Brigade of the Royal Marines to replace 16 Air Assault Brigade in the Helmand Province of Afghanistan. The Marines decided on a more 'hearts and minds' approach than the Airborne had been using. Their aim was to engage the people of Helmand Province in tribal and village *shuras* – or discussions – through the central Afghan Pashtunwali code, a 5,000-year-old code of conduct based on honour (*namuz*) and shame (*haya*), under which the conducting of defensive roles in warfare or failing to exact revenge is seen as shameful and lacking bravery (*tureh*).

Instead, they would find themselves fighting.

On the Marines' first patrols out of Camp Bastion, it became clear that the 'Airborne and Furious' or 'cloud punchers', as the Marines called the Air Assault Brigade, had taken a firm and aggressive stance towards the inhabitants of Lashkar Gah, due to the threat from improvised explosive devices in vehicles or strapped to suicide bombers. The Marines tried a more relaxed posture and engaged with the local population. However, within days of their arrival the threat became a reality. On 19 October, a mobile patrol in Lashkar Gah was hit by a suicide bomber and Marine Gareth Wright, the top cover from 45 Recce Troop, was killed. From then on, the Marines' message to the Taliban became, 'Either give up fighting and join in with the reconstruction efforts – or die.'

The Brigade Reconnaissance Force was stationed at FOB Price, a small piece of real estate in the town of Gereshk, 32 kilometres (20 miles) north-east of Lashkar Gah. They shared this with 'an odious group of American weekend warriors known as the ODA' – Operational Detachment A, a Special Forces A-Team – according to the BRF's Sergeant Steve King, 'who firmly believe that their role in the grand scheme lies somewhere between that of Delta Force and the CIA.'

They were known to the Marines as the 'Tennessee Shooting Club'.

'The only thing they are missing is Clint Eastwood as their OC,' said King.

In the UK, the BRF were told they would have all the equipment they requested before deployment. Failing that, their opposite number, the Pathfinder Platoon of 16 Air Assault Brigade, would hand it over to them. Unfortunately, no one had informed the Pathfinders and the Marines deprived them of nearly all the stores and equipment that they had brought from the UK, including vehicles, optics and weapon systems.

No sooner had the BRF settled in than they were told that they were to abandon their initial engagement strategy and adopt what was known as 'advance to ambush'.

'The routine was as follows,' said King. 'Identify a

potential trouble spot, drive towards it, get shot at, return fire – proportionately, of course – then drive away very quickly, sometimes with the added bonus of incoming indirect fire. It took a ferocious engagement of just under an hour for us to realise that maybe we needed to change tack.'

The terrain of Helmand proved difficult to negotiate in the fleet of worn-down WMIK armed Land Rovers that they had inherited from the Pathfinders – they were losing them at a rate one per day, due to mechanical failure. However, the local populace in their patrol area were generally friendly and they set about trying to win hearts and minds once more.

Meanwhile, Y Squadron were thrown in at the deep end. Within 24 hours of landing at Camp Bastion, the 1st Detachment – callsign RRT2, comprising Sergeant Thompson, Corporal Gordon and Marines Thomas and Wadsworth – found themselves being airlifted to Sangin's platoon house, which was taking incoming mortar fire at the time.

'After a quick check zero and issue of ammo, we had our bergens packed full of batteries and were sat in the Chinook ready for the off,' said Marine Wadsworth. 'And breathe... four very flushed faces staring at each other, after only 12 hours' acclimatisation. With our day sacks on and bergens underslung as they were too heavy to carry, we were Sangin-bound.'

They practically had the Chinook to themselves and, on the way, Sergeant Thompson took them through the standard operating procedures. Marine Wadsworth was just beginning to think that things were OK when they neared Sangin.

'The aircrew made their guns ready,' said Wadsworth,

'and I glanced around, noticing rather a lot of spent cylinders on the floor. Our worst fears were realised when the air-crewman shouted in my ear, "Sangin is under contact, two minutes, P1 casualty, we have to land." A steep dive later and we were over the compound. The underslung dropped, a lurch forward, and we were down. We were off huddling the deck. Visibility was nil for a few seconds. Then it cleared and we found ourselves in an open field.'

After a quick number check, they moved off across 200 metres (218 yards) of open ground. The ominous sound of rounds landing ensured that they covered the ground at lightning speed. They moved swiftly across the 'pipe range' into the headquarters building, past the mortar position that had already fired 160 rounds that day.

'Marine Thomas and I had gone to retrieve our bergens and Scarus containers,' said Marine Wadsworth. 'This is the point where we had a close encounter with our first 107mm rocket. Crossing the courtyard past ANP house, the ominous whistling of incoming ordnance saw the kit ditched and the two of us diving for cover. *Boom!* 100 yards [91 metres] away, but close enough.'

Perhaps they were lucky. In an effort to increase their electronic footprint, other detachments of Y Company were sent to other unappealing destinations, such as Garmsir and Nowzad.

Next in were 42 Commando. With them was 23-year-old Marine Iain Kentish from London on his first operational deployment.

'As the Hercules was coming in,' he said, 'I was looking out of the window and was amazed at the vastness of the desert and how the Afghans survived in such a biblical barren land. It reminded me of the scenery in the film *The Life of Brian*.'

'As soon as we came off the plane the heat and dust hit the back of my throat,' said 20-year-old Marine Ben Wadham from Bodmin in Cornwall. 'The hot air from the Hercules engine intensified the heat and this made me think how hot it really was.'

The first on the ground were L Company, with elements of M Company attached. L Company were to relieve 3 Para in Sangin, while the M Company elements were deployed by Chinook to Kajaki, 80 kilometres (50 miles) to the north.

'I was in the second helo to land,' said Corporal Tim Hughes. 'As I was sat by the door gunner, I was able to watch the scenery as we circled "the dam", the name that we gave to this area. The scenery can only be described as awesome. It's just a shame that the area couldn't be better explored due to the mine threat.'

This was home for the next two weeks. They had ten-man rations to eat and drank purified water from the dam.

'There was nothing there when we arrived, apart from sangars,' said Hughes. 'But we made it our own, building a gym and a shower. It eventually became our home. There was also a house at this location we christened "Honking House", from the Soviet invasion. When the Afghans finally overwhelmed the Soviet invaders, it was the scene of barbaric torture. This acted as a stark reminder to a previous existence, while the sound of mortars landing at regular intervals reminded us of the real reasons that we were there.'

The hydroelectric dam at Kajaki was of major strategic importance. Once completed, it would provide power to more than two million people across Helmand Province. To finish it, the contractors needed a secure environment so they could bring in the civilians to work on the dam in relative safety. This was impossible when the Taliban were still a threat. For the moment the forward party would reconnoitre the situation, then, in early December, M Company Group of 42 Commando would arrive in strength.

Back at FOB Price, K Company took over vehicle and foot patrols.

'The Company experienced its first hostile engagement with the Taliban when they came under small-arms and mortar fire,' said Major Neil Sutherland, 'but through a combination of direct and indirect fire defeated the Taliban aggressors.'

'We were told to hit the ground running,' said Lieutenant Colonel Matt Holmes, 'which we've done, having had a number of successful engagements with the Taliban within days of arriving. We are robust, highly capable and have unrivalled firepower at our disposal – Javelin [missiles] proved effective on day one.'

Next came Operation Omer, the redeployment of troops by road convoy to relieve the Paras in Musa Qaleh. Elements of K Company moved forward to a desert rendezvous. They were supported by artillery, attack helicopters and fixed-wing air cover, ready to respond if the troop convoy was attacked. In fact, the operation ended with the commanding officer holding a *shura* in the desert with tribal elders. Meanwhile, J Company stayed back at FOB Price, patrolling in and around Gereshk, where they had a number of successful engagements with the Taliban.

By 28 October 2006 – the Royal Marines' 342nd anniversary – 45 Commando and the Commando Logistic Regiment were also in-theatre. Soon the whole corps were to see action.

Juliet Company of 42 Commando were involved in

Operation Slate to protect the town of Gereshk. With Whisky Company of 45 Commando, who were also in-country, they were to set up a number of checkpoints and defensive positions around the hydroelectric dam that provides power to the town. The operation was led by 2 Troop. After a horrendously early start, they left FOB Price, heading for the dam and the place where they would spend the next 36 hours.

'They say that no plan will survive contact with the enemy,' said Lance Corporal Wright, who was with 2 Troop, 'but our plan didn't even survive the *journey* to the enemy. Through no fault of the driver of our Viking, we took a hard left-hand turn with a deep irrigation ditch to our left.'

As the vehicle turned, the ground gave way, dropping the Viking down hard on its side. The section in the rear of the wagon, under Corporal 'Coconut' Kibbler, found themselves pinned down and unable to open the rear hatch. Luckily, Troop Sergeant Nige Quarman spotted their predicament and waded waste deep into the water to release them. As result, he had to put up with wet boots for the next day and a half.

By the time Two Troop arrived at their designated position, One and Three Troops of Juliet Company were already in position, forming a defensive cordon to protect the engineers who were working on the dam's defences. Soon after, incoming mortars and RPGs began to rain down on both Juliet and Whisky Companies' positions. The Marines soon spotted the enemy mortar positions and started replying with their own 81mm mortars.

Mortar support was so much in demand that 42 Commando's Mortar Troop had to be augmented with six barrels and 22 more personnel from 45 Commando, giving it 23 barrels and 71 personnel, supporting six different locations, making it the biggest mortar troop in recent times. They also supported the Danish Recce Squadron and the Estonians on long-range desert patrols, hitching lifts in whatever vehicles were available.

While the mortar men kept the insurgents' heads down, Two Troop moved off to provide a mobile cordon to intercept the Taliban mortar crews if they attempted to move positions.

'We had barely left the security of the cordon, when sharp-eyed Corporal "Nobby" Hall called the convoy to a halt after he spotted a group of Taliban moving directly towards us,' said Wright. 'However, upon debussing it was quickly realised that his hardcore foreign fighters were actually a herd of camels.'

The target discarded, Two Troop forded the Helmand River and moved to the prominent Spot Height 852 – or 'Viking Hill', as it came to be called. Earlier that morning, AH-64 helicopters had attacked the hill after a group of Taliban fighters had been seen on the top. Now, Two Troop were to clear the hill and gather any intelligence left. But after they reached the top and began to move forward, they started to receive effective enemy mortar fire. As they were unable locate a firing position or a forward controller to bring down mortar fire of their own, they were ordered to 'bug out'.

'As we hastily made our way off the Spot Height into dead ground and back towards the Helmand River, we heard the unmistakably scary sound of RPGs whizzing past our Vikings,' said Wright. 'As our top cover gunners began to return fire, the unthinkable happened, my vehicle was hit.'

Once the vehicle had juddered to a halt there was

nothing else to do but debus. Kibbler led the charge and they all emerged unscathed.

'Our Viking gunner was still putting the rounds down,' said Wright, 'and with the rest of the Troop returning to give us support we moved quickly into all-round defence and secured the wagon.'

The situation was far from ideal. They were isolated in deep vegetation along the edge of the river and it was obvious that they could not hang around. But Corporal Ash Oates and his section had debussed from their Viking and made their way on foot to begin the rescue mission. Wright's Viking crew reported that the wagon could not be recovered without support. With enemy movement in the area, they quickly decided to destroy the vehicle and get out of the killing zone. They gathered up all the essential gear and everything else they could carry, and then destroyed several thousand pounds' worth of kit to deny it to the enemy. Phosphorous and HE grenades were then thrown into both front and rear cabs, and they moved away from the contact area.

As they left, Marine 'Button' Moon fired an ILAW [Improved LAW] missile into the Viking to finish it off.

'Fifteen seconds later we had established that the Viking armour is actually "bombers",' said Lance Corporal Wright.

The ILAW bounced off and disappeared over Spot Height 852. With that they piled into – and on top of – the other Vikings, and moved off with everyone accounted for. Minutes later, they stopped to watch as a passing F-18 Hornet dropped a 225-kilo (500-pound) joint direct-attack munition (JDAM) onto their abandoned Viking, destroying it – along with Two Troop's bergens.

'Two Troop arrived back at the cordon area, none the worse for their contact with the Taliban,' said Wright, 'to spin some exaggerated dits and have a bit of banter at the expense of the guys from the Viking crews, who looked decidedly unhappy at the loss of their favourite toy.'

They also heard the news that One Troop had been in contact with small arms, mortars and RPG fire on and off all afternoon. And there were repairs to make.

'Having lost all the sandbags around his position from a passing mortar, Corporal "Tug" Wilson looked like he was digging to Australia,' said Wright.

With the sun setting fast, Two Troop were sent to reinforce the inner cordon around the dam, where they were met by the company second-in-command, Captain Bruce Anderson. No sooner had they moved into position than they came under enemy mortar fire, which rained down just 30 metres (33 yards) from them.

'With "Jockanese" screams of "incoming" coming from the 2IC [second-in-command] we quickly dug in, and settled down for a long night,' said Wright.

Enemy mortars also fell within 30 metres (33 yards) of 42 Commando's mortar line, but the enemy positions were quickly located and silenced.

Once the engineers had finished their work, Two Troop moved off just before first light to secure two bridges, so that the convoy could move safely through town and back to FOB Price. Then, the Viking-less Two Troop had a short yomp back to camp, where kit insurance claim forms awaited.

Other operations around Gereshk regularly brought J Company face to face with the Taliban, who engaged them with small-arms fire, mortars, rockets and IEDs. On 17 November 2006, Corporal A J Wilson was on patrol with Juliet Company in the town of Habibollah Kalay, which lies approximately 5 kilometres (3 miles) north-east of

Gereshk, along the Helmand River and canal. The town itself is dominated to the north by a large levee running east to west, and the remains of an ancient fort made from red sandstone, appropriately known as the Red Fort. Habibollah Kalay had long been considered a pro-Taliban area and a stronghold for foreign fighters. The people there had little contact with Coalition forces and lived at the mercy of the local Taliban commanders.

After Juliet Company had established a number of checkpoints on key routes into Gereshk in Operation Slate, they sent out a reconnaissance patrol into the town. The company moved into the outskirts of Habibollah Kalay from the north, with two manoeuvre troops and a fire support group (FSG). In Phase One, Two Troop under Captain Gordon Sweeny were to secure the western side of the levee. Then One Troop under Captain Chris Burr were to move along the eastern side, supported by the WMIK vehicles of the FSG, led by Captain Anderson.

The company broke out of the cover of dead ground and Two Troop moved forward to secure their objective on foot. Once they were firmly in position, One Troop pushed forward on foot towards the Red Fort. Having cleared a number of deserted compounds and old enemy positions, they had just reached their objective when they were engaged by RPGs and small-arms fire.

One section on the right-hand side under Corporal 'Tug' Wilson identified one of the enemy firing points and pushed forward into a walled compound to engage it. On the left, Corporal Mick Cowe's section were engaged by another enemy position with small-arms fire and RPGs. With One Troop receiving substantial incoming fire, Corporal 'Tommo' Thompson from FSG pushed out to the flank in his WMIK and began engaging with .50-calibre and machine-gun fire. At this point, the company positions to the rear of One Troop and company headquarters began to come under effective enemy mortar fire.

The enemy had clearly set up a number of positions and fired a salvo of RPGs at One Troop, which resulted in 'some private moments for a few people', according to Corporal Wilson, 'Marine "Geri" Halliwell being one.'

Halliwell was in the process of firing his 51mm mortar when he noticed an RPG winging its way towards him. Quickly on his feet, he just managed to jump up as the RPG passed under his legs and detonated 30 metres (33 yards) away in some rocks. Corporal Thompson in his WMIK also began to receive accurate RPG fire and was forced to move three times as RPGs whizzed past the sides of his vehicle.

With Two Troop pushing up to secure One Troop's western flank and Corporal Reggie Reddrop's section securing the eastern side, they heard the reassuring roar of aircraft overhead. It was a JTAC team attached to company HQ, who had called in close air support. On top of that, Two Troop had identified in-depth enemy positions, and British 81mm mortar barrels under Sergeant Andy Waiton now went into action.

By then, One Troop had been in contact for over 40 minutes. They had neutralised a number of enemy positions and it was clear that the enemy were moving location after almost every shot. Wilson's section had received a number of accurate airburst RPGs over their position and, with ammo running low, they called forward their Viking, which had been providing fire support, to get them out of there. But, as the Viking manoeuvred, its rear cab rolled over. So Corporal Reddrop pushed forward to the contact, and joined Corporals Cowe and Thompson as they covered the recovery of the Viking and the withdrawal of One Section on foot.

With Corporal 'Drinky' Drinkwater's WMIK and Two Troop engaging in-depth enemy positions, the OC began the process of withdrawing. All their Vikings now recovered, One Troop broke contact and got the order to mount up in their vehicles from Captain Burr. Then the rest of Juliet Company broke contact and moved back to FOB Price, ready to fight another day.

When Zulu Company of 45 Commando returned to Afghanistan, they was initially stationed at Kabul. Then, at the beginning of November, they were moved to Helmand to take part in operations down south. At Camp Bastion, they were given 13 Vikings and were told to interdict and disrupt enemy activities in the Garmsir area, as well as reassure the local population and generally improve stability in the area.

The 90-kilometre (56-mile) trek south proved more eventful than expected. The wheeled vehicles were not able to tear up the terrain like the Vikings and regularly had to be dragged out of the soft wadi bottoms. During one encounter of wheel to soft sand, the ever-observant Captain 'The Ham' Hamilton asked the tanker driver, 'Are you aware you have a large luminous orange panel on top of your vehicle?'

On the first night, as Sergeant Kenny Everett dug a shell scrape, he noticed the bright lights of Camp Bastion filling the sky and realised that what was intended to be a four-hour drive could well turn into an epic journey. It did. It took two days before they arrived at the 79 Battery Mobile Outreach Group gun line outside Garmsir.

Once on the ground, they started an extensive patrol

programme that included interdiction operations on the main supply routes and river crossing points. The Taliban did not seem to know how to react to the presence of dismounted troops, whose actions were not as predictable as those in vehicles they had been used to seeing. They seemed to disappear into the shadows when heavily laden foot patrols shook out with 51mm mortars, anti-tank weapons and Javelin missiles hanging out of their day sacks, while Vikings stood off in support. The stalemate was broken when One Troop, using the thermal imagery from the Javelin sighting system, spotted the enemy moving into an ambush site and manning a crew-served weapon. A well-placed Javelin missile took the sting out of this group's tail.

Next, as the result of a contact by Information Exploitation Group recce, an operation was hatched to disrupt enemy activity and destroy their positions south of Garmsir. This involved two troops and the squadron headquarters of the Light Dragoons, the Viking Troop and a seven-man fire support team.

At first light on 5 December, they were in position on the line of departure. The troops advanced across the river with fire support from the Scimitars and snipers on the dominant feature in the area nicknamed 'JTAC Hill'. Zulu Company moved south, clearing all the compounds and buildings along the way. This met with light resistance for most of the morning. By lunchtime, it was clear that the enemy had been reinforced. The company then encountered a much more determined and effective adversary, who held their ground in the face of overwhelming firepower. Some elements even attempted a counter-attack, getting to within 20 metres (65 feet) on one flank. The Marines countered by calling in close air support, Apache gunships and 105mm artillery.

Once they had achieved their aim, it was time to extract. C Squadron and Four Troop held the enemy at bay as Five Troop pulled back, followed by One Troop, who, finding themselves fighting on three sides, had to blow a hole in a compound wall to disengage. The withdrawal provoked a new burst of heavy enemy fire. The OC's Viking moved up to resupply Four Troop to guarantee a constant high weight of fire in retaliation. Throughout this withdrawal the tactical air controller and Forward Observation Officer stayed in place with the forward troop, calmly acquiring new targets as more enemy closed in, using never-ending trenches like rat runs to infiltrate the area the best they could.

The contact lasted for ten hours. Even when the company were back in the district centre (DC), they continued to receive sporadic fire throughout the night and the following day. Subsequent damage assessment indicated that the enemy had sustained a very significant number of losses and casualties, in an area in which they had previously assumed they had total freedom of movement.

Zulu Company also suffered casualties that day. Marine Adam Edwards sustained a gunshot wound to his arm, and Marine Jonathan Wigley died from his injuries despite being medevacked out to Bastion. They returned to Camp Bastion in time for the camp ceremony for Wigley.

At 04.00 on 13 December, loaded with extra ammo, India Company of the Command Support Group left from Lashkar Gah and headed for the frontline at Garmsir, in Operation Sandbag. It was still pitch black when Corporal Williams led his vehicle, call-sign 'Topaz 60', out into the unforgiving desert where, according to Corporal Graves, 'He tried to find every bog he could to make sure our journey was as eventful as possible.' They hit one such bog within an hour of leaving Lashkar Gah and were stuck there for the best part of two hours.

'The first two vehicles got through and, to the delight of the OC, Major Jules Wilson, it was his Land Rover and trailer that got stuck,' said Graves.

As the cover of darkness began to lift, extricating the vehicles became urgent.

'In the end we had to use all of our tow ropes and borrow a few extra from another call-sign who had decided to take the hard ground that surrounded the bog we were in,' said Graves.

After a few failed attempts they managed to free the vehicles and continue on their journey. They arrived at the gun line around 10.30 with wet boots and muddy trousers, 'all bombed up and ready for action', only to discover that the corps had ordered a five-day ceasefire in the Garmsir district.

'The DC is not exactly Butlin's,' explained Captain 'Bomber' Harris of OMLT Ops Company. 'It forms the basis of a government – controlled enclave, surrounded by the River Helmand to the west, and Taliban narcotic strongholds to the south and east. The area is known as the "green zone", due to fact that all the fields, canals and irrigation ditches had been heavily shelled throughout the previous five months so that there was now a distinct "buffer" between the Taliban positions to the south and our own line of troops in the DC. Locals have been forced out of the area due to the heavy fighting and instability – something we have tried to address throughout our time by reassuring them, supporting local projects and attempting to broker ceasefires to allow them a degree of relative stability.'

The current ceasefire was holding, so, after one night on

the gun line, India Company moved into the district centre.

'Our arrival in the DC was uneventful,' said Corporal Graves, 'yet the evidence of harsh fighting was all around with empty cases on the ground and bullet holes splattered across the mud walls. The first thing we all noticed when we arrived was the lack of civvies in the area. The place was like a ghost town from an old Western flick. It was very eerie.'

With the ceasefire fully in force, their initial task was to reinforce the compound defences with lots of razor wire, a stack of sandbags and the traditional Bootneck 'gash sweep' (rubbish heap). Soon, the compound was ready to be defended and lived in for as long as they needed to.

After Marines had filled what seemed like every sandbag in the theatre, the ceasefire lifted and they were subjected to the occasional burst of AK-47 overhead.

'The real change in mood came when the OC tasked the interpreter to make a loudspeaker announcement, which went something like this: "Taliban, Taliban, Taliban, your weapons are weak, our soldiers are stronger than yours and you will die if you do not surrender," ' said Corporal Graves. 'To say this upset them a little bit is an understatement, as their reply was in the form of AK-47 fire, and four RPG rounds missed the eastern sangar by about a metre, and exploded behind our compound.'

While all this was going on, Marine Dallas Turner, one of the company's snipers, spotted two Taliban shooters moving around behind a wall and dropped one of them from 1,050 metres (1,150 yards).

'A few more bursts came our way after that and I replied with some HE from the 51mm mortar,' said Graves. 'Rumours have it from intelligence that the guy Dallas shot was a high-ranking Taliban officer – let us hope so.'

Captain Adam Rutherford was with Two Troop of the BRF at Garmsir. At three o'clock one clear, cold morning in December they were poised to attack. The moon has just risen above the hills, casting its light across the frosty desert surface and Rutherford was concerned that it was too bright. Then he saw two shadowy figures race across the open ground between scattered compounds, but no words were spoken. Twelve fighting vehicles were lined out in fire-support positions recced the previous evening. The MILAN crews were dismounted and were scanning with thermal imaging. The heavy machine gun teams had acquired their arcs and, a short distance behind, the Ground Assault Troop were making their final adjustments. As H-hour approached, they waited in silence, deep in thought.

'Where did I put my spoon?' wondered Captain Rutherford. 'Why do I always get menu C?'

Dogs barked in the distance. Then the still was shattered by wild small-arms fire from the enemy position. The 12 MILANs responded, ripping apart the outer walls of the compound. The holes they made were blasted by waves of heavy machine gun and general-purpose machine gun fire. The Taliban's response was brief and fruitless. Right on cue, a B-1B bomber delivered two laser-guided 907-kilo (2,000-pound) bombs into the compounds. The ground assault troop rapidly closed in for a damage assessment. The first target was 100 per cent destroyed and only 15 per cent of the secondary remained. With Operation Penver completed, Captain Rutherford gave the word to withdraw.

In southern Afghanistan, 45 Commando also found themselves deployed as Operational Mentoring and Liaison Teams – OMLTs or 'omelettes' – with the Afghan

National Army (AMA) based at Camp Tombstone, the American base near Camp Bastion in Helmand. One team went out on patrol around Garmsir, where they came under small-arms fire daily. During one heavy, hour-long contact, Marine Jonny 'Purple' Hart's head camera caught the moment of his being shot in the backside. The clip is thought to be flying around the Internet. Later in the tour, after being caught in an ambush, Corporal 'Fen' Fenwick gave thanks for ballistic matting as he received blast injuries only to his lower legs – rather than in more sensitive areas – after a direct hit by an RPG.

Next, they were to make a sweep up the Panjwayi Valley with the ANA.

'It was with some trepidation, and the faint strains of "Ride of the Valkyries" dying away from the speakers of the US psyops truck, that we put our best foot forward and walked out of the Sperwan Gar firebase and onto our start line,' said Corporal Richie Akhurst, who had recently joined OMLT B as a medic. 'It's not often you can do an advance to contact, look over your shoulder and see your grot [quarters], as well as groups of Canadians standing on the roofs eating toaster pastries and settling down to the big show. Surreal just doesn't come close.'

The joint UK–ANA team under Colour Sergeant Tam Laird and 336 ODA – one of the US Special Forces – had been tasked with capturing Zangabar Gar, a range of low hills known to be a Taliban stronghold and a nest of enemy activity. The last time it had been captured, a reported 900 Taliban had been killed, and earlier probing patrols made by Laird and Corporal 'Raffs' Rafferty had met with serious opposition.

'Everyone felt they were in for a real tear-up this time and cheerfully christened this gig "Operation Certain Death",' said Corporal Akhurst. 'Not the first or the last time that this name has been used on this tour, I'm sure.'

The advance began without a hitch, and some good artillery preparation onto Zangabar Gar 'gave me a bit of a warm and fuzzy feeling, but we were still patrolling in the "brace" position,' said Akhurst. 'We were by now surrounded by the infamous bombproof grape houses that dot the landscape, each one a natural bunker, but we received no incoming.'

Signals Intelligence steered them towards enemy targets. Unfortunately, they could also spot the Taliban correcting their aim. But the advance pushed on and there was still no contact. The foothills were secured without a fight. Once in position, they spent an hour or two waiting for the counter-attack. It came just before last light with a couple of mortars and small-arms fire from the north and south.

'True to fashion the Taliban had good cam and con [camouflage and concealment] and were not pinged [discovered],' said Corporal Akhurst 'This didn't stop the ANA turning good rounds into empty cases, making a lot of noise and not much else.'

The next day dawned with F-18 strikes close by and they scrambled for a good spot to watch the B-1 907-kilo (2,000-pound) bombs hit the next targets, Zangabar 1 and 2. Then they mounted up for a sweep of compounds to the west. With the Apaches strafing ambush lines around them and 225-kilo bombs (500-pounders) levelling everything else, they continued unopposed.

'We'd joked about getting here and the Taliban having all gone home,' said Akhurst, 'but this was getting ridiculous. They were there but didn't engage us and the ANA were beginning to think perhaps this war-fighting lark wasn't all that bad after all.'

By the end of the day, they had reached Zangabar Gar and not a bullet had been fired.

'It was then decided that after taking all this ground we were not going to hold it but "retire" to another compound as the CS team were concerned that they wouldn't get their twice-daily resupply,' said Akhurst. 'The compound where we "retired" to just happened to be about 10 metres [11 yards] off our start line that morning.'

But then delivering supplies to forward troops in Helmand could be a dangerous business. Corporal Dobson was out on a 'desert mule' convoy out of Camp Bastion with Marine 'Arnie' Arnold, when they were warned over the radio to be extra vigilant.

'Just before we reached our destination we were told to move off the track as intelligence suggested that the track we were on was no longer safe,' said Corporal Dobson. 'Buttocks clenched, we moved off through a number of small desert villages and settlements with great care and vigilance.'

As they were passing a settlement, there were a number of individuals outside a small dwelling. To avoid any confrontation the convoy broke track and moved off over some irrigation channels. As the last vehicle in the convoy reached the channel, there was an explosion on the track where the convoy would have been if it had continued on its original route.

The convoy pushed cautiously on around numerous mud huts and narrow streets until suddenly the warning 'contact front!' came screaming over the radio.

'Instantly, the force protection boys put down a huge weight of fire to allow the convoy to extract to a safe area,' said Dobson.

Air cover was on standby not far away, and within

seconds attack helicopters were swarming overhead with an awesome demonstration of firepower. The convoy went into all-round defence positions and awaited the return of the force protection vehicles. After some quick checks, the convoy moved off again, but, as it rounded a corner, some small-arms fire began to land nearby. This time the drivers' feet were pressed firmly to the floor and the convoy sped forward, as the top cover suppressed the firing point, until it reached the safety of a coalition-held compound.

Juliet Company of 42 Commando continued patrolling along the length of the Sangin Valley to the north and east of Gereshk, as part of the Mobile Operations Group, going out for five to ten days at a time.

'You will not find the term *combat recce patrol* in any pamphlet and it's not taught at Lympstone [the Commando Training Centre in Devon],' said Corporal Mick Cowe of Juliet Company. 'What it basically entails is tipping up in the back yard of the enemy and waiting for a reaction.'

The aim was to conduct a combat recce of additional checkpoints in the vicinity of Habibollah Kalay, the scene of bitter resistance in previous actions. J Company Group, along with two 105mm guns from E Troop, 79 Battery, were split into northern and southern groups. The northern group, consisting of One and Two Troops and the company tactical headquarters, mounted in Vikings and two WMIKs, were to patrol along the Nahr-e Boghra Canal. The southern group were to establish a gun line to the southwest of Gereshk, with Three Troop as a fire support group, providing an overwatch of the target area and preventing reinforcements coming from the Taliban stronghold of Zumbelay to the east.

'At the time this was the most ambitious operation carried out by the company and the only time a deliberate action had been conducted in a known hostile area of the "green belt",' said Corporal Cowe.

Final checks on ammunition and weapons were done and the OC was ready to move. The normal banter between the section commanders came to an end. J Company all felt that something was going to happen that day, though nobody could have guessed what actually lay ahead.

The day started badly for Sergeant Willie Whitefield. In a minor collision, the bar armour protecting his side of the Viking cab was ripped off. It lay in the sand, a mangled heap. Shaking his head, Whitefield remounted his wounded steed and set off.

'Those who know Gereshk understand that anything can happen east of the dam,' said Cowe, 'so it was no great surprise to find a body lying in the road close to the release point.'

It turned out to be a missing civilian contractor, executed by the Taliban.

With Three Troop set to overwatch, Corporal Coles's WMIK provided arcs over the dam to the north while Corporal Bailey's WMIK faced east. They stood out in silhouette as the sun rose over the sleepy compounds and signs of life began to appear. A thrown Viking track delayed the move in by 20 minutes, but, as dawn was breaking, the northern group continued its move along the canal to the target area, where mist still blanketed the ground, with Corporal Thompson's WMIK in the lead.

At 06.47, the group were engaged on three sides by a heavy weight of accurate mortars, RPG and small-arms fire from numerous firing points. One Troop found themselves trapped in a Taliban ambush on a single-track road. Corporal 'Tug' Wilson fell out of the Viking cab into a ditch, as an RPG exploded on his vehicle. He spent the next hour and a half bare-headed, shouting at his Viking commander, who was otherwise engaged, to throw him his helmet. The Viking commander merely screamed back at him to 'shut the bleeding door properly'.

On the main canal track, Two Troop had neutralised one RPG firing point and pushed forward to engage the enemy on One Troop's right flank. After moving about 200 metres (218 yards), they were engaged by a further two firing points. This stage of the fight was to last about two hours – winning the initial firefight alone took 25 minutes. An observer from Three Troop said it was 'an awesome display of firepower, and utter carnage within a grid square – everyone was firing'.

The young Three Troop commander, Second Lieutenant 'Pickles' Law, who was looking on in awe at the amazing spectacle of tracer rounds, mortar and artillery fire that filled the sky over the canal, felt guilty that he was not in the thick of it – only to find that he was. An RPG whistled a couple of metres over his Viking and one of his WMIKs reported ten to 15 enemy 200 metres (218 yards) to the east. They were reinforcing a well-defended trench, and engaging Three Troop with RPG and small-arms fire. Soon, a hellish rate of fire was loosed by both sides. Enemy rounds struck the steering block and gun mount of Corporal Coles's WMIK, and RPGs whistled past Corporal Bailey's head as he gave target indications to his gunner. All three troops were now in contact and fighting separate Taliban positions.

As direct fire from the 0.5 calibre was not successful in suppressing the enemy engaging Three Troop, Marines Talbot and Moncaster crawled out of cover to fire a Javelin missile at the trench, calmly locking on to a heat source as enemy fire landed between them. With the trench system neutralised, the Javelin team crawled back into cover to enjoy a brief respite in the contact.

Along the canal the fighting was intense. Corporal Thompson's WMIK crew were all 'smoking', and they were soon down to 20 per cent ammunition. Marine Beagles was firing the Minimi from the driver's seat and Marine 'Afghan' Steve Davies was knocking down a building with the .50 calibre. By this time 'Tommo' was deaf – he had burst an eardrum.

Corporal Mick Cowe shouted fire-control orders to Lance Corporal Coe.

'Bang the ILAW down there, John,' he yelled.

Grenade rounds were fired into the compounds and irrigation ditches, to suppress enemy firing points there. Now smiling, Sergeant Whitefield and Marine Sam Vocea loosed salvos of 51mm mortars. The Viking and WMIK crews provided devastating covering fire and had to be resupplied by the troops as they were running through ammunition at an incredible rate. While seen stretching to reach his GPMG, the diminutive Corporal Ads Lison was heard shouting: 'I've done five grand already.'

An RPG exploded next to Corporal 'Kibbler' Matthews and his section, with shrapnel hitting Matthews in the arm,

'Later at FOB Price,' Corporal Cowe said, 'it would require Savlon and a plaster.'

The situation remained dire. Studying the extraction routes, Marine 'Fatboy' Farr said, 'I hope we aren't pinned down here much longer. That canal looks fucking cold.'

The OC Major Ewen 'Col. Kurtz' Murchison's Viking was also hit by an RPG, but he continued calling in mortars, artillery and air support. At one point, artillery fire hit targets between the two close-combat troops. But every time a target was neutralised, another popped up.

'At Company Main, CSM Marty Pelling was organising the ammo resupply,' said Corporal Cowe. 'LMA Al McNeil and Marine Coleman put on their gloves and had the crash bag ready.'

It was now daylight and attack helicopters began circling the area. Dozens of empty ammo liners littered the ground. The trees to the front were virtually cut down by the weight of fire, and the compounds and fields were smouldering. One Troop had fought their way out of the initial contact point and Second Lieutenant 'Pig Man' Hughes was issuing orders to assault an enemy compound. Turning to Tug Wilson, Mick Cowe pointed out that he might want his helmet for this.

Under a heavy weight of suppressing fire, One Troop advanced and conducted a 'hard-knock' clearance of a number of compounds with HE and phosphorous grenades. Asked for a grenade to lob into a compound, Corporal Cowe replied, 'Here you go, mate, use two.'

The last compound proved to be a high-priority Taliban hideout with a substantial weapons cache and IED factory. The weapons, ammo and equipment were taken back to FOB Price to be examined by the Weapons Intelligence Section.

At the same time, Two Troop were ordered to push on to a Taliban firing point at the sluice gate, which channels the Helmand River into the canal. But, as the troop moved east, they were suddenly engaged by numerous firing points to the north, east and south, including one on the sluice itself. Second Lieutenant 'Dickie' Sharp's men dashed into the alleyways and compounds, and returned fire. Supported by Apache gunships firing chain guns and Hellfire missiles, Two Troop engaged the enemy positions.

By now everyone had either had a near miss – Marine

Steve Dounias fell off an assault ladder as an RPG detonated on the wall supporting it – or they had had some sort of surreal experience; Corporal 'Nobby' Hall's section claimed to have witnessed a dead Taliban stand up after he had been shot. But still the sardonic wit flowed. After a heavy exchange of fire, Sergeant Nige Quarman said he thought 'we may have wound them up a bit'. Although they were winning the gun battle, Two Troop were still surrounded on three sides and the word was given to withdraw. The Royal Engineer attached to the troop whose job is was to assess potential checkpoints said that they were not to worry that he did not actually reach the site. He would write the report saying it was unsuitable due to excessive incoming fire.

As Two Troop pulled back, the enemy were trying to use dead ground to crawl closer to Three Troop's position, firing a heavy weight of RPGs and small-arms rounds.

'Enough was now enough,' said Corporal Cowe. 'The enemy were clearly not playing the game and so inorganic weapon systems were brought into play.'

Corporal Heath, who remained exposed throughout the contact calculating target grids, brought 81mm and 105mm onto the enemy trench and compounds. Then a B-1 bomber had the final word. JTAC Corporal Larry Lamb co-ordinated the dropping of a range of ordnance. Finally, a stick of three 907-kilo (2,000-pound) bombs silenced the trench.

'Nasty,' said one of the Marines, 'but problem solved.'

The company withdrew on foot, clearing compounds on the route back. The Viking provided fire support and, when the Marines reached a safe distance, artillery fell on the enemy positions that were still firing.

After the action, Corporal Cowe said, 'A lot of

different emotions came out during the first few hours. No one showed fear at the time. The funniest thing was that, even at the height of battle, everyone was shouting at each other saying how "hoofing" it was, laughing, giggling and making a joke of the situation. You may as well laugh when things get tough. You'll only cry if you don't. Bootnecks are good at that and it's a great pressure relief.'

The other thing he remembered was the noise of battle – 'but something inside your body kicks in and you get on with the job in hand; everyone switches to autopilot and the training takes over'.

During the course of the four-hour battle, there were many individual acts of bravery. The commanders called the shots. Their instructions were followed to the letter and the men of Juliet Company returned to base unscathed.

To get construction work on the hydroelectric damn at Kajaki back on track, M Company Group of 42 Commando arrived there in force in early December. They began pushing the Taliban back on all fronts. Nightly engagements using heavy machine guns were very much the norm, along with mortar exchanges. According to Captain Rob Thorpe, on a 'good night' in Kajaki, the Mortar Troop would fire about a hundred rounds of high explosives at enemy positions. Corporal Alex Heath spent the five weeks at a remote, heavily mined outpost in Kajaki, the only mortar fire controller (MFC) providing critical force protection to a site of strategic significance.

'It was a perfect location for me,' he said, 'overlooking the villages, dramatic mountain scenery and the rolling desert with awesome 360-degree arcs out to a good 10 kilometres [6 miles].'

The action began within a few hours of their taking over the position and did not stop for the next five weeks. The contact was almost daily and lasted anywhere from minutes to several hours.

'As a recently qualified Bravo MFC, this gave me an awesome opportunity to hone my skills,' said Heath, 'and I was soon calling in all types of fire missions: high-explosive to adjust and neutralise targets, smoke to screen the enemy or mark targets for air attacks and, at night, co-ordinated illumination missions... After the best weeks I've had in the corps yet, I was regrettably recalled to Bastion. However, I now sleep soundly at night knowing that the Taliban will be needing reinforcements at Kajaki, thanks to 42 Mortars.'

When Corporal Lewy Stallard of the Royal Marine Reserve was told that 45 Commando was to take on the role of the Operational Mentoring and Liaison Team, it conjured up images of playing Lawrence of Arabia to battle-hardened Afghan hill tribesmen. Within a fortnight, he found himself at the OMLT compound on the dominating high ground in Kajaki, with Warrant Officer Second Class Rick Groves and Sergeant Lee Mildener. Sitting in the Sangin valley at the foothills of the Hindu Kush, they overlooked the infamous hydroelectric plant.

'While the intelligence briefs seemed to focus solely on guys swimming in the reservoir, the reality on the ground was far different,' said Corporal Stallard. 'It is arguably the busiest of the fixed locations, and stand-off engagements take place daily with the Taliban conducting hit-and-run-style operations, only to find the wrath of 42 Commando or the ANA close on their heels.'

The remnants of past fighting were all too apparent. As well as the seemingly endless minefields, burned-out armoured fighting vehicles and shattered buildings, the locals had chilling stories to tell.

Stallard's next deployment was out to FOB Robinson, on the outskirts of Sangin town. There he was to take over the S4 mentor job from the heavily bearded Sergeant Stan Stamford. Many of the British troops grew beards to fit in with the locals, but Stallard's attempt at growing facial hair was a non-starter. He was to advise 90 Afghans on the importance of rationing and getting requests in early. It proved to be a thankless task.

'My faith in the ANA became stretched to breaking point here, especially when one of the commanders proceeded to try to strike a deal with the local Taliban,' said Stallard. 'Food and safe passage in return for British night-vision gear and weapons. Needless to say he was quickly removed.'

But the rest of the ANA proved their worth and did not shy away in subsequent contacts. One such contact occurred on Christmas Day, when Marine 'Melzy' Mellon got the rounds down with the heavy machine gun while dressed as Santa Claus. After that they moved onto Garmsir.

'Our arrival allowed Zulu Company to probe further south and allowed us to give our trigger fingers a good workout,' said Stallard.

Mentoring of the ANA took a back seat there, with self-preservation a more pressing concern. Again, the ANA proved themselves willing to stand their ground and take the fight to the enemy, even if their methods raised one or two eyebrows. Stallard's comrade Jonny Hart, who had already been shot in the backside, managed to survive three RPG attacks – one when he was the driver of a WMIK hit by the RPG that injured Corporal Nick Fenwick.

On 28 December, Whisky Company of 45 Commando

took over from the ANA at FOB Robinson. As they completed their takeover from the rapidly departing ANA, they realised that they had quite a task ahead of them to build up the defences. The inadequate perimeter wall and shed-like sangars the ANA had left offered little protection from the gullies that led up to the position.

'Also, no patrols had left FOB Rob since the previous summer,' said Second Lieutenant Matt Hills, 'so we were keen to get out and dominate the ground.'

But their first task was to improve their force protection and living conditions. The in-house engineers from 42 Field Squadron quickly rebuilt the sangars and provided basic ablutions for the living areas. A bit of DIY also improved the quality of life; the men built makeshift gyms, bread ovens and a boulder wall.

Patrolling started without delay. Because no UK patrols had been out in the area for a while, the local farmers were a little nervous when they saw the Marines. As well as familiarising the Marines with the local area, these initial patrols served to build trust among the locals.

'Civilian and military co-operation became the main effort,' said Hills. 'Before long we had every man and his sheep knocking on the gates for a chat and a cup of pusser's tea.'

But it would not be plain sailing. Their first major incident came in mid-January, when a group of Taliban ambushed a vehicle patrol. They started the attack with an RPG and one of the British vehicles broke down in the killing area. The enemy still came off significantly worse. There were nine confirmed enemy dead and more wounded, with no friendly casualties.

News that more ANA were about to join the Marines at FOB Rob evoked a mixed response. Whisky Company thought that their worst fears had been confirmed when they saw an Afghan soldier dribbling a football down the ramp of the Chinook that had brought them. But out on patrol the Afghans proved to be professional, and they managed to pick up bits of intelligence that would otherwise have been lost in translation by the Marines' interpreters.

On 21 February, 23-year-old Marine Jonathan 'Dutchy' Holland was killed by a landmine while out on patrol in Sangin. Holland was the longest-serving member of Whisky Company, and one of its true characters.

'Marine Holland's legacy will live on at RM Condor for quite some time,' said Lieutenant 'Monty' Montgomery, his Commanding Officer at Camp Tombstone. 'His tales of pink BVs and impromptu canine grooming sessions had even the padre struggling to keep a straight face at his ramp ceremony.'

Then, as the weather warmed, the frequency of attacks increased, with 107mm rockets and mortars raining down on FOB Rob almost daily.

'Although accurate, reports that one rocket managed to wake up Corporal Slunker have yet to be confirmed,' Corporal Stallard quipped.

Then they figured out what the problem was.

'Does the mast have to be at that height?' Corporal Gordon of Y Squadron was asked. 'The Taliban are using it to aim at.'

'There's perhaps a degree of truth to this,' Gordon admitted. 'However, recent attacks with 107mm rockets have been with the level of accuracy that would shame any graduate of the Taliban weapons training school.'

However, at 20 metres (65 feet) in height, the Odette mast gave the best chance to intercept intelligence and allowed them to support operations in other areas. And, as the Taliban generally used the same firing points, it allowed the artillery to respond with plenty of 105mm shells.

Y Squadron were also listening in at Kajaki, and Corporal McGonnel was sent up there a little over 12 hours after getting back into Camp Bastion from R&R.

'I arrived at Kajaki in the darkness just before dawn,' said McGonnel. 'The sun rose to reveal some dramatic mountain scenery and lift my post-R&R blues. I was taken up to one of the peaks held by M Company, called Athens, and instantly picked out my accommodation, the one bristling with antennas.'

The mountainsides were littered with mines and the rusting hulks of former Soviet hardware, relics from another era – a reminder that the people who live here have always been well acquainted with war. The detachment consisted of McGonnel, Marine 'Naggers' Andrews and a couple of crazy Afghan interpreters – Boris, the self-styled 'king of Kajaki', and Rashid.

'We became the new local Samaritans,' joked McGonnel, 'always ready to listen.'

The radio intercept post shared Athens with the Mortar Troop. They fired off 81mm rounds daily, shaking the listening post so that little pieces of the roof fell on the RRT (Radio Receiver/Transmitter) boys' heads and kit. But a steady stream of chatter could be heard from their little room.

'We listened and reported as the Taliban endeavour to plot our doom from somewhere on the plain below,' said McGonnel.

Their information was passed onto the M Company patrols and to the analyst cell at Lashkar Gah, to help build the wider intelligence picture in the province.

Since M Company's mission was to try to enhance security

in Kajaki, and consequently increased stability and employment in the area, the dam was crucial. But it was surrounded on three sides by a strong Taliban force, and had a reservoir to the rear. Elements of the company, including a section from Recce Troop, moved up onto the three hilltops that dominated the surrounding area. From there, the company began fixing the Taliban in areas where they had previously enjoyed freedom of movement. Meanwhile, the rest of the company group established themselves at FOB Zeebrugge, situated on low ground near the dam.

The company began a series of framework patrols, allowing coalition forces to dominate the ground. Then M Company, with 59 Independent Commando Squadron of the Royal Engineers, built a permanent vehicle checkpoint at a crucial road junction as a base for the Afghan National Police.

Once a commanding presence had been established, the company began conducting a series of deliberate attacks and company-level fighting patrols to force the Taliban onto the back foot.

Captain William Mackenzie-Green and Ten Troop led an attack on an enemy stronghold named Nipple Hill, 3 kilometres (2 miles) north of the dam that the Taliban was using for a mortar base.

'In the early hours one morning M Company moved off to remove the enemy from the hill and surrounding compounds,' he said. 'As the first streaks of daylight caught the top of the hill two enemy sentries were seen with weapons.'

With the lead troops only 300 metres (328 yards) from the base of the hill and in limited cover, a mortar strike was called in. Then, with bayonets fixed, the lead troop moved across the open ground.

'As soon as the first mortars went in we fixed bayonets,' said 20-year-old Marine Ash Hore. 'The feeling of adrenalin was awesome.'

They quickly cleared the enemy trench system and a bunker.

'Afterwards it felt great, but at the time it was "honking",' said 23-year-old Marine Bispham.

'The two assaulting sections "pepper-potted" for 300 metres [328 yards] with the gun group behind,' explained Corporal Jack Scott. 'They went straight up the hill. Right on top there was a bunker. We could hear a communications radio inside. The room was cleared with a grenade. When we entered, the radio was still working. We gave the radio to our interpreter and from then on we could hear everything they said. One group was saying, "The Brits are coming" "How many?" "... I think they have sent all of them for us."'

As they crested the hilltop, the forward troops came under heavy fire from small arms and rocket-propelled grenades. Soon most of the company were engaged. With the aid of two attack helicopters and two troops acting as fire support, the lead section broke into the nearest compound.

To the flank was Lance Corporal Owen.

'I was in the lead vehicle and we saw eight blokes dressed in black robes with weapons,' he said. 'Two or three of them stopped to fire at us at the top of the hill. Our guys on foot were halfway up the hill. We were engaged with gunfire. I dismounted my general-purpose machine gun to engage them. As our ground troops came in I changed my directional fire to give fire support.'

'With their will to fight broken,' said Captain Mackenzie-Green, 'the Taliban turned and fled.'

Nevertheless, during the following six hours, M Company were engaged in many separate firefights, but continued to move forward methodically, clearing each compound in turn. During one of these engagements, Marine Tom Curry was killed while leading his troop in an assault on an enemy compound.

'Without thought for their own safety,' said Mackenzie-Green, 'the Marines never faltered and continued the attack despite the loss of one of their finest.'

Corporal Scott took away another memory. 'Faces lighting up with tracer,' he said. 'That's something I'll never forget – the redness of the tracer round as it passes between you and your oppo. It was like *Star Wars* [George Lucas, 1977].'

Having again pushed the Taliban back – and unearthing numerous weapon caches – M Company withdrew to the dam. They took with them a badly wounded Taliban fighter who later died in custody – but not until the on-site British medics had tried everything in their power to keep him alive.

'Why did you try to save him?' asked a local.

'That's what makes us different from them,' a Marine replied.

The problem was that, even after taking heavy casualties, the Taliban continued to fight rather than give ground; so in the New Year M Company decided to attack the enemy command post. At 21.00 on 1 January 2007, Second Lieutenant Bertie Kerr, commander of Two Troop, told his men of the attack.

'Listen up, guys!' he said. 'We leave tomorrow at dawn. Get some scran down your necks and then get some sleep. I want you up at 04.00 hours. We leave at 04.45 hours.'

They were sheltering from the cold night wind behind the

remaining walls of the deserted police compound in Kajaki, which had been shot up and mortared to hell by the Taliban. Crowding around the fire, they took it in turns to heat up their boil-in-the-bag bacon and beans in a huge kettle they found there.

'It's my 21st birthday today,' said Marine Thomas Curry – known to everyone as 'Vinders', as in *vindaloo*.

'Twenty-one! Bloody hell! What a way to spend your 21st, eh?' said another Marine, offering Vinders his hipflask. 'A slug of single malt to celebrate, Royal.'

'Congratulations, Vinders,' said Lieutenant Kerr, who was just two years older than Curry and only three weeks out of officer training. 'And happy New Year, too. You know what, though?' he added. 'I really wish I was at home with the girlfriend right now going down the pub.'

After the bacon and beans – and a tiny drop of whisky – they crawled into their sleeping bags for a fitful sleep to the accompaniment of the distant sound of small-arms fire.

At 04.45 the following day, they were up and ready for action. 'OK, lads,' said Lieutenant Kerr. 'Let's go. Move!'

It was two hours before dawn and bitterly cold as 20 silent silhouettes shuffled out of the police compound. There was a three-quarter moon, enough to shed some illumination over the rocky landscape.

'Keep to the shadows, guys,' said Kerr through his headset. 'The Taliban could be anywhere.'

This was his first command and, at Kajaki, he was at the sharp end of the war in Afghanistan.

The men of Two Troop moved slowly and silently forward in single file, snaking through the shadows with their SA80 assault rifles at the ready. Each man kept 9 metres or so (30 feet) behind the man in front, just in case someone stepped on a landmine – or was hit by mortar fire or a rocket-propelled grenade. They were heading for the 'Shrine', the Taliban base on a piece of rocky high ground just north of the river and overlooking the dam, whose turbines had yet to turn. The Marines figured that, if they could destroy the Shrine, they would knock out the Taliban command structure. This would prevent the insurgents hijacking road traffic and, by showing the locals that there was no hiding place for the rebels, encourage civilians to work on the dam. That morning a hundred men of M Company were involved in the daring dawn assault. And Two Troop were out in front, the designated point.

Under cover of darkness, they climbed the steep southern slope of the Shrine, halting just short of the summit. There, Kerr consulted Sergeant Pete McGinely and Corporals 'Jacko' Jackson and 'Sully' Sullivan. Then the whispered order was issued through his headset: 'Go firm. We wait here until it gets lighter.'

The men took cover among the rocks and waited.

At 06.25, the pale, morning sun painted the landscape a bright beige.

'We're bloody exposed here,' whispered Kerr.

The summit of the Shrine was closer than expected. The men made their SA80s ready. They put a bullet in the chamber, but left the safety catch on. They fixed bayonets.

'Keep low, lads,' said Kerr. 'Don't skyline yourselves. The enemy is out there somewhere.'

At 06.45, they heard the crack of gunfire.

'Jesus – we've been spotted!' shouted Lieutenant Kerr. 'Incoming – take cover!'

The glowing pink streaks of tracer passed over their heads.

'Keep your heads down, lads!' yelled Kerr.

As the Taliban's aim improved, the crack of gunfire

266

turned into the buzz of what the Marines called the 'Afghan bee' – the sound of a bullet as it whistled passed your ear. There were swarms of them.

Pinned down on the exposed upper slopes, the Marines had no choice but to try to crawl downhill to safety.

'On your belt buckles, lads,' said Kerr.

As soon as they got far enough down the slope and into dead ground, he planned to make a run for cover. There they would regroup and establish a firing line.

As fresh bursts of Taliban tracer scarred the now bright blue sky, a bullet whizzed passed Kerr's ear, causing him to lose his cool for a moment.

For two hours the incoming fire did not let up. By then, Ten Troop had arrived at the base of the hill and had opened up with everything they had in the hope of drawing the Taliban fire. Air support had been requested, but it would take some time.

Despite the screaming bullets, Kerr could hold off no longer.

'OK, lads! Go for it!' he yelled. 'Down to the ridge!'

They leaped to their feet and sprinted 180 metres (200 yards) down the slope, where they regrouped.

An hour later, Two Troop had established a firing line just above their defensive position and started to lay down effective fire. But the Taliban were dug in and in a strong position and shooting back with disconcerting accuracy. The mortar troop behind them fired a salvo, laying down a screen of smoke to cover their movements. But then came the sound no one wants to hear. It was the sickening sound of a bullet hitting flesh and bone. It was followed by a muted scream. Marine Richard Mayson had been hit – a bullet had gone straight through his wrist, shattering the bone. The wound threatened a serious loss of blood. Lieutenant Kerr tended it while Marine Hoole whipped out the morphine syringe from behind Mayson's body armour and jabbed it into his upper thigh. Then they applied a field dressing.

'We'll soon have you out of here, mate,' said Hoole. 'Look on the bright side, mate. Think of the dits you can spin down the pub. The birds'll be all over you!'

Mayson smiled at the prospect and, minutes later, Sergeant McGinely helped the wounded Marine down the hill to safety.

To everyone's intense relief, at 10.05, an Apache helicopter arrived and fired a Hellfire missile into the Taliban position. A direct hit, it killed eight. The rest fled. M Company advanced back up the hill and took the position. They spent the rest of the day checking the nooks and crannies of the Shrine, proceeding cautiously for fear of booby traps. Then they moved through numerous deserted compounds to the north that had been used by the Taliban as fire bases and weapons caches. For the time being, the Taliban were nowhere to be found.

Twelve days later, Two Troop led another assault. This time 21-year-old Thomas 'Vinders' Curry was killed.

Zulu Company of 45 Commando were back in action at dawn on Monday, 15 January 2007, when they staged an attack on the Taliban base of Jugroom Fort, south of Garmsir. Mounted in Vikings, Z Company crossed the Helmand River to the south-west of the fort, supported by C Squadron of the Light Dragoons. The BRF had already secured the crossing point. The Marines then dismounted and engaged the Taliban with small-arms fire.

The attack was supported by elements of 29 Commando Regiment, Royal Artillery, elements of 59 Independent Squadron, Royal Engineers, elements of 32 Regiment, Royal Artillery, and attack helicopters and aircraft. Earlier,

India Company, alongside the Afghan National Police, had conducted an attack further to the north of the fort.

As part of this operation, One Troop of India Company were to move forward and attack four objectives simultaneously, in order to mislead the Taliban into believing a large-scale assault was being mounted from the north, diverting attention from Zulu Company's southern approach.

'One Section, I want you to move 1.5 kilometres [a mile] forward of our frontline to Objective Snowdon,' Corporal Pete Harvey of One Troop, India Company, was told. 'On H-hour I want you to fire two ILAWs into this suspected sentry position, then fire into the adjacent enemy compounds with everything you've got, to make the enemy think there is a large-scale attack happening from the north. Oh, and en route you'll need to clear Strip Wood.'

'What could be easier?' he thought as his section moved up to the line of departure at JTAC Hill.

'As we crossed the LD into the Taliban's back garden we had a nervous feeling in our stomachs,' said Corporal Harvey.

One Section led the troop, before breaking off and moving along a riverbank, heading for Strip Wood. This was a known enemy firing point and home to a recently discovered trench system. Clearing the wood, they continued south until, using thermal imaging, they identified a heat source 200 metres (218 yards) ahead.

'Minutes seemed like hours as the snipers observed, eventually engaging the source with two .338 rounds,' said Corporal Harvey.

They continued pushing forward until they identified two Taliban in a well-defended bunker 50 metres (55 yards) away. Harvey and Marine Cain moved in to observe, but they had to back off when one of the occupants got out of the bunker. They moved back to the riverbank to see if they could find their way around the right flank, but the bunker was so well concealed it would have been impossible to approach by stealth.

'I was informed this was now my objective,' said Harvey, 'so I positioned the fire support and ILAW team and waited for H-hour.'

For the men of One Section, H-hour could not come quickly enough. On Harvey's orders, the two ILAW men fired at the bunker. The first, fired by Lance Corporal Woods, scored a direct hit, going in straight through the window. The second, shouldered by Marine Cain, was less successful.

'Firing on the third attempt and missing the target, it was last seen heading for Pakistan,' Harvey said.

Fire support suppressed the bunker as they started taking fire from the east. But green Taliban tracer was soon coming in too close for comfort, and they pulled back to Strip Wood. With artillery and mortars suppressing the Taliban depth positions, they were told to return to assess the damage. They found that the bunker was well constructed and they had done well to defeat it in the initial contact. The roof had collapsed, killing the occupants.

'Our mission was a classic commando raid,' said Harvey. 'A small group of determined men moved into the enemy's rear, unleashed hell and extracted back to fight another day.'

They made their way back to the troop reorganisation point at JTAC Hill under the cover of fire support from Three Troop, mortars and artillery. Then they pulled back to Patrol Base Delhi, where they could relax while listening to the sound of Zulu Company's attack further south.

It seems that the India Company's diversionary tactic had not worked. The main force soon met ferocious Taliban fire from all sides and, after five hours of fighting, Z Company had to pull back across the Helmand River. As the Marines regrouped there, they discovered that Lance Corporal Matthew Ford was missing. They then planned a daring rescue mission. Initially, they were going to use Vikings, but it was concluded that the Apache WAH-64 attack helicopters would provide a quicker and safer means of getting him out and back to safety. Four Marines were strapped to the small side 'wings' of two Apaches, two to each helicopter. The men involved were Regimental Sergeant Major Colin Hearn, Captain Dave Rigg of the RE, Marine Chris Fraser-Perry and Marine Gary Robinson.

A third Apache provided aerial cover, and further units laid down a mass of covering fire. When helicopters reached their landing zone, the four men on the wings got off. Some of the aircrew also dismounted to provide additional firepower and to help in the recovery of Lance Corporal Ford.

'It was a leap into the unknown,' said Lieutenant-Colonel Rory Bruce of the RM. 'This is believed to be the first time UK forces have ever tried this type of rescue mission. It was an extraordinary tale of heroism and bravery of our airmen, soldiers and Marines who were all prepared to put themselves back into the line of fire to rescue a fallen comrade.'

Sadly, although Lance Corporal Ford was recovered, he died and was listed killed in action. He would not be the last to lose his life. As this book went to press, operational deaths in Iraq have topped 170. By the time you read this, there will, no doubt, be many more.

GLOSSARY

AAC: Army Air Corps
AAMS: Air Assault Medical Squadron
ABU: Amphibious Beach Unit
ADT: Air Defence Troop
AFV: Armoured fighting vehicle
AGC: Adjutant General's Corps
ANA: Afghan National Army
ANP: Afghan National Police
APC: armoured personnel carrier
APOD: Aerial point of debarkation
BERGEN: A type of backpack used by armed forces
(possibly from the trademark Bergens, a Norwegian
manufacturer)
BLUE ON BLUE: Refers to an action, an accidental
attack, by allied or friendly forces as opposed to the
enemy (*a blue-on-blue attack*)
BPT: Brigade Patrol Troop
BRF: British Recognisance Force
CAM AND CON: Camouflage and Concealment

Cimic: Civil–military co-operation
CSG: Command Support Group
CVR(T): Combat Vehicle Reconnaissance (Tracked)
dit: Tale, story
EFP: explosively formed projectile
EOD: explosive ordnance disposal
FAC: forward air controller
FOB: forward operating base
FSG: fire support group
GOSP: gas–oil separation plant
GPMG: general-purpose machine gun
HE: High Explosive
helo: helicopter
H-hour: appointed time for an attack or other military event (*H* for *hour*) (*see also* L-hour)
humint: *hum*an *int*elligence
IED: improvised explosive device
IG: Irish Guards
ISAF: International Security Assistance Force
JDAM: joint direct-attack munition
L-hour: actual time at which deployment for an operation begins (*see also* H-hour)
medevac: *med*ical *evac*uation, or an aircraft used for such
MFC: mortar fire controller
MILAN:a French/German anti-tank missile (*Missile d'infanterie léger antichar*)
MMS:Manifold Metering Station
MSG: Manoeuvre Support Group
NBC: nuclear, biological and chemical
NVGs: night-vision goggles
OMLT: Operational Mentoring and Liaison Team, nicknamed *omelette*
OP: observation post

OSG: offensive support group
ping: discover, spot (an enemy)
psyop (or PSYOP): psychological operation
PWRR: Princess of Wales's Royal Regiment
QDG: Queen's Dragoon Guards
QRL: Queen's Royal Lancers
RAMC: Royal Army Medical Corps
RAR: Royal Anglian Regiment ('Anglians')
Red Caps: nickname for Military Police
REME: Royal Electrical and Mechanical Engineers
RHA: Royal Horse Artillery
RLC: Royal Logistic Corps
RMP: Royal Military Police
RMR: Royal Marine Reserve
RPG: rocket-propelled grenades
RRF: Royal Regiment of Fusiliers
RTR: Royal Tank Regiment
RV: predetermined meeting point (*rendezvous*)
SAM: surface-to-air missile
sangar: small, temporary, fortified position, originally built of stone but now more often made of sandbags and similar materials
SBS: Special Boat Service
scran: food
Scud: type of tactical ballistic missile developed by the Soviet Union
SEAL: US naval Special Forces, abbreviation of *sea, air, land (team)*
shock and awe: term used to describe gaining rapid dominance using overwhelming decisive force; made popular during the second Gulf War, it has now entered popular culture
Sigint: signals intelligence

SOC-R: Special Operations Craft-Riverine
SOP: standard operating procedure
TA: Territorial Army
TAA: tactical assembly area
TAC: Tactical Air Controller
USMC: United States Marine Corps
UXO: unexploded ordnance
VCP: vehicle checkpoint
wadi: steep-sided, usually dry watercourse in arid regions
yomp: long-distance walk, usually across rough terrain and often with a difficult load

BIBLIOGRAPHY

Beck, Sara, and Downing, Malcolm (eds), *The Battle for Iraq: BBC News Correspondents on the War against Saddam and the New World Agenda* (London: BBC Worldwide, 2003)

Collins, Tim, *Rules of Engagement: A Life in Conflict* (London: Headline, 2005)

Elgood, Giles, *Twenty-One Days to Baghdad: A Chronicle of the Iraqi War* (Upper Saddle River, NJ: Reuters Prentice Hall, 2003)

Fowler, William, *SAS Behind Enemy Lines* (London: Collins, 2005)

Katovsky, William, *Embedded: The Media at War in Iraq* (Guildford, CT: Lyons Press, 2003)

Keegan, John, *The Iraq War* (London: Hutchinson, 2004)

Mervin, Kevin J, *Weekend Warrior: A Territorial Soldier's War in Iraq* (Edinburgh: Mainstream, 2005)

Rew, David, *Blood, Heat and Dust*, (North Somerset, UK: Avonworld, 2005)

Rooney, Ben, *War on Saddam* (London: Robinson, 2003)

Ryan, Mike, *Special Operations in Iraq* (Barnsley, UK: Pen & Sword Military, 2004)

Woodhall, Philip, *Iraq and Back* (Victoria, British Columbia: Trafford, 2005)